PASSAGES
of
MARRIAGE

OTHER BOOKS BY THE AUTHORS

Day By Day, Love Is a Choice (Serenity Meditation™ Series)
Richard and Jerilyn Fowler and Brian and Deborah Newman

Free to Forgive (Serenity Meditation™ Series)
Dr. Paul Meier and Dr. Frank Minirth

Kids Who Carry Our Pain
Dr. Robert Hemfelt and Dr. Paul Warren

Love Is a Choice: Recovery for Codependent Relationships
Dr. Robert Hemfelt, Dr. Frank Minirth, Dr. Paul Meier

Love Is a Choice Workbook
Dr. Robert Hemfelt, Dr. Frank Minirth, Dr. Paul Meier,
Dr. Deborah Newman, Dr. Brian Newman

Love Hunger: Recovery for Food Addiction
Dr. Frank Minirth, Dr. Paul Meier,
Dr. Robert Hemfelt, and Dr. Sharon Sneed

Love Hunger Weight-Loss Workbook
Frank Minirth, M.D., Paul Meier, M.D.,
Robert Hemfelt, Ph.D., and Sharon Sneed, Ph.D.

One Step at a Time (Serenity Meditation™ Series)
Dr. Frank Minirth, Betty Blaylock, Cynthia Humbert

A Walk with the Serenity Prayer (Serenity Meditation™ Series)
Dr. Paul Meier, Dr. Frank Minirth, Dr. David and Janet Congo

PASSAGES *of* MARRIAGE

FRANK & MARY ALICE MINIRTH
BRIAN & DEBORAH NEWMAN
ROBERT & SUSAN HEMFELT

A JANET THOMA BOOK

THOMAS NELSON PUBLISHERS
NASHVILLE

Published in Nashville, Tennessee, by Janet Thoma Books, a division of Thomas Nelson Publishers, and distributed in Canada by Word Communications, Ltd., Richmond, British Colombia, and in the United Kingdom by Word (UK), Ltd., Milton Keynes, England.

Scripture quotations are from the NEW KING JAMES VERSION of the Bible. Copyright © 1979, 1980, 1982, Thomas Nelson, Inc., Publishers.

Library of Congress Cataloging-in-Publication Data

Passages of marriage / Brian Newman . . . [et al.].
    p.   cm.
"A Janet Thoma book."
ISBN 0-8407-7582-2 (HC)
ISBN 0-7852-8187-8 (PB)
    1. Marriage—United States.   2. Interpersonal relations.
3. Communication in marriage—United States.   I. Newman, Brian.
HQ734.P24   1991
646.7'8—dc20   91–24125
                                                                          CIP

Printed in the United States of America
2 3 4 5 6 7 — 98 97 96 95 94

To our parents

Roy and Frances Holt
Ike and Olive Minirth

Bob and Norma Bowles
Danny and Jerry Newman

Francis and Nell Winters
Bob and Ivas Hemfelt

CONTENTS

PART FIVE: THE FOURTH PASSAGE
Renewing Love, the Twenty-sixth through the Thirty-fifth Years

PART SIX: THE FIFTH PASSAGE
Transcendent Love, the Thirty-Sixth Year and On

ACKNOWLEDGMENTS

The authors wish to thank the many people who helped make this book possible. Many thanks to Sandy Dengler whose writing talent brought the illustrations, thoughts, and notes from the authors to a consistent and readable form. We also thank Janet Thoma for the many hours she spent guiding, editing, and directing the completion of the manuscript. We recognize Jennifer Farrar and Susan Salmon for their editorial assistance and attention to the details that helped make the book complete. Lastly, we acknowledge our children: Rachel, Renee, Carrie, Alicia, and Elizabeth Minirth; Rachel and Benjamin Newman; Katy, Kristin, and Robert Gray Hemfelt, for the special part they add to our passages through marriage.

PART
ONE
Where Are You?

1

IS YOUR MARRIAGE STUCK AT SECOND?

*C*arl Warden hated to see a grown man cry, himself least of all. But the tears ran freely down his cheeks now, as Beth Anne came down the aisle. Praise God, she was beautiful! Warm, clear, suntanned skin against the white gown; long golden hair like her grandmother's, tumbling in loose waves; that uncertain, innocent smile. She was as beautiful as Annie had been on her wedding day, almost as beautiful as Bess had looked. Beside him, Bess gripped his arm and squeezed.

His granddaughter getting married—how old does that make you feel?! He glanced over at his daughter, Annie. The mother of the bride still had that look of I've-got-it-all-together that had made her such a source of pride to Bess and Carl all these years. She watched her daughter, dewy-eyed, as Beth Anne approached the altar.

Annie had outdone herself with this wedding. All the details, the special little touches, the attention to small things—they added up to perfection. Yes, that was Annie. Carl could feel assured Annie had done it all too. Rob provided for her well enough, but he never lifted a finger to help with anything like this. You couldn't call him lazy, but you couldn't call him a go-getter, either. In all the years Annie and Rob had been together, Carl could never get a really good, warm feeling for his son-in-law.

The wedding went off without a hitch; again, that was Annie and her planning. She even had the limo drivers wearing identical neckties as the wedding party moved across town to the reception at the Northside Country Club.

Bess shook her head as she crawled into their own limo. "Can you imagine this?" Carefully she lowered herself in the seat. "When we got married we didn't ride around in limos."

"Naw," Carl chuckled and settled in beside her. "But as I recall, our wedding vehicle cost more than this does."

She laughed out loud. "True. A city bus costs more!"

The reception, too, hummed along flawlessly, like a well-oiled machine. Carl enjoyed being a guest of honor at a fancy "do" like this—one of the fringe benefits of old age. He shook hands with more people in two hours than he'd met in the last three years. Among them was an old business associate, Louie Ajanian. Louie, a widower, had remarried recently, and he still looked in the throes of young love. Carl had never seen him quite this cheerful. Her name was Margaret.

Carl also met Julia Karris at last. Beth Anne had been talking about her good friend Julia for years. Beth had described Julia's woes with the ex-husband, the present husband, the kids. Too bad about all the problems. Julia was such a charming woman, graceful, dark-haired and beautiful.

Julia grasped his hand firmly. "Beth Anne is just gorgeous! You must be so proud."

"As an understatement, that'll do," Carl smiled.

"She's so lucky." A wisp of sadness edged her voice. "My mom never attended my weddings—either one of them—let alone my grandparents."

While the string quartet tuned up, Carl sat under a parasol and thought about this whole business. There was Louie, as happy with his bride as a pup in a dog food factory. There was Julia Karris, unlucky at love twice over, but still trying to make a match work. Here was Annie, who seemed to hide problems, if she had any—he bet she did. And Beth Anne, just starting out. . . . He looked across the pool at Bess. Too bad every man in the world couldn't marry a woman like Bess. It would sure solve a lot of troubles. Then the string quartet began a waltz and Beth Anne with her Alan led it off.

Carl finally managed to draw Annie aside as the event wore down. He gave her a warm squeeze. "Perfect, end to end," he crowed to his daughter. "You even arranged for the right weather." He led her to a little bench along the edge of the expanse of green lawn. "Bet you're going to be glad to relax, after all this."

Annie's face darkened. She tried to smile; no smile came. "Dad—" She took a deep breath, and her eyes skittered about everywhere, anywhere except her father's face. "This wedding kept me busy, you might say. But now . . . now I have—I don't have anything to do. It's just Rob and me in that house." She turned to him.

"Your marriage is solid, Sugar Anne. What are you saying?" Carl tried to read her face; all he saw was fear. "You always said you'd be glad when the last child moved out."

"It's—" She waved a hand in the air, trying to pluck words that would not come. "Our marriage has changed somehow, Dad. He's not the same person. Or maybe I'm not. We don't have anything in common, or . . . I'm not even sure I love him anymore. And now it's only me and him, me and something I don't think I want. What am I going to do, Dad?"

Everyone's marriage, like Annie's, changes with time. So often, the changes are not for the better.

WHO'S SORRY NOW?

Our very nature throws into marriage certain clinkers that we do not recognize and cannot anticipate. Those clinkers are generated by our families of origin—by the way our relatives did things, said things, and hid things. Dr. Hemfelt likens them to time-release capsules. Things can be chugging along comfortably. Suddenly, with no warning, one of those time-release beads goes off. The union is not what it was, and something has gone dreadfully awry.

Yet these clinkers, and the other inevitable changes in a marriage, can be turned from bad to good once you recognize what they are. A marriage that appears dull and mundane can be made to sparkle. A hopeless situation can emerge into bright promise. A good union can be made better. It all depends upon finding and managing the sources of trouble, the clinkers and changes. We want to help you do that.

Hints of Trouble

Couples who approach professionals in our clinic never come in because everything is going well. Rather, they sense trouble. They feel unmet needs. Their symptoms, the surface clues to underlying problems, show up in our case files again and again, however unique they may seem to the couples experiencing them. Because no marriage is perfect, every couple weathers these problems to some extent. But when the problems loom too large to handle and threaten the union, trouble will follow.

Look over the following hints of trouble in light of your own family relationships. Do more than a few of them mar your happiness right now?

Chronic Financial Distress

Why can't Harry get ahead? He doesn't overspend. His wife, while not frugal, is not extravagant, either. Yet his ship of finance wallows up to its gunwales in debt. By this stage in life, Harry ought to be a unit manager, if not a store manager, but he's still clerking and stocking shelves. Harry knows why he can't get ahead. He's had to change jobs five times in the last ten years because of unfeeling, incompetent bosses. One of the places he worked for even sent him to the company shrink to talk to him about his attitude problem. *His* attitude!

Then his wife cajoled him into marriage counseling for unrelated reasons. After a year of counseling at the Minirth-Meier Clinic in Dallas, Texas, Harry is still in debt, but at least now the bill collectors don't call him at home and work every day. He's working things out. He says, "I went to a financial counselor long ago. But what I learned from him simply didn't work until my marriage smoothed out." He grimaces. "And I didn't even know it was wrinkled."

Not all financial distress points to marriage problems, of course. We do, however, consider chronic financial difficulties a factor to look at closely. We also look closely if a person experiences constant or recurring vocational failure. This often points to some individual psychological problem or anger in the marriage. Maybe the husband wants to be married. Yet a part of him longs for someone to take care of him. He buries that desire, but he unconsciously sabotages job after job. That's a warning signal. The husband is saying, "Yes, I've told you I want to be a breadwinner, but part of me feels that someone needs to take care of me." The man may never have felt he was well taken care of at home. Maybe he was the child who never got the attention he deserved. Now he and his wife will have to work through these issues before they can establish a good relationship.

In-law Problems and Involvement

A related financial clue we address is any monetary dependence of the married couple upon the in-laws.

"But they prepared for us with trusts and legacies!" the couple might protest.

"Absolutely. And we're all in favor of it. Inheritances as frosting on the cake are marvelous. What we look for, rather, is the prospect that the couple requires that legacy in order to survive financially."

Far more telling is a situation wherein the in-laws provide financial or intense emotional support long beyond the wedding, after the couple should have cut the economic and emotional apron strings and become independent. When newlyweds are engaged in a multigenerational family business, this particular red flag marks a lot of gray areas, some wholesome and some not.

In fact, in-law problems in general suggest that unfinished business—incompleted passages—lie in the background. And though we will discuss unfinished business in detail later, keep in mind for now this broad generalization: Severe in-law friction indicates a cross-generational problem that, if not resolved, will fester in the present generation and infect the next ones.

Family Imbalance and Stress

Jason and Jennifer fight every day. They wish they didn't because it upsets the kids, just as their parents' fights used to upset them. But they realize bitter fighting is the mark of any marriage, the only way to resolve differences. Because Jennifer is right in most disagreements, she makes sure the kids are lined up on her side of the fence. And they are on her side because Jason is unnecessarily strict with them. They naturally resent that, preferring Jennifer's more easygoing ways. The fighting, of course, has moved into the bedroom, and Jennifer hasn't enjoyed their sexual expression for months. Oh, sure, Jason comes over now and then, but it's not fun anymore.

In one fell swoop, Jason and Jennifer illustrate what we look for in family imbalances: chronic fighting, sexual dysfunction, factional alliances within the family ("them" against "us"), and problems with and about kids.

Emotional or Psychological Dysfunctions

Jocelyn, a former model, fought a chronic depression for three years. Her husband sympathized, but he couldn't really understand her attitude. After all, he wasn't depressed. Their marriage was fine, their economic situation stable, the in-laws a thousand miles away. Obviously, he pointed out, it was her problem. Only when he entered into counsel with her and changed some basic attitudes and behaviors did her problem disappear.

Any emotional or psychological difficulty in one marital partner will invariably influence, and be influenced by, the other partner. Always.

Other similar symptoms we look for are anxiety, chemical dependence and addictions, and driving compulsions such as extreme perfectionism, workaholism, spendaholism, and such. Threats of suicide obviously raise red flags.

WHAT IS YOUR MARRIAGE
TRYING TO TELL YOU?

All these symptoms are merely the surface fluff. Their presence in your marriage, and their presence in the couples we counsel, say that something far deeper is going on. In this book we want to plumb the depths of problems, rather than bandage the surfaces. These depths, the inner workings of marriage, can be compared to the dynamics of a softball game, believe it or not, which are not all that different from the dynamics of marriage.

The Dynamics of Marriage

The city league softball player steps up to the plate, shoulders his bat, and watches intently. Here comes the pitch. . . .

"It's a solid hit into deep right field!" the announcer screams exuberantly. The ball is still airborne as the player rounds first. It drops into tall grass—*very* deep right field—and a portly fielder scurries after it. The player passes third, homeward bound.

Wait! He failed to touch second! As his team groans in unison, he runs back to stomp second base. What would have been a home run ends up only a double, all because the runner failed to clear second base satisfactorily. Marriage is like that. We call the bases "passages."

When Doctors Newmans or Minirth or Hemfelt deal with a marital problem, they deal with three entities: the husband, the wife, and the marriage itself, as if the marriage were a living, breathing organism. We have found that if a marriage is not growing, it's dying, just as any living organism. When a marriage gets hung up in a passage, it ceases growing. Growth is, therefore, critical.

By definition, then, *passages are predictable and necessary stages, involving the physical, the emotional, and the spiritual.* Through them, partners journey toward the lifetime goal of growth as individuals and as a couple.

In our personal lives and in our professional practice, the six authors of this book have identified five distinct stages, passages through which marriage passes. The developmental stages through which a child passes from birth into adulthood are well known. Similarly, a marriage matures from developmental stage to stage—from passage to passage—according to the number of years it has existed. Remarriage may differ somewhat; because the partners have been married previously, they might telescope a passage into a briefer time or extend a passage beyond its normal life span.

The Passages of Marriage

Not counting courtship, which by definition is a passage of premarriage, we divide the lifetime of a married couple into five distinct units. Although some people hasten ahead of time into the next passage, or linger a little longer than average in one passage or another, in general, marriages hew pretty close to this outline. The passages are these:

- The First Passage—Young Love, the first two years
- The Second Passage—Realistic Love, the third through tenth year
- The Third Passage—Comfortable Love, the eleventh through the twenty-fifth year
- The Fourth Passage—Renewing Love, the twenty-sixth through the thirty-fifth year
- The Fifth Passage—Transcendent Love, thirty-six years and thereafter

As the marriage moves from one of these passages to another—from base to base toward home plate, if you will—it also moves through specific conditions common to the human race. Crisis and conflict, intimacy, forgiveness, children, and memories form some of them.

Each of the passages through which every married couple travel, like bases on a softball diamond, must be appropriately dealt with if the next one is to count. And the tasks that accompany these passages must be completed before the next tasks commence. By tasks we mean attitude changes one must make and jobs one must complete in order to maintain an intimate marital relationship.

Should a runner skip over a base, inadvertently or on purpose, dire problems result. Should a runner get stuck on one base, the only way he can leave is by walking away scoreless. That's infinitely less satisfying than making it to home plate, for the aim of the game from the very beginning is to make it home.

Carl and Bess Warden, married forty-eight years, were making it home. As painful as eventual separation and death would be, the Wardens both would know the peace and satisfaction of being able to say, "We did it."

One of every two married couples will never know that satisfaction.

During their long life together, Carl and Bess Warden did not talk to marriage counselors or become involved in marriage therapy of any sort, though counsel might have helped them navigate the difficult passages more easily. Yet Carl and Bess did not simply muddle through. They worked diligently at their marriage, and to the very end enjoyed the fruits of a growing, timeless, abiding love.

You may be thinking, "But my marriage is so different; nobody has a husband like Joe (or a wife like Janet)."

Don't be so sure.

WHAT IF MY MARRIAGE DOESN'T FIT THE PATTERN?

Remember the age-guessing booth at fairs and carnivals long past? A rather rough-looking man with a four-day stubble would offer to guess your age within three years. If he guessed, he won and you paid him. If he missed, you won and he paid you. And he almost always won. Why? Because age makes itself known in certain ways, and the trained eye can see those ways in every person.

A marriage also ages in certain ways regardless of the persons involved, regardless of the circumstances. The same patterns prevail even though yours may be a most unusual union. In fact, what is "normal"?

Mary Alice and Frank Minirth know their marriage could probably never be considered normal. "When we married, we were both in school," Mary Alice explains. "Frank, in medical school, studied day and night. I had two years yet to complete my degree, so I was studying too. It wasn't a normal start-a-family situation.

"My first job was as a teacher in inner-city Little Rock. Definitely not normal! Frank worked a twenty-five-hour day completing his internship. Then, getting a practice started—not normal. Possibly, there's no such thing as a normal marriage."

Your own situation may be less stressful than the Minirths', or more. You may be fishing off the Alaskan coast or working in a bank in Topeka. What's normal?

The passages themselves are the norm, the common denominators of any marriage. They are universal. They form the skeleton upon which problems and pleasures attach.

Each of the authors of this book is at a different passage: Brian and Debi Newman in the Second Passage, Robert and Susan Hemfelt just approaching the Third Passage, and Frank and Mary Alice Minirth in the Fourth. All six of us will give you our personal expertise and experiences as well as our professional insights. In addition to counseling couples and leading marriage enrichment seminars, psychotherapists Brian and Debi put their advanced degrees to work on the staff of the Minirth-Meier Clinic. Dr. Minirth, psychiatrist and a cofounder of the clinic, takes special interest in marriage and family dynamics. Dr. Robert Hemfelt, psychologist, is well known and respected as a leader in the study of codependency and multigenerational issues.

If you've been a married couple for many years, we want to help you examine yourself and your marriage. Have you successfully completed the passages so far? Is there something you ought to back up and re-cover? Would your happiness and contentment be fuller if you did so? Our years of counseling tell us yes.

If your first marriage ended in divorce, do you now see the underlying reasons why it failed? At the bottom of most divorces, trouble came when one or both partners got hung up in a passage and failed to complete its tasks.

This book is meant to be read over and over again. If you are reading this book early in your marriage, we invite you to reread pertinent sections as you pass through those particular passages. Particularly in later years, points that escaped you will become clear. This book is meant to help over the long haul.

If you are reading this book at a later passage in your marriage, we advise you to read through the early passages. We have counseled couples whose marriages were in the Third and Fourth Passages, but their relationship was actually stuck in one of the tasks of Passage One or Two. In counseling we walk them back through these earlier passages so they can examine their marriage history. Then we show them how to complete these earlier tasks by rewriting their marriage contracts.

If you know chess or backgammon, you recognize that the strategy changes as the game proceeds. Your goals at the beginning of play are not the same as those at the end. It's that way with marriage too. The original contract ceases to serve and must be rewritten. We'll discuss how to do that so your marriage will stay on a solid foundation.

We will also examine closely the role prior generations play in your marriage now. Yes, even grandparents dead and buried can be shaping your marriage. Very rarely do counselors and theorists consider the multigenerational impact of victories and defeats in prior generations. We shall do so and show you how to assess the influence of the past in your present situation.

In Parts 2, 3, 4, 5, and 6, we will examine each passage in detail. We'll see just how every marriage changes shape with time. We will help you know where you fit and how far through these stages you've progressed.

We will suggest ways to avoid fruitless friction and damaging conflict, and even how to turn conflict into a positive experience. Then, we will look at the tremendous payoff a good marriage returns.

Let's begin at the beginning with Young Love, the passage so often lauded by prose and poetry.

PART
TWO

The First Passage:
Young Love,
the First Two Years

2

CAN TWO INDEPENDENT PERSONS BECOME ONE UNIT?

You've seen it in encyclopedias, if not in actual use. It looks like a kind of walking stick, something a proper gentleman would take out on a stroll through the park. When the gentleman wishes to sit down he unfolds the top of his walking stick into a seat of sorts and there perches, his weight on the single-legged stool and both heels firmly pressed into the ground. It looks dreadfully uncomfortable, but actually, it's not bad.

Geometry buffs understand why a stool sits best on three legs; three points define a plane. They also define a stable marriage. A four-legged stool will wobble if all four legs are not exactly even and sitting on a flat surface. A one- or two-legged stool cannot stand alone. But you can perch a three-legged stool on uneven ground and sit securely. You can tip a three-legged stool forward while you're milking, the better to manage a bored cow who's finished eating. A three-legged stool adapts solidly to any situation.

Every marriage exists as a three-legged stool. One leg is the husband; another is the wife. The third leg changes through time; it might be the kids, or the job, or buying and furnishing a home, or, as in Annie Warden's case, arranging a perfect wedding. That third leg always gets kicked out. The kids leave home. Retirement ends the job. Annie's daughter's wedding became history. Suddenly the stool's remaining two legs only have each other. That prospect terrified Annie, you remember, as it does many middle-aged couples.

"I remember," one of our clients recalled, "the night before our youngest child went to college. I sat on the sofa looking across the room at my husband in his recliner, and I thought to myself, *What in heaven's name will we ever talk about when the kids are gone? Do we have anything in common besides them?*

Right in the beginning, as in the Fourth Passage of marriage, the stool is two-legged, and therefore unstable. The happy newlyweds are certain that in each other their lives are complete. They don't think they need a third leg. Their lives don't have room for one. As a result, the marriage bond at first is extremely fragile and easily hurt, as are the marriage partners.

THE FIRST TASK: MOLD INTO ONE FAMILY

The first task newlyweds must accomplish if they are to complete the First Passage—to mold two absolutely different, independent persons into one unit—won't come easily. It didn't come easily for Carl and Bess Warden two generations ago, or for Annie and Rob. Beth Anne and Alan will also find some rough sledding.

Unity vs. Individuality

A couple of days after Beth Anne and Alan returned from their honeymoon, they came over to Bess and Carl Warden's to pick up some spare furniture.

Carl and Alan talked a while of occupations and former occupations. "I don't know," Alan said, "if Beth Anne ever mentioned I used to break horses."

"Nope." Carl Warden smiled. "But I figured there had to be some reason you wore boots to your reception."

"I was gonna wear them to the wedding, but Annie blew the whistle."

"I'd guess breaking horses is pretty rewarding," Carl mused. "You're doing something productive, and no two situations are alike. So you have to be creative in how you deal with them."

"That's it exactly. The easiest job is to take a two-year-old filly or colt and teach it the bare essentials. Then you hand it over, green broke, to a professional trainer who teaches it a specialty, like barrel racing, cutting, or maybe just pleasure riding. I do that myself sometimes, but it takes a lot of work."

"What's the hardest job?"

"Breaking a team to harness." Alan sipped lemonade. His voice told Carl that here was his first love—after Beth Anne, of course. "Now take your average Belgian or shire. Each horse weighs about an even ton. Tie two of 'em close together. Two tons of horse wouldn't be so bad if they weren't operated by two separate brains. Horses have personalities and likes and dislikes just the same as people do. If you get two horses that don't particularly like each other, or two horses that think along different lines, it takes about half of forever to work them into a well-matched team. And you never do get two that think alike."

Carl nodded sagely. "You know, Alan, you're talking as much about marriage as teams of horses."

Take two headstrong individuals and forge them into a unit without sacrificing their individuality. What a formidable task! To get through the passage of Young Love with flying colors, you, as well as every other newlywed, have to master this task. Several things help in completing it.

On the Plus Side . . .

A powerful tool comes built into this task of Young Love: excitement and enthusiasm. Raw, exuberant energy. Louie Ajanian married Margaret Holtz late in life. Louie is fifty-eight and Marj fifty-four. Louie, widowed three years before he met Marj, was a veteran of thirty-four years of marriage. Because Marj's first husband deserted her eight years into their union, she developed a strongly independent personality. She had to, with four kids to raise. Regarding their attitudes toward marriage, Louie and Marj are poles apart. And yet, both are just as excited about their new union as are Beth Anne and Alan.

On the Other Hand . . .

One thing seriously hinders the move to unity: the possibility of breakage.

"Breakage?" exclaims the new couple. "What could break? We're young and indestructible and in love."

Regardless of what the couple think (or imagine), their intimacy in the beginning is superficial. True intimacy grows only as a couple get to know each other better. Persons in a new relationship have not had enough chronological time to do that in depth. This is true no matter what the actual age of the persons involved. Teenagers and seventy year olds suffer equally. They feel compelled to walk on eggs, as it were, when dealing with each other. "Will this upset her?" "How will I tell him about _____?"

Alan explained this about breaking a team of horses to harness: "The only way you get a horse team used to being driven together is by harnessing them up and working them. A large part of training is just getting out and driving them." A new couple, regardless of chronological age, has simply not logged enough time in harness to develop deep intimacy.

Often a new couple inadvertently strain their fragile intimacy by loading it with burdens it cannot carry. "This is the intimate relationship that will solve all my other relationship problems from the past. I will finally receive what I need." Friction with parents, failed prior relationships, perhaps even failed marriage—all melt away in the brilliant heat of this new and encompassing love.

Julia Karris, Beth Anne's friend who was so unlucky in love, unconsciously put that kind of weight on her marriage to Jerry Karris. She told us, "Rick Astin, my first husband, is a charmer. Oh, what a charmer! He's really good-looking. In fact, our son is going to grow up looking a lot like him. Rick has this mellow baritone voice that could coax the shell off a coconut. So persuasive. And he's got a bottomless supply of self-confidence. He tells you something and you just know he's going to deliver. He doesn't, but he's such a con artist you don't realize he's ripping you off."

"Ripping you off?" we asked. "You mean emotionally?"

"Emotionally, financially, every which way. He takes. He soaks up. And he goes out looking for more. He never gives."

"And you married Jerry because he's a giver."

"Yeah. After all those empty years with Rick, I deserve to get a little back."

We learned also that Julia's parents, wrapped tightly in their respective career ambitions, had each assumed the other was providing Julia's nurturing. She could not remember a single instance when she sat on a parent's lap to have a story read. She does, however, remember her children's book-plus-cassette tape sets, nearly a hundred of them. Her tiny little tape player read to her as she turned the pages. By talking about her childhood extensively, we led Julia to see that here was another love hunger, another lack, she was expecting Jerry to fill. The past is much too onerous a burden for one relationship to endure, so the couple must deal with some of those time-release capsules we mentioned in Chapter 1.

Putting Original Family Patterns Behind

Pulling up roots exists in another dimension. The bride and groom have successfully left home. They're on their own. But the home has not left them.

The old patterns from home color nearly everything in the new marriage. Do you open gifts on Christmas Eve or Christmas morning? Do you make your bed immediately upon rising or when you go through the house tidying up? Which is right? The way you did it when you were growing up is right, of course. Any other way, though not exactly wrong, isn't right either.

Obvious examples such as those above seem overly simplistic, but far more subtle "rights" and "not rights" color our day-to-day living. What's more damaging, they color a mate's perception of the spouse. We find in counsel that "what's right" often forms the basis of habits the mate considers annoying:

- "Her table manners are atrocious. Elbows on the table, using her knife with her left hand. . . ."
- "He leaves the cap off the toothpaste tube. That drives me right out of my tree."

To these complaints the mate usually responds, "What's the big deal? You'd think I was robbing a bank!"

Can you see the subtle traps? More importantly, do you see this sort of thing in your own marriage (or, if you are divorced, your former marriage)? How much of your mate's petty annoyances are founded on the way *you* were raised? The question is worth considering in depth and at leisure. You can "cure" a mate's annoying habits by either changing the habits or changing your annoyance. Identifying the source of the annoyance often ameliorates it.

Debi Newman recalls a rocky bump in her union with Brian. "From an early age Brian did a lot of the cooking and grocery shopping. Even cleaning. He's very good at what you normally associate as a housewife's chores. In my house, Mom did most of that and she didn't need any help.

"When I was single, if lettuce was on the grocery list, I'd grab a head of lettuce. They all looked alike to me. After we married, Brian and I would push the grocery cart down the aisle together, very romantic, shopping. I'd toss a head of lettuce into the basket. He'd take my choice out of the cart, put it back, and choose another.

"I found that terribly threatening. Brian, the husband, was better at a job that was traditionally supposed to be mine, and he knew it. He really did pick the best lettuce.

"It took me a long time to realize, and then to accept, that the roles tradition assigns to a marriage are nothing more than guidelines. My mom did all the shopping in our home. Brian's family of origin was much different, giving him a much different body of experience from mine. He was reflecting his background just as my attitudes reflected mine. It's healthy,"

Debi grins. "We eat better lettuce. But it's also healthy in that we can appreciate each other's unique gifts better now. From that original bump to my ego has come increased intimacy."

Patterns from your childhood also influence major decisions, such as household financial matters.

THE MONEY PIT

For example, who will handle the finances in the new family? Julia Karris talked about her first marriage. "My mom balanced the checkbook, paid the bills, all that stuff. Dad said if she was willing to, he didn't want to be bothered. She was good at it."

"Did it cause conflict?" we asked.

"Not really. They both preferred the arrangement. In Rick's family, his dad did all that. If his mom wanted to write a check, she had to ask for the checkbook and tell why she wanted it."

"And Rick wasn't about to give up the purse strings."

"You got it. In the first six months we overdrew the checking account five times, because we both carried checkbooks and never talked to each other before writing big checks. What a mess!"

Indeed, what a mess. Differing perspectives and lack of communication caused serious problems for Julia and her first husband. "This is how it's supposed to be done, because this is how a family always does it." Those perspectives came directly out of the family of origin. They always do.

Julia Karris correctly identified that her attitudes toward money came out of her family of origin, as did her first husband's and her present husband's—time-release capsules of the most invidious sort. You would probably agree that yours do also. But what to do about it?

We asked Julia to take a careful look at her parents' marriage through a series of inventories similar to the ones in *Getting Ready for Marriage*, a workbook written by Jerry Hardin and Dianne Sloan (Nashville: Thomas Nelson, 1991) to help couples lay the foundation for a happy, healthy marriage. Although this particular workbook is designed for couples contemplating marriage, the principles work well for use in marriage recovery and enrichment, especially during this initial Young Love passage.

The workbook contains several categories of statements. One series reflects the couple's parents' attitudes and habits. Julia and her present husband, Jerry, answered a series of true-false questions. Each question had two spaces for answers: You answer according to your own gut feelings, and you also answer as you believe your mate would.

To the statement, "I think credit card balances should be paid off each month," Julia answered "false" (meaning, she explained, that there are times you want or need something without ready cash) and she anticipated a "false" for Jerry too. After all, he often paid the card balance over a period of months.

After both Julia and Jerry completed the questions, we compared the answers. How much of each person's attitude was shared by the other? How well did each know the other's opinions?

Not always very well, in Julia and Jerry's case. Jerry wanted to pay off credit card balances each month. He couldn't always swing it, but paying off before interest accrued was his goal. It was important to him. That and similar questions revealed not only that Jerry and Julia had never shown each other their divergent views of money but also in what ways they diverged. It is one thing to know you disagree with your spouse; it is much more helpful to know exactly where and how much you disagree.

How about You?

How about you and your spouse? Even if you are in the Second or Third Passage of marriage, you may be stuck in the area of family finances. This excerpt from *Getting Ready for Marriage* might reveal some ghosts from your or your spouse's past. Check the statements that apply to you:

_____"My parents were extremely cautious about going into debt."

_____"In my family we seldom used the air conditioner at home so we could save money."

_____"My parents frequently fought over how to spend their money."

_____"Having the latest styles of clothing was very important in my family."

_____"My father usually left a good tip for the waitress/waiter in a restaurant."

_____"My mother would give us money and say, 'Now don't tell your father.' "[1]

A second series of questions, then, reflects each of the couple's present attitudes:

_____"It is important to me that we have a budget and try to live within it."

_____"I think we should shop for lower prices whenever possible."

_____ "It would upset me to find out my marriage partner had money or debts I didn't know about."

_____ "I am unconcerned about money and tend not to worry about financial matters."

_____ "I want us and our children to have the latest fashions if we can afford them."

_____ "I think it is okay to ask our parents for financial help."[2]

Can you see any similarity between your answers to the first six statements and your answers to the second set? Are some of these financial matters causing any tension between you and your spouse?

With this knowledge, the couple can now sit down and answer a third group of questions together, such as "Who will manage our money?" Neither Jerry nor Julia had really thought about that, each assuming the other would not see it as a divisive issue. "How many credit cards are *too* many?" was another question. Julia didn't think you could have too many.

"What about spending for recreational activities?" Julia rated the need and pleasure of the moment most highly; Jerry hoarded for the future. "This is the future!" Julia protested. "Tell me that when you're sixty-five," Jerry retorted. The purpose of this bank of questions is to bring the couple together into a shared attitude toward finances.

Julia and Jerry's attitudes were actually not all that wildly divergent; the differences were subtle, wedging between them quietly, causing discord on some occasions but not others. Probing questions and careful attention to the answers revealed the differences so that they could be examined in the clear light of day. Only when Julia and Jerry both knew where the differences lurked could they hope to talk them through and resolve them.

ATTITUDE CHECK

If you are in this passage you might want to review your own attitude toward finances as a couple. Consider these questions together:

1. "Will we both work after children are born?"
   _____ yes _____ no
2. "Should we have separate bank accounts?" _____ yes _____ no
3. "Should we have separate savings accounts?"
   _____ yes _____ no
4. "Should we have insurance—life, medical, car, household?"
   _____ yes _____ no

"How much insurance do we need?"

5. "How many credit cards are *too* many?" _____³

Finally we often suggest that a couple enter into a financial covenant with one another, just as we did with Jerry and Julia, even though they may be in a later passage of marriage. Are you and your spouse willing to establish a covenant, which will help eliminate any ghosts from your past? Consider a verbal or written agreement like the one below:

_____"I agree that money will never be more important than our relationship."
_____"I agree to let you know if I think that either of us is becoming irresponsible about financial matters."
_____"I agree to stay within the budget we plan together."
_____"I agree that from our wedding on, money is ours and the problems and joys it brings are also ours to share."
_____"I agree that credit cards can be a major problem, and I'll always talk to you before making a purchase over $_____."
_____"I agree to work with you until we agree on how to pay, and who will pay, the bills in our marriage."[4]

This type of agreement between you and your spouse will help you to eliminate financial ghosts from your past. We often suggest that a couple explore their family ties in many other areas, such as communication, attitudes, and religion. If your exploration of family finances has revealed some ghosts from your past, you might want to work through *Getting Ready for Marriage*. This type of introspection is the first step toward completing the first task of this passage. Two other steps are necessary to mold you into one family unit: saying good-bye to any pain from your childhood and shifting your priorities to your new family.

SAYING GOOD-BYE

Part of pulling up those old family roots is saying good-bye to the pain of your childhood.

Pain from Your Childhood Family

Books, such as *Love Is a Choice: Recovery for Codependent Relationships* (Nashville: Thomas Nelson, 1989), deal at length with a curious phenomenon Minirth-Meier counselors see constantly. That is, the more dysfunctional and unsatisfying a child's family of origin has been, the harder it is for the child to leave it. Logic suggests that if the original family failed to serve that person's needs, leaving home is the solution. But human beings do not operate on logic. More than 80 percent of our decisions are made below the conscious level, in the deep recesses of thought and sub-thought where logic never goes.

Julia Karris's mother worked ten-hour days advancing herself as a mid-level manager in a bank before coming home to the housework. Julia's father put in his eight-hour shift, then spent another three or four hours taking hands-on computer courses at the local technical school. After all, his wife was still at work anyway, so why rush home?

For all practical purposes, abandoned, Julia couldn't wait to get out of the house and on her own. Yet, once married, she called Mom and Dad three and four times a week. She dragged Rick and the kids over to the house every Sunday afternoon. In short, she kept her roots deeply ensnared in her family of origin, seeking nourishment that never had been and was never going to be.

Julia had been out of her parents' house long before she met Rick. She had made her own living, having cut economic ties with her parents. Yet emotionally, she was still her parents' little girl, still under the family-of-origin roof.

We frequently find adult children who, like Julia, have remained over-involved with their parents. Frequently, too, the parents become so enmeshed in their children that they are loathe to give them up. Such was the case of a newlywed named Marla. Her father died when she was nine. As she matured, an only child, she and her mother descended into a frenetic love-hate relationship.

Marla married to get away, but not very far away. She and her husband lived across town. Marla's mother felt free to pop in on them any time, for any reason, or for no reason at all. "Oh, don't bother," she would say as she barged in. "It's only me." Unfortunately, Marla had become so codependently involved with Mom that she didn't realize how badly Mom was overstepping and destroying their personal boundaries.

Wearied beyond patience by this invasion of his privacy, her husband found a job in Minneapolis and summarily carted Marla off a thousand miles from her mommy. Six months later the widow retired. To Minnesota.

Few young adults are so unhealthily enmeshed with parents, but even in the most benign of relationships, friction sparks. Usually the problems, however mild, start in courtship. Conflicts erupt in wedding preparations. What is actually happening is that daughter is pulling away from mother, son is breaking out from under his parents' roof and aegis. It is a healthy and temporary friction, unavoidable, necessary. Shifting from the old, familiar family to a new and untried family causes a wrenching jolt. As earthquakes dissipate the energy of shifting continents, so tensions and flare-ups ease the shift to the sometimes frightening new lifestyle.

Normally, the difficulty will be fleeting. Annie smiled grimly. "Beth Anne was a real pill her senior year of high school. Threatened to leave home early, chafed against every rule we had. She was out on her own less than a year when the phone calls and letters got more frequent. She started coming home from college some weekends . . . and bringing her laundry, of course. I thought for a while, around graduation, that we had lost her. But she came back, and our relationship is warmer than ever."

SHIFTING TO THE NEW FAMILY

Marla in Minnesota had to become a tightrope walker. You've seen the high-wire balancing acts at the circus. Some of them feature a comic performer, a person who, although highly skilled, pretends to be a novice. As he steps out onto the wire he wobbles crazily; the crowd giggles. He "falls", bouncing on the wire; the crowd gasps. He extends his arms and waves them up and down, lurching back and forth. The crowd waits for the inevitable fall.

The audience understands this parody of proper balance because a novice would do exactly those things—wobble precariously, flail wildly, fail to find the center of balance, move in fits and jerks rather than smoothly. Novices in marriage also do those things as they seek a comfortable balance between all their new and altered relationships.

In shifting to their new family and in putting original family patterns behind, the couple in the first flush of young love must completely reshape all their other relationships. Finding the new balance point is inevitably rocky. You've never seen such wild flailing and tilting! They have to bring new balance to . . .

Relationships with the Family of Origin

A traditional Navajo husband will never look at his mother-in-law or speak to her. And think of all those stale Henny Youngman mother-in-law jokes. In-law conflicts and adjustments, though, are far more delicate, and can be far more rewarding, than the jokes and customs suggest.

Here you are in a whole new family, all of whose members know your spouse better than you do. They fit together like an old shoe; you feel like a cellist in a drum and bugle corps. There is no formula for adjusting to the in-laws. Each case is individual, each situation unique in its way. That makes finding balance all the harder. The balance becomes nearly impossible until both newlyweds successfully pull up roots from the old home.

To all these tugs between the couple and the in-laws, you can add the new relationship with siblings. Brothers and sisters are no longer the main same-generation support people. And yet, their roles, though changed drastically, should not diminish. More balancing.

Then there are the many other relationships that you had before you were married; they, too, will change.

Relationships with Single Friends

She still wants to run around with her single girlfriends, shopping, perhaps, or just doing what they used to do together, and for the best of reasons: These are her friends. He yearns for his boys' night out with the old, familiar buddies, where guys can be themselves in all their take-me-as-I-am glory.

And how about a foursome or party? It used to be, the guests had to be compatible with only the host or hostess. Now the guests have to be compatible with the couple. In a foursome, he and she both have to mesh satisfactorily with she and he. It isn't easy. Finding other couples who fit well as couples becomes quite a complex process, with lots of false starts and disappointments.

Speaking of singles, both partners must say good-bye to past romantic relationships and dreams. The infamous bachelor party symbolizes the joking but not-so-joking "This is your last fling, pal" end of an era. Raucous as such parties are, they are sad too. The groom-to-be rightfully grieves his loss of the past even as he rejoices in the many advantages his future promises.

The balance is never perfect. Personalities clash. The newlyweds find themselves embroiled in far more than just love spats. The second task of the Young Love passage is to deal with the inevitable conflict that's part of any relationship.

3

WHO'S IN
CONTROL?

*C*arl Warden sat on neighbor Bert's front porch as Bert boasted, "Meg and I had a perfect marriage. We never fought."

"Wish I could say that," Carl sniffed. "Bess and I, we've had some go-rounds, let me tell you! We keep it honest, though, and it all worked out."

"Not us, no sir." Bert's rocking chair squeaked with every oscillation. "Meg was the proper wife of Scripture. Submissive."

Carl thought about that a few minutes and shook his head. "Bess has a mind of her own, and when she thinks I'm wrong, she doesn't hesitate a bit to point it out. I would've made some major mistakes if Bess weren't as strong as she is." Carl didn't say any more, but he reflected, *God's blessing to me that she doesn't let herself be a doormat.* And the recollections of Bess's solid, stubborn love nearly brought tears to his eyes.

THE SECOND TASK: OVERCOME THE TENDENCY TO JOCKEY FOR CONTROL

The second task is one which will resurface off and on throughout all the passages of marriage. Each spouse will ask, "Who's in control here?" as different situations arise, from the choice of a restaurant for a Friday night date to the purchase of a new home. The source of conflict will change, as will the couple's methods of responding to it, but conflict itself is present in all relationships.

Unfortunately, too many couples think, "We must squelch conflict, lest it damage this relationship." The couple instinctively know the relationship is untested and unhardened. Yet here's an equation we've learned to be valid:

$$1 \text{ person} + 1 \text{ person} = \text{conflict.}$$

Its corollary:

$$1 \text{ person-in-love} + 1 \text{ person-in-love} = \text{conflict anyway.}$$

Conflict is inevitable, no matter what the ages or backgrounds. The new couple are not far enough into their relationship to know that conflict, because it is inevitable, is nothing more than a normal part of marriage. How the couple deal with that conflict, however, can make or break the union. Often their ability to handle conflict is stifled by their fragile egos and dreams.

Fragile Egos

If the couple as well as the relationship are young in years, they don't know themselves well yet. An older couple such as Louie and Marj Ajanian won't have such fragile egos. The sum of their years is more than a century; they know by now what they can do and who they are.

Even the well-established ego gets bruised at the beginning of a marital relationship.

Both parties are equally affected, of course. The man, too, enters marriage with a lot of insecurities. "Will she get tired of me? Continue to love me? Can I satisfy her—and keep on satisfying her? Can I handle this new responsibility? Especially, can I provide financially for her?"

One of our clients voiced those insecurities: "I felt vulnerable. If I flubbed up, if I didn't do everything expected of a man, my ego would really take a beating. I wanted to be the dream husband, the Clark Gable of married men."

Fragile Dreams

Not even Clark Gable the actual man could equal Clark Gable the dream image. No matter how well the partners think they know each other, when courtship becomes marriage, some disillusionment sets in.

Debi Newman explains it from experience. "Brian was so romantic! In July, six months before our wedding, he sent me six red roses. August, five months before the wedding, five roses. And so on until one rose a month before. January when we got married, nothing. And for the next three years I got nothing.

"Brian was still very nice and thoughtful toward all the other people in his life. I felt sort of left out. We've each given on this issue; he's more attentive, and I've learned to be content in his love, without a rose a month."

Not just expectations transfer from courtship into marriage. So does every unresolved issue. Conflicts the couple thought would disappear, little things in their engagement, blossom into big things in the marriage.

ATTITUDE ADJUSTMENT IN CONFLICT

The couple in the throes of Young Love, not yet fully comfortable with each other, will instinctively guard what they say and do. They know (although they might not articulate that knowledge) that the greater the openness, the greater the potential for conflict. What they may not realize is, the greater the openness, the greater the potential for improved intimacy.

In forty-three years of marriage, Bert and Meg never achieved anything near deep intimacy. Although Bert would tell you quite truthfully that he loved his Meg, he could not tell you what Meg thought, how she responded to a situation ("Oh, I don't know, I guess she just sort of accepted it"), what she felt or when ("Frankly, she got to be something of a cold fish after a while"), or whether she even had any hopes and dreams ("Never mentioned them, so I guess she didn't have any"). And yet, every human being not only possesses a wonderful capacity for deep intimacy, every person craves it. Intimacy feeds happiness and contentment. We were made for it.

When Carl said he and Bess "kept it honest," he referred to their mutual desire to avoid dirty fighting. Conflict approached wrongly causes not intimacy but pain and alienation. Separation. It's a lady-and-the-tiger situation. In a famous short story, a man must choose between two doors. If he opens the one, a willing and lovely lady awaits him. Behind the other door waits a hungry tiger. The story is an allegory of life, and it also typifies conflict. Behind one door, intimacy. Behind the other, separation. But there's an infinite difference here. The man could not know in advance which door hid what. You can.

Causes and Symptoms

Boy, do you feel rotten! Sneezing, a runny nose sore from so much blowing, no energy, aching all over. . . . You take cold medicine, but unlike many medicines, cold medicine does nothing to cure the cold. All the king's horses and all the king's men have not been able to cure the common cold. The medicine alleviates the symptoms somewhat—the nose does not run so fast and so far, the sneezing lessens, the aches abate. But the causative agent, the cold virus, follows its merry course unhindered.

The germs cause the symptoms. Instead of that nasty cold, should you contract one of certain treatable kinds of pneumonia, the appropriate antibiotics will stop the cause—the pneumococcus germs—and thereby the symptoms as well.

Married couples assume that conflict in their union causes separation. Actually, conflict is usually not a cause; it's a symptom. The wedge has already been driven in somewhere, somehow, and conflict has resulted. We've learned that if you can find and deal with the issue causing separation—the germs, by analogy—the conflict, the symptom, takes care of itself.

Not always, though, can you do that. Sometimes you can merely treat the symptoms. However, if you handle the conflict well, improved intimacy and contentment result, and the cause emerges, to be healed.

"Aha!" you say. "So if I let 'er rip and encourage conflict, my marriage will grow stronger. Good! I love to argue."

That's not what we're saying at all! We're saying that you can turn the friction inevitable in any honest union into an asset. Food is a good illustration. We must have it; eat or die. And yet, used wrongly, food becomes the center of all sorts of problems, from anorexia to obesity.

As the marriage matures, moving from passage to passage, the couple's attitudes toward conflict will change. The symptoms—the conflicts themselves—will change somewhat. So, therefore, will the means of dealing with them.

Frank Minirth puts it this way: "Part of the idealism in the first stage is, 'We're not supposed to be fighting.' I was small as a child, and very lonely growing up. I met Mary Alice, and she was the most beautiful thing. She looked just like Snow White. How can you fight with Snow White?

"Also, fighting is a fearful thing. You just know it will destroy that fragile relationship. At first we didn't know how to handle it. We learned together how to argue without hurting each other, to grieve the past, and take up the new."

THE RESOLUTION

Although the couple's attitude toward conflict matures and changes, the three ways to handle disagreement remain the same: a) compromise, b) agreement to disagree, and c) love gift.

Compromise

Everyone gives in a little. That's what Frank and Mary Alice Minirth decided to do when they purchased a vacation home. A friend of the Minirths' tells about their compromise: "Frank is a country boy. He likes animals; he likes rural living. Mary Alice is strictly a city girl. They have a property in rural Arkansas—I mean, *very* rural Arkansas. Cabins, horses, wild land. As you approach, you see no power poles, no hints of modern conveniences at all. It looks like a hundred and fifty years ago. But inside the cabins are up-to-the-minute kitchen appliances, right down to the dishwasher and microwave. The outside is Frank's concept of country living; the inside is Mary Alice's. It's a lovely compromise and works beautifully for both of them."

Agreement to Disagree

Early in their marriage the Newmans agreed to disagree. Brian remembers one incident clearly: "Debi was making pancakes for breakfast, shortly after we married. She tossed the flour into the blender, and then an egg and some milk. That just floored me! That's not the way you do it. You mix the dry ingredients thoroughly and separately. You blend the egg into the milk. Then you slowly add the dry ingredients to the egg-and-milk until you get a perfect batter."

Debi adds: "I could have backed off and done it his way, but the potential was there for me to bury my anger—to be resentful. That wouldn't have done either one of us any good. I stuck with my way. We didn't resolve it by compromise or giving in. We simply agreed to disagree."

Brian continues: "Her pancakes turned out just fine. You know, though, a strongly controlling man might not be able to eat them when they weren't made the way he thought was 'right.'"

The symptom in that case was a disagreement over method. The cause was, again, a family-of-origin habit. Brian grew up with a certain concept of what's "right." Debi didn't mind a bit taking shortcuts.

Debi explains: "When one spouse is very controlling, it's important that the other not constantly cave in just to avoid conflict. That's an open door to unhealthy polarization. The controlling spouse becomes all the more controlling, and the other begins to lose identity and self-esteem. The situation—giving in, I mean—certainly generates anger, and that's not good for either the spouses or the marriage."

Does that mean one should never give in? Not at all!

Love Gift

A love gift is, essentially, exactly that: giving in. A love gift says, "For whatever reason, I'm giving on this issue. I may feel as strongly as you do, but I'm willing to give."

Obviously, a love gift must be given without anger or it will not be a healthy response.

Debi Newman recalls this illustration: "A situation came up when we were engaged that nearly wrecked us before we even married. I wanted to apply for a job as secretary. Brian worked as a janitor in the same building. He saw how the men treated the position of secretary—their attitude—and the way they flirted with the secretaries. He felt extremely threatened and insecure, and he thought a couple just starting out shouldn't be in a threatening position of that sort. I wanted the security of a steady job, and didn't feel I had many options.

"For a while we thought it really was the end of the relationship. Compromise wasn't possible; either I took the job or I didn't. I finally made the decision to give in on this issue. I didn't understand everything Brian was feeling; I definitely didn't agree with him, but I chose not to apply for the job out of love for him.

"God worked in all of this. He helped us with the anger and forgiveness, and I got an even better job. Surviving that crisis put us on a much deeper level of intimacy."

None of these three is appropriate to every situation. Sometimes, for example, compromise is wisest; at other times it's not possible. Should a couple become locked into one of these three approaches to the exclusion of the other two, problems follow.

Carl's friends Bert and Meg illustrate this. Meg gave in every time. And that's where a love gift became, with time, a cop-out, no longer either love or a gift.

THE NUTS AND BOLTS
OF CONFLICT RESOLUTION

There is no cookbook method to deal with conflict, and for good reason: In the heat of disagreement, when your very self is on the line, you don't think of following rules. And if you do think of it, you don't want to anyway, lest by following the rules you lose.

There are, however, some guidelines to prevent conflict from causing separation.

As you consider those guidelines, use as a specific example the last conflict you suffered with your spouse. It needn't be a big one—maybe it was an argument over how you spend your time. Sometimes one spouse or the other acts as if he or she is still single. The person hasn't made changes in his or her relationship with single friends as we suggested in the last chapter. "You're not playing golf again with the guys this Saturday," the wife moans. "You played golf twice this week after work. We never spend any time together." And there begins an argument.

As we go along, apply the guidelines to the particular instance you select. You'll study who said precisely what (it's amazing how often statements are misheard and misread), what the underlying feelings and needs are, what went wrong and how you might handle the situation better when it pops up again. Because most conflicts are born of the same problems, they do keep popping up, again and again.

Know Thyself

First, understand and be aware of what's going on inside yourself. Divide a piece of paper in half vertically. On one side list the things you say out loud, such as:

"I see you less now than I did when we were dating."
"Who's more important to you, the guys or me?"
"I don't matter to you; you don't really love me."

On the other side of the paper list the thoughts you are thinking:

He wishes he wasn't married.
He'd rather be playing golf with the boys than spending time with me.
I feel lonely (abandoned).
I have no control over this situation.

Often you won't admit these thoughts, but you know they are there and now's the time to own up to these feelings.

Now think about why you might have felt that way and complete the following statements. For example, at a pause in a wild argument, when vitriol had reached an emotional level, one of our clients suddenly sensed his old inadequacy fears kicking up. He was deeply, viscerally afraid of seeing himself as a loser. The self-revelation forced him to yield somewhat, simply to beat down that ogre from his past, inadequacy.

"I felt *(lonely)* _____ during this argument."

Can you remember the last time you felt that way? *(For instance, "I always felt lonely when my parents went on long business trips and left me at home." Or, "My father was a workaholic and he never spent much time with me.")*

"I felt this way when _____

_____."

Are these two situations similar? _____ yes _____ no
If so, how? *(For instance, the feeling is the same: "I feel as if I've been abandoned. Those feelings from childhood might be making me feel worse now.")*

_____

_____

You obtain insight into conflict in marriage through this type of introspection, through feedback from others, through willingness to grab hold of nuggets of truth others give you. You may have to wade through a lot of dross to find those nuggets. You don't have to buy it all, but do look for them. As you open yourself up to understanding, you set a precedent for how you'll resolve conflict.

Brian did that. "I told a friend about the pancake incident not long after it happened. 'Brian,' he said, 'that is an amoral issue. There is no right or wrong. Don't let amoral issues become bones of contention.' He said a lot of other things, too, but that stuck with me."

Think

Have you ever analyzed a television series episode? Try it sometime. You'll find an unvarying pattern. For example, there's the one-hour adventure story: In the first two minutes, a lot of attention-getting things happen. They want you to stay at that spot on your channel selector. The plot gets rolling in a hurry, drawing you into the story. The first commercial break happens at, literally, an odd moment. The second, though, will occur on the half hour. Just before this break, the hero will be in the utmost danger, the ultimate pits—whatever—for the producers want you involved enough that you won't switch channels during all those commercials. If there is any character development, it will happen during the third segment, "garbage time." After the third commercial break, just as it appears the villain might win, the action will lead to a flip-flop as the hero comes out on top, an exciting finish, and the wrap-up. Every time.

This is one of several reasons Americans no longer feel any strong need to think. Television, by rote formula, does all the work of thinking for us.

Some shows even do the philosophizing for us in the wrap-up. We need not bother to look for deeper meanings; they are clearly explained. Yet unless people are trained in the ability to look at options and to think, they can't resolve conflicts.

"Okay," you say, "so what's to think about?" For starters, think about what your spouse's position really is. Use debating skills. Anyone surviving a high school debating course knows that you must be able to debate either side of a question, if you're to present your own side effectively. You must know where the other side's strengths and weaknesses lie. Take a moment and mentally fill in these blanks:

"My spouse kept saying *("You don't appreciate all I do for you or how hard I work.")* _____
_____."

"His (her) position has some merit, in that *("He does work hard and some of the times he was playing golf he was with clients.")*
_____
_____."

"He (she) seemed to be feeling *(angry, afraid)* _____."

Often the husband realizes that the wife is right. He has been spending a lot of time playing golf. So he becomes defensive because he feels guilty. He is, in fact, having difficulty making the adjustment to a married relationship where he has to consider someone else's desires.

Finally, think about those time-release capsules. Could some other situation be feeding your husband's or wife's anger?

"I suspect that some of these feelings might have been prompted by something else besides our argument *(such as, a difficult situation at work or a domineering mother who tried to control every minute of his or her time)* _____
_____."

Frequently we are so busy formulating our own position and mentally framing the perfect riposte, we miss the other person's position completely. This type of introspection forces us to think also of just how our own side looks. (For instance, Charles Darwin, when making major decisions, would list all the pros and cons side by side. He used the method only to clarify his thoughts, and not as a guide, for although the cons far outweighed the pros, he boarded the *Beagle* anyway, and became one of the best-known figures in history.)

While you're enumerating various sides, study your own.
In your recent fight, for instance, what did you say more than
once? *("You don't really love me, and I'm not sure I even love you.")*

Do you really know that your husband or wife doesn't love you? Do
you have the power to read his or her mind? We always advise couples to
stick to the facts, not their assumptions, which might well be inaccurate.

Think about the second part of that statement now: "I'm not sure I
even love you."

How might that have been misconstrued? *("He or she might see those
words as rejection and a threat to our marriage.")*

Do you say these same things at other times when you and your
spouse fight? ____ yes ____ no

It's natural to throw grenades back and forth in an argument. If both
parties know themselves, however, they can call a halt to general accusations and talk about their true interior feelings. This will *never* happen if
you speak in absolutes:

"You *never* stay home with me."

"You would *always* prefer playing golf with the boys rather than
spending time with me."

Absolute statements usually guarantee defensiveness because they are
so overstated. A husband might play golf with the boys on Saturday and
once or twice during the week, but the other four nights he is at home with
his spouse.

We also advise couples to be wary of character assassinations. The wife
in this example might say, "You're a totally selfish person. You never think
of anyone but yourself."

We suggest that couples ask themselves an important question as they
are fighting: "How would you feel if your spouse said these things to you?"
If you can take a moment to do this, you will readily see that you were
caught in the trap of making absolute statements or dealing in character
assassination.

Evaluate your own need to control. At the heart of the golfing argument is that question, "Who's in control here? Who sets the schedule?
What time is mine? What time is yours? And what time is ours together?"

And much of each spouse's reaction is motivated by fear. It's scary to yield some control of your life to someone else. It's difficult to work out time-sharing in a marriage.

If you have by nature a strongly controlling personality, your potential for conflict is greater, for you feel the urge to control what you cannot control—your spouse's attitudes, feelings, and actions. We find this equally true for men and women.

And what about your husband's need for control? In the golfing example, the husband is probably feeling, "You're trying to control every part of my life." He's just as afraid as you are.

Finally keep a clear head about just how big this fight really is. Not all disagreements are created equal.

Susan Hemfelt recounts this from her past: "My parents disagreed in a civil manner in front of us kids, but it was never a strong fight. They drew the line between disagreement and a screaming mimi. Their philosophy was don't fight in front of the kids.

"Oh, we knew they disagreed sometimes. But we also knew growing up that they respected each other. They were united but not rigid about it. I mean, some things were privately negotiable. But they never dragged us kids into it."

If you were looking at that fight from the perspective of six months from now, would it rate as an enormous barrier or an insignificant pothole on the road to happiness?

Stick to the Basics

Think also about the basics. Vince Lombardi watched his Green Bay Packers lose several games and decided to go back to basics. He waved a pigskin aloft and announced, "This is a football."

Julia Karris wanted to buy her stepdaughter, Kinsley, the latest shoes for school. Jerry insisted that $69 was too much for a pair of shoes the fourteen-year-old was going to outgrow by Christmas.

Julia explained the prestige attached to that particular brand.

Jerry remained unimpressed. He lauded frugality.

So far, both were sticking to the basics.

Then Julia pointed out how much Jerry spent for fishing equipment. He countered with the amount of "free" time she gave the department store. She complained how stingy he was, and he fumed that she shared the same spendthrift ways that alienated him from his first wife. Basics had just gone out the window.

Caught in the middle, young Kinsley felt certain she was the cause of her parents' fight. She could not see, nor could they, that they had strayed from the basics. They were dragging in issues from the past, things which had nothing whatsoever to do with the wisdom of purchasing a pair of shoes.

When Carl and Bess "kept it honest" as they fought, Carl meant essentially that they thought about the basics. *They kept to the issue at hand.* If the price of a pair of shoes were at issue, they argued the cost and value of the shoes. And that brings up another key point Julia and Jerry were missing.

Keep Your *Self* Out of It

Keep out of it? But we're the ones fighting!

Issues and persons are two different things. *Argue over issues, but never allow your conflict to get personal.* As much as you can, keep emotions out of it. Given its own way, the need to win will gain full control of your emotions and rob your rational processes. Disagreement then becomes a brute dog-fight, invariably shredding love and egos. Dogs don't fight in support of ideas. They fight each other. A constant equation is

$$\text{Conflict} - \text{rational processes} = \text{explosion}.$$

Brian Newman says: "We see it constantly in couples we counsel. Once a conflict becomes emotional, reason goes out the door and the conflict is never going to be resolved. We help the couple keep it from becoming personal, by any of several ways."

Get Creative

Part of being creative about conflict is being able to see options. There is, for example, the obvious but rarely used option, to simply cool off a while.

Debi explains: "So very frequently when we talk to Christian couples, we hear the passage, 'Be angry, but do not sin; do not let the sun go down on your anger.' The man and woman interpret it that their anger has to be resolved quickly, and so they deny their anger. Or else, they take it to bed with them. Lights out may be the first time the couple is really together.

"We try to help them see that dealing with anger does not always mean getting rid of it or resolving it right away. That's simply not possible in every instance. By all means, address the anger before the sun goes down. But you might have to address it by agreeing not to deal with it now; you'll deal with it tomorrow. Then set a definite time tomorrow. You may not be able to sleep any better, but it gives you breathing space."

Frank Minirth agrees: "Don't lie in bed, tired and frustrated, and expect to hash it out, whatever it is. You don't have the ability to look at options then. To be creative in dealing with conflict, you must be fresh enough to think."

Breathing space. Time out. Most people need to dispel the physical rush with which anger and frustration can overload the rational circuits. Throw rocks, mow the lawn, do something physical to sap off the adrenaline that anger ignited. Indeed, you may have to postpone discussion more than once if the flame isn't banked right away.

Cooling off time is not wasted time. There are many helpful things a couple might want to do during such a time out.

Write your spouse a letter. Don't mail it. It serves its purpose just by being written. Flush it down the toilet with military honors.

Defuse the Situation

One couple hit upon a diversion by accident. In a particularly acrimonious set-to, the bride of seven months wailed, "All I know how to do is love!" Now one or the other will pop that quote into the middle of an argument and they both end up giggling. Situation defused.

Another couple take their clothes off if argument rains hard and heavy. It is very difficult to argue angrily in the nude. The sheer incongruity of the situation works against anger.

Reflect now on that fight we've been picking apart in this section. Should something have been done to prevent its escalation? What could you have done?

"I could have *(called time out by going outside to do some yard work* or *I could have given up trying to control the situation)* _____
_____."

Sometimes fights are the only way two people express their true feelings. In the golfing argument, that is exactly what happened. Both spouses had a problem that needed to be aired and resolved. Did that happen in your incident? The next time the issue surfaces, what are three different ways you can redirect it—making it not a fight but a negotiating point?

For instance, if the couple in our example argument worked through their fears—his about her controlling him as his mother did and hers about being neglected as a child and the natural fear of giving up some control of their lives in the intimate relationship of marriage—they can then negotiate a workable solution. The wife might say, "If you play golf once—or at the most twice—a week, then you and I also need to have a date where you are investing some time with me." Unless their underlying fears are shared with one another, however, this healthy resolution will never occur.

Think about your incident now. What can you do next to redirect the argument to make the experience beneficial to you and your spouse.

I could:

1. _____
2. _____
3. _____

THE BOTTOM LINE

Although you cannot always expect perfect resolution, you must always look toward eventual resolution. The alternatives are easily seen in these mathematical equations:

$$\text{Conflict} - \text{resolution} = \text{separation.}$$
$$\text{Conflict} + \text{resolution} = \text{intimacy.}$$

The argument unsettled, the opinion unvoiced, the issue unresolved—all such un's become wedges between a couple. If a couple separate, we have found that separation actually began long before it surfaced; in fact, sometimes from the very beginning of the marriage.

One source of conflict that arises in this First Passage of marriage is sexual conflict. In the next chapter we will look at the third task of this passage—to build a sexual union—which will eliminate much of this conflict.

4

IS YOUR BRAIN AFFECTING YOUR SEXUAL EXPERIENCE?

Steve Pauling was a hunk. Mm-MM! His new wife Sally matched his good looks in every way. Her strawberry-blonde hair bounced and shimmered. She could slop around in a tank top and cutoffs or strut in a formal evening gown; everything she wore flattered her beautiful shape. When Steve and Sally married, their friends called it the Ken and Barbie wedding. Members of the wedding party sniggered as they agreed that they would have to separate the gorgeous couple with a fire hose when the honeymoon was over and Steve had to go back to work.

Six months later, Sally and Steve sat in our office. Married half a year, they were engaging in sex once a month. Or less.

"I hate it," Sally moaned. "Every night I hide in a flannel nightgown all curled up on my side and dread the thought that maybe he'll reach for me. I can't stand his touch. I can't stand . . ." She shuddered.

"In the beginning, when our relationship first turned physical, it was great." Steve squirmed, uncomfortable. He didn't discuss sex well at all. "A couple of weeks after the wedding, it all nose-dived. I mean zip. Nothing."

"I think I know what caused it," Sally offered. "In college I dated this guy who—well, I guess the term is date rape. The third time we went out, he forced himself on me. He kept insisting and arguing and finally just did it. He said that's what adults do when they date, and he wasn't going to be denied just because my religion made me too prim. I'm sure that's what caused this."

"Why are you so sure?" we asked her.

"I think about it so much, especially when Steve touches me. That's how I know."

Thoughts that intrude themselves the way she described can be a good indication. And we certainly know that a traumatic event such as rape—yes, date rape is rape—can profoundly influence the marriage relationship. But the answers were not nearly so cut-and-dried as Sally believed.

You see, Sally's mind, which controlled her thoughts and memories, had, quite literally, a mind of its own. We knew it could well be that the traumatic memories of that date rape covered a deeper, more severe reason for their sexual dysfunction. And as we discovered soon, it did indeed. First, Sally and Steve had to learn something about the body's most important sex organ.

THE THIRD TASK: BUILD A SEXUAL UNION

In *Passage to India*, an Englishwoman and an Indian man discuss arranged marriages. "But what about love?" she asks, in essence. His reply: "We were a man and a woman, and we were young."

Letting nature take its course would be sufficient were sex primarily biological. It is not. Unlike other biological needs—food, shelter, water—the sex drive is profoundly influenced by factors outside biology. Physical factors such as drugs or alcohol, fatigue, stress, and physical disabilities alter sexual response. But the most active sex organ, and the least appreciated, is the brain. It does its thing largely beyond the conscious level. Personal problems and distractions, fear, misconceptions about sex ("hang-ups," if you will), and the emotional states of both parties are subconscious mental factors.

Today, newlyweds come to bed armed with all sorts of "safe sex" information but very little about what really happens emotionally and physiologically so we'd like to review those aspects of sex now. By understanding them, you more easily can sort out just what part your brain is playing in your sexual expression. And you will know how the human body responds.

The Anatomy of Sexual Intimacy

Picture a sexual episode in four phases: Desire, Excitement, Orgasm, and Resolution. A graph of the man's and woman's experience will differ in shape, for their stimuli and timing differ. "A man is turned on by what he sees, a woman by what she hears." You may have heard that before. The man can complete a satisfying sexual episode in a few brief moments; a woman requires ten minutes or more. The man and woman who understand these and other differences and adjust for them will enjoy a far firmer and more satisfying union than will the couple who disregard nuance and detail.

Desire

The first phase, Desire, begins with thoughts of the spouse. Here, right at the beginning, we find differences between men and women. The sights, the sounds, the smells, an occasional kiss excite the man. Words, actions, touch, and her relationship with her husband encourage the woman's desire. His primary fear, now and later, is that his sexual performance might fall short, failing to bring his wife to orgasm, failing to complete a satisfactory episode for them both. Her fear centers upon being unwanted sexually.

If problems appear during the early phase, Desire, they are almost always the result of personal or relational problems. Ninety percent of the time it's not a physical malfunction. We will talk about these problems in the second part of this chapter so we can cover them completely.

Excitement

During the next phase, Excitement, the skin flushes. The man's scrotum and testicles shift. His penis rises to erection. So does her clitoris, as she releases a slippery, wet lubricant.

The sexual experience levels out now, which is actually a part of the excitement phase. Unless he prolongs it, a man's plateau can be extremely short. The woman's progress ambles across a relatively long plateau of some minutes. To reach orgasm, most women need their men to stroke their clitoris manually for five to fifteen minutes as their desire builds. Rather than diminishing the man's ultimate pleasure, this lengthened plateau increases it. Sometimes when men wait, bringing their women to full excitement, they enjoy a more intense and pleasurable orgasm.

If the problems appear during the second phase of love-making, Excitement, the couple usually sees a physician to rule out physical causes. Alcohol and drugs, including prescription drugs for such things as blood pressure, can cripple sexual performance. Fatigue and stress splash cold water on the fires of desire. Often, so does obesity, not for physical reasons so much as for psychological ones—the man or woman feels unlovable and unsexy.

Hormonal problems, certain diseases, and medications—we make certain that doctors have ruled out any physical reasons for the body's lack of sexual response. Fifty percent of the time they will be emotional or psychological, to be resolved through counsel.

"After medical causes have been ruled out, we dig for the underlying problems," Debi Newman says. "We also use some reverse psychology. It works especially well for people having problems in this middle phase. I give them an assignment. 'This next week,' I say, 'I want you to shut yourself off in a room. Find complete privacy. Undress, massage each other, be together, touch in nonsexual areas. Tell each other what feels good. If your shoulder is tense and your partner massages it, and it feels good, tell your partner that.'

"It's an exercise to show the couple how very important communication is to sexuality. Then I tell them, 'But don't have sex. This is a nonsexual exercise.' Once you tell them they can't, they usually do. It's not just human nature. You're lowering their anxiety about it. This relieves anger and stress. Even if it doesn't result in unblocking their sexual responses, they at least have the intimate experience of touching, saying what's pleasurable. They talk their way through it, and that's a positive gain."

Orgasm

Now man and woman arrive at Orgasm. He achieves ejaculation. She experiences a thrilling tingle of pleasure rippling across her. Man and woman need not reach the top simultaneously; remember, they do have different experiences.

If the sexual dysfunction surfaces in the third, the ultimate phase—Orgasm—physiological problems may well be the cause, particularly for men who have difficulty maintaining erection. Specific dysfunctions include impotence, wherein a man folds before achieving ejaculation—that is, fails to maintain erection. He may fail to obtain an erection at all. Failure to adequately control the timing of ejaculation is called premature ejaculation. The woman may fail to achieve orgasm or reach it only very occasionally. Her outer vaginal muscles may spasm, tightening down so intensely that he cannot enter at all.

"As before," says Debi, "we look for underlying causes. However, many times we find the problem is that women, and men too, don't understand their body and its sexual functions. Each rather naturally believes, 'My spouse feels and responds as I do. What pleases me will please my spouse.' As you've seen, that's not true. In those cases, education can help a great deal. Simply explaining the function of the clitoris and how to stimulate it can sometimes solve the problem.

"The wife must tell her husband what is bringing her to a state of orgasm and how he can help her get there," advises Debi Newman. "He should also guide her into what is pleasurable for him. Open, honest exchange is absolutely essential."

A lot of fiction embellishes the fact of sexual union, and it can damage or delay sexual satisfaction for newlyweds (oldlyweds, too, for that matter). For example, "A good spouse never says no." Or he fears his masculinity comes into question if he doesn't perform on demand, and she fears that if he doesn't get it here whenever he wants it, he'll seek it elsewhere. In counsel we find women who feel that good girls must remain passive. But it is normal for the woman to initiate sexual activity and to participate fully.

A lot of misinformation centers around Orgasm. "It's my spouse's fault if I don't have one." Maybe it is, but don't bet the ranch on it. Probably what you both need is more openness in talking about it. A man might decide a woman is incapable of it anyway, so why try. Another couple might feel that if the performance isn't athletic, it's not erotic. The man who falls victim to one or two episodes of impotence might quit trying altogether.

And then there are the romance novels and the cinema and the sheets-and-bare-shoulders TV movies. "Oh, wow, that's exciting and fulfilling and dramatic! How come we're so clumsy and awkward? Why isn't it the singing, zinging thing the novelists describe?" Keep in mind that good sex, like good golf, takes practice. Also remember that the media are not training sources; they are fantasy machines. They project a larger-than-life view of sex in order to promote the fantasy. They want to leave you breathless and wide-eyed, not better informed. The cops and robbers don't shoot real bullets in those movies, either. It's an elaborately staged set-up. Your love life is the real thing and, pursued with élan, will provide infinitely better pleasure and intimacy than any manufactured fantasy.

Resolution

In Resolution, man and woman again take widely different routes. As his sexual organs return to their nonexcited condition, his body savors a rich feeling of well-being. He toboggans from mountaintop down to flat land rapidly. It's over, and his sex interest is pretty much centered on the orgasm. He will go into a refractory period now, meaning that he will not achieve orgasm again quickly. In very young men, refraction may last fifteen minutes; in older men, three days or a week or a month.

The woman doesn't follow that pattern at all. She is capable of multiple orgasms, and her primary sex interest centers on the closeness and emotional union the sex act provides. She will descend the mountain at a much more leisurely pace as her primary and secondary sexual organs return to their nonexcited states.

Now that we've walked through the phases of sexual intimacy, let's take a careful look at the effect that misunderstood sex organ, the brain, can have on any one of these phases, particularly the first phase, Desire.

THE BRAIN AS A SEX ORGAN

Sally and Steve Pauling hit trouble right in that initial phase, Desire. Sally turned off just thinking about him. She immediately identified one problem she would have to work through with guidance, that date rape. That's abuse. But there was more.

Sally and Steve's extremely conservative upbringing made sex a nasty thing no one indulged in if they were nice and clean and good, the way their families expected them to be. Both members of this couple illustrate the problem factors we find most common.

The major factors that can influence your sexual experience are personal problems within one of the spouses and relational problems between the couple.

Problems within a Spouse

Personal problems within one of the spouses are often related to what we call "sexual taboos," another of those old time capsules from the past.

Sexual Taboos

Possibly the most common dysfunctions a new couple must combat are the sexual taboos they learned in childhood. Those deep-seated precepts, such as, "It's wrong to be sexual inside a family." Another unconscious message is the equation

$$Sexy = illicit.$$

And the reverse is also seen as true:

$$Illicit = sexy.$$

Therefore, if I'm sexy, I'm being illicit or dirty or immoral.

Soon after marriage, one or both partners shut down. One or both of them experience physical problems with intercourse or their emotional satisfaction freezes up. Sex has become domestic. And yet, because married couples are supposed to be sexual and the precept is buried too deeply to find, sex goes on, muted by the conundrum. Possibly damaged. But it goes on.

We counseled a woman in her early twenties who was trapped in the first phase of sexual intimacy, even though she had entered the second phase chronologically. She loved her husband, and was strongly attracted to him physically during courtship. But as soon as they married—in fact, within days of the ceremony—her desire went away. Oh, she dutifully continued the sex, but she received no satisfaction, felt no desire. She had no idea where the problem came from. We went back through her history to explore stated and unspoken messages. By process of elimination, the taboo "It's wrong to be sexual inside a family" emerged. Her parents had slept in separate rooms for many years, and every time she went out on a date during her dating years, her mother warned her not to get pregnant. As soon as we dealt with her sexual taboos by replacing them with the correct message that sex in a marriage is legitimate, that sex is the God-given means of union between man and wife, her inhibitions melted. The new message was something she had always known in her head. But the silent hidden message shouted down that head knowledge.

Frequently, we counsel couples whose premarital sex was far more satisfying than any they're experiencing in marriage. It's a function of that same old sex-is-dirty attitude. Since sex outside the union is perceived as wrong, the sex-is-dirty feeling is strongly reinforced. Suddenly, the couple say a few wedding words, throw a whiz-bang reception, and sex isn't dirty anymore. The head can make the switch, but the heart gets thrown for a loop.

During that big trend when couples were living together, another sexual taboo we call the incest inhibition wreaked havoc. Couples would apparently do well with several years of living together. Confident that they were compatible, they would formalize the union, then divorce in a few months or a year. The incest inhibition that said, "It is wrong to have sex within a family" had remained silently buried until the couple actually became a family.

In the area of sexuality, as in the areas of many decisions within the new family, those time capsules from your childhood family may begin to affect your sexual intimacy.

Those Time-Release Capsules

They came in for counsel regarding sexual dysfunction. Edith could not bear to let her husband see her any way other than fully clothed. When they first married, everything was grand except for one little quirk: Any time Edith's husband saw her undress, or asked her to undress, or looked at her, she would become extremely uncomfortable and have to cover up. They made love in total darkness. He dismissed it at first, chalking it off to shyness in the new union. But her problem intensified, and by the second year of marriage she wore a heavy robe to bed. She could not tolerate his looking at her.

"You feel uncomfortable now. What feelings made you uncomfortable when you were young?" We started at the beginning and moved forward through Edith's life, exploring feelings and events. Her father had never sexually molested her or ever touched her wrongly or made unseemly remarks. But every now and then she'd catch Dad staring at her. His look made her squirm even now as she described it. Yet it wasn't actually leering. Repeatedly, Dad would burst into the bathroom or bedroom without knocking, catching her in states of semi-undress. There was always some legitimate reason; at least, he always had an excuse. And after all, he was her father. Even though there was no episode of molestation, Dad's interest was inappropriate and she sensed it even in childhood. Recognizing and grieving that covert abuse helped her master her inhibition.

Analyze your parents' lifestyle carefully. Do so with your grandparents' also, if you're familiar at all with it. Here are a few of the statements from *Getting Ready for Marriage*. Check those that apply to your family of origin:

_____ "In my family, sex was not discussed."

_____ "My mother and father hugged and kissed in front of the children."

_____ "My parents slept in separate beds."

_____ "My parents believed that a marriage should be faithful and permanent."

_____ "My family used affection as a reward for good behavior and withheld it for bad behavior."

_____ "My mother thought intercourse was a wife's duty."

_____ "I received excellent sexual information from my parents."

_____ "I never felt free to ask my parents anything about sexual issues."[1]

Look back at the statements you checked above. Are there any actions or attitudes in your childhood that might be influencing your married life? Think about your own attitudes toward sexuality by checking the statements below:

_____ "It is important to me that we greet each other affectionately after being apart all day."

_____ "I like to be held and touched without always having intercourse."

_____"I am easily embarrassed when I am nude."

_____"Sex is too embarrassing for me to talk about."

_____"I think that sex outside of marriage is okay."

_____"I believe sex should be honored within the marriage covenant."

_____"I think it's okay to use sex as a weapon or reward."

_____"I think that the woman should do whatever the man wants."

_____"I feel free to talk about my mate and our intimate sex life with my friends."

_____"It is all right for the woman to initiate sexual activity."

_____"I believe that a man should take the lead in sexual intercourse."[2]

Do you see any patterns from your childhood reflected in your present life? More important, do you see conflict in your marriage now because your spouse doesn't like your way of doing something? Or were there such conflicts in the past that are now apparently resolved? Maybe they aren't. Burying them is not the same as resolving them.

Talk about these issues with your spouse. Then consider a sexual relationship covenant, like the one below:

_____"I agree that we may differ on some things, and I agree to respect your opinion and feelings."

_____"I agree to be open and honest about our sexual relationship."

_____"I agree that the only way I can really please you is to let you guide me, and I am willing to do so."

_____"I agree not to use sex as a weapon or reward."

_____"I agree not to criticize or make fun of my mate's sexuality."

_____"I believe that God's teaching and guidelines about sexual relationships are important and agree to make them a part of our marriage."[3]

We've found that verbal or written covenants, such as this, form the foundation for an honest sexual relationship that undergirds any strong marriage.

A final personal problem, one that is extremely devastating to sexual intimacy, is previous sexual abuse.

Sexual Abuse

We have never yet seen an exception to the rule that a woman abused in childhood will suffer some degree of sexual dysfunction in adulthood. Problems within the person include damage done by sexual abuse and other traumatic sexual experiences. Such damage almost always affects marital sex. In these cases professional counseling is almost always necessary. We also recommend reading the book, *The Wounded Heart*, by Dr. Dan Allendar (Colorado Springs: NavPress, 1990).

Persons coming from a home where sex was thought of as nothing but dirty, or never mentioned at all, have trouble later. Fear or revulsion of sex and sexuality cause problems.

Problems in sexual intimacy also evolve from relationship problems between the husband and wife.

Relationship Problems

As we said before, the relationship between the young couple is fragile, and often sexual issues from courtship or earlier—such as abortion—can damage the couple's sexual experience.

Abortion

The nitty-gritty of Sally and Steve Pauling's sexual problems emerged in the third session. We were talking about children when Sally blurted out, "We'd have a baby now if we hadn't . . . never mind."

Alerted, we explored what that sentence had left unspoken. Sally and Steve both grew up with conservative religious beliefs that forbade sexual relations outside marriage. Despite that, they became physically intimate some months before their wedding. Sally got pregnant. Steve, unwilling and unable to deal with fatherhood at this stage in his life, encouraged Sally to have an abortion. At the time, it seemed the only way out. After all, it was perfectly legal. Had the baby come to term, it would have been born the week they entered counsel.

Here was the main issue, buried beneath the unrelated issue of date rape. Steve had refused at the time to discuss what they were doing or to talk about it after it was done. When Sally desperately wanted his support, he considered the matter finished. With counsel, she came to understand her intense resentment toward Steve, that he had not been there for her emotionally when she needed him most. She finally saw that her sexual shutdown was her only weapon, a sexual weapon, to express her resentment and punish him for his apparent coldness.

An abortion in the woman's past will sometimes cause disruption in sexual intimacy. It's supposed to be over with. Done. The wedding was going to take care of it, but the issue remains. Usually, he doesn't appreciate what the woman is going through and forgets about it, failing to recognize the intensity of her feelings. She expects him to share her grief and sense of guilt when he doesn't even recognize it as a baby. Conflict.

We know from our practices that if married persons do not resolve the special problems generated by an abortion in the past, they separate right in the beginning, emotionally if not residentially. They don't trust each other. They are hurting. The man feels threatened and the woman is carrying all the load. As we mentioned, the husband usually doesn't want to admit it was a baby. That leaves the woman to handle all the emotional, psychological, and physical trauma for both of them. Typically, he won't talk about it; threatened by her anger, he may not listen if she tries to talk about it, or he thrusts it aside. Frequently, he's reluctant to deal with the mistake at all. So he is not open to sharing what the woman is going through. It becomes a formidable barrier to intimacy and a bar to any further movement through the passages.

The first thing we do when counseling couples with an abortion in their past is to help them resolve the responsibility fifty-fifty. Then we can lead the couple into mutual grieving and mutual forgiveness. It sounds simple, easy, even glib. In reality, it is immensely difficult and painful. It takes time, as you will see in Passage Three when we talk about the grieving process and show you how to grieve losses in your marriage relationship.

Still another source of relationship problems sometimes makes itself known about now: infertility. The Pill, lauded enthusiastically as the great emancipator of women, possesses a dark side. Women assume they can turn fertility off and on through its use. Yes, they can turn it off with a high degree of safety. But, no, fertility does not automatically return when the Pill is discontinued, as medical researchers have discovered.

When baby-making time comes, in many cases nothing happens. The couple experience anxiety and doubt. Sex becomes a mechanical thing to a specific end. Assume just the right position; do it at exactly the right time. The man begins to feel used. So preoccupied is she, the woman neither feels very sexy nor comes across as such.

Problems will be generated by the marital relationship itself where anger, frustration, and resentment reside. "Conflict and lack of communication are frequent reasons for dysfunction," Debi explains. "Below the conscious level, the person yearns to get back at the spouse for real or perceived faults and slights. He or she uses sex as a tool. Often the person simply cannot perform and may not consciously know why. Withholding sex and pleasure is perhaps the only weapon that person has."

If you harbor resentment or bitterness, in other words, your sexual activity will suffer, one way or another. This concept is so important we will explore it throughout the passages of marriage.

Sex, we have found, mirrors the marriage's general health. When heavy problems and lasting dysfunctions persist, the sexual life suffers. The husband says, "If things went better in bed, everything would be all right," even as the wife says, "If we had our financial affairs in order, sex would be a lot better."

Any stressor shoving at your marriage right now can affect your sexual intimacy. Yet we don't want to suggest that every slight irregularity reflects a sexual problem. During the first two years, obviously, a great deal of sexual adjustment takes place. It is not at all uncommon for couples during that first year or two to go through phases when they shut down. They may go overboard for a few weeks and then go dormant for a few more. As a short-term dysfunction, it's not really a dysfunction. They're working out a rhythm. When problems persist, though, and cannot be talked through, we urge professional counseling.

Finally, we always counsel couples to commit to lovemaking and romance in their marriage.

Commit to Lovemaking

Commit to lovemaking, not just as a recreational option available to married folks, but as a channel to deeper intimacy. It's one of the nicest things you and your spouse can do for each other.

But there is lovemaking and there is lovemaking.

Debi Newman points out, "There is fun sex versus meaningful sex. The world and media teach fun sex. It's exciting. In some cases the world even teaches to try different partners, which of course we certainly never would. Sex is uniquely designed for the marriage union. Outside marriage there's no commitment. That's not real intimacy. It's all physical, all on the surface. Outside the marital context, pleasure is its only goal.

"In contrast, meaningful sex is a special relationship with a particular person, an expression of emotional oneness as well as sexual release. Intimacy is the goal as well as pleasure. Sex and intimacy are not synonymous. Real intimacy is not truly available when you seek only pleasure. Intimate marital sex provides an emotional intensity greater than just the physical orgasm. Call it soul orgasm or emotional orgasm. Good marital sex gives physical pleasure secondarily."

Debi's advice is not limited to new marital partners in this First Passage. Couples should be talking about sex throughout the marriage. Sexual intimacy is a journey. Partners who focus only on pleasure are bound to be disappointed eventually because there is only so much pleasure in the physical experience. Those who focus on intimacy find that the pleasures of sex never pale.

Commit to Romance

"But you just said that," you remind us. "'Commit to lovemaking.'"

No, we didn't, not exactly. Romance and sex are not synonymous. Romance deeply enhances sex, and sex vividly fulfills romance. Sex is lovemaking; romance is love-nurturing. Romance is holding hands, a heartfelt kiss that happens spontaneously, a rose on her pillow, a light in the window when he's coming home late. Romance is dinner for two. Most of all, romance is listening, truly listening, to the quiet of each other's heart.

As Frank Minirth puts it: "We have to move beyond Stage One. We have to move through it, but at the same time, hold onto it. We ought not lose all our idealism.

"How do you hang onto the romance, the idealism? Behavior helps. Do the same things you did when you dated. Walk together, hold hands. Feelings drive our behavior, but behavior also drives our feelings.

"People get in trouble when they become disillusioned. When they see it's not perfect, they tend to bag it. Don't throw out idealism and romantic love, but hang on to it in the face of reality and imperfection. Work through the realism and other stages, but don't forget romantic love. That would be a shame!"

5

ARE YOU MAKING RESPONSIBLE CHOICES?

Frank Minirth sits back in his chair and shakes his head sadly. "I'm dealing with a case right now. The husband is divorcing. He has a wonderful family with three kids, a good wife. He's leaving all that because he found someone else. He's back in that First Passage again, searching for romantic, idealistic love. He never made it past Young Love.

"In my office this man goes on and on about what's wrong with his wife. He's projecting his own frustrations and shortcomings, you see. I can't imagine him completing the First Passage and making it into the Second with his new love, either."

THE CHOICES TREE

As Dr. Minirth's client clearly illustrates, completing the First Passage isn't just a feel-good-if-you-do-it option. Fail to complete it and disaster lurks in the wings, ready to grab centerstage.

It's not too flattering a picture, but imagine this client as a squirrel clambering about in a tree. Its claws scratching in the bark, it scampers up the main trunk. Soon the squirrel has two options: Climb out this first major limb, or continue up toward the other limbs. Should the squirrel move out onto that bottom limb, a large part of the tree is out of reach, for it can't get to the rest of the tree from here. The squirrel makes a choice between this branch and the next.

Frank's client has come to a major fork in his decision tree. People who care can encourage him to make the choices that will lead toward fuller branches and happier times. They can warn him away from the dead-end branches, but he may not let himself see the dead ends. In counsel we can point out what we see about the branches. With this book we hope to show you some of them and where they lead. In the end, though, he—and you— make the choices.

THE FOURTH TASK:
MAKE RESPONSIBLE CHOICES

It helps the squirrel considerably to know in advance where the various branches can lead. Every decision tree is unique to the person moving through it, but all such trees share some dead-end branches in common. Dr. Hemfelt uses the tree allusion frequently in counsel to help patients recognize and make sound choices. Consider some of these branches and deadwood in relation to your own marriage. We'll make them very general so you can interpret them according to your situation.

The Urge to Run vs. Hanging Tough

A number of fears hit newlyweds between the eyes during the first few years of marriage:

"What's the big deal about intimacy? You say that this or that leads to greater intimacy as if intimacy were a goal. Not to me, it's not. I want my space, and my wife can keep hers. Too much intimacy messes up a relationship."

That's fear talking. To be intimate is to be vulnerable. Many people, men and women alike, are afraid of that kind of vulnerability. Other fears are just as common. For instance, the young married sometimes thinks:

"I'm stuck. I just bought into one sexual partner for a lifetime. I just blew any chance to do better!"

Fear of entrapment turns up frequently as we talk to clients. Such fears bring divorce or abandonment to the minds of most newly marrieds sooner or later. Bailing out is definitely a dead-end branch, but in the face of fear it may well look inviting. This includes threatening to bail out too. ("That's it. No more. I'm going home to Mother.")

As Dr. Hemfelt points out, the urge to run has never been easier to indulge than in the twentieth century. "There are few—if any—moral, social, or even ethical stigmas attached to divorce. We've lost the powerful peer pressures that used to keep people married."

Bolt or stay? These are the two major choices, and there is no undoing the damage if you take the wrong fork.

Resisting Change vs. Going with the Flow

Here is a major limb on the choices tree that pops up frequently in marriage: to adjust and compromise or to resist change and pretend things are working.

A case in point: Gretchen and Tim Heusen. Gretchen and Tim both grew up in fairly affluent families. Eight months into their marriage, they were begging Daddy Heusen and Daddy Mullins to help them get their credit cards under control and cosign for their house. Wisely, Daddies Heusen and Mullins conferred together before addressing the newlyweds and saw the problem.

The daddies knew that newlyweds almost always take a big drop in their standard of living, and logically so. Their earning power is as yet nowhere near where it will be someday, their accumulated assets negligible because they've not had time to accumulate much. Gretchen and Tim, however, chose to pretend their circumstances had not changed. They could not adjust to the new reality and, as a result, had acquired heavy debts beyond their ability to pay.

Their story has a happy ending, though not an easy one. Daddies Heusen and Mullins sat down together with the kids, showed them how to consolidate debts, and offered advice on how to live more economically (both dads knew a trick or two in that department; both had started with nothing). The couple was smart enough to listen to their fathers' counsel. Six months later, when Gretchen and Tim showed they were adjusting to the new reality by making good progress at paying off their debts, their dads bought the house themselves. Today, they rent it to the kids as an income property. When Gretchen and Tim have built up enough savings for a down payment, they'll be able to buy it.

Here is a case where the squirrel started out along one branch, realized it was the wrong one, and turned back to make a different choice. The Heusens were able to adjust their lifestyle expectations.

Mary Alice Minirth talks about another aspect of adjusting. "Throughout our marriage, Frank and I have been careful to reserve time for each other. It's not easy. A lot of times we've had to improvise—to be flexible. For instance, during his years of internship and getting started in practice, the kids and I would go over to the hospital to eat supper with him. It was the only break he had at a reasonable hour. Today, we may go out for breakfast before he does his radio show. Spur-of-the-moment things like that keep the romance alive and well. You have to roll with the punches; you have to be ready to improvise."

A third way newly marrieds will find themselves at this fork is when the new starts to wear off. People in courtship try to keep their best foot forward. Still somewhat uncertain about their relationship, newlyweds maintain their best behavior. That stuff never lasts. Both partners must be ready to adjust to the surprises as the real spouse emerges bit by bit.

What adjustments did, or does, your particular situation require? How comfortable are you about adapting to them?

The last task of this First Passage of marriage deals with the passages of marriage themselves. Sooner or later, you and your spouse must recognize your parents' incomplete passages or they will join those other ghosts that can haunt your relationship.

THE FIFTH TASK: DEAL WITH YOUR PARENTS' INCOMPLETE PASSAGES

We have some good news and some bad news for you. The bad news: All the unresolved issues of the prior generations, those time-release beads that have been accumulating down through the years, are visited upon you. These time-release beads are different from the family patterns we discussed in Chapter 2; those were simply attitudes or methods of family life. These issues can be very destructive to your relationship. Yet they often lie so deeply buried beneath your conscious mind that you cannot tell they are there. You cannot escape them either.

The good news: Although others failed to work out these issues in the past, usually because they didn't realize they were there, you can go back and untangle them. Recognizing the issues foisted upon you by prior generations is half the battle. Over and over, our patients and clients tell us how very liberating it feels as they see what is happening in their lives.

The prior generations leave many kinds of unfinished business for our generation and our children's to mop up—or suffer with. Not all unfinished business consists of incomplete marital passages. Unfinished business is anything the parents started and did not complete; dreams they entertained but did not fulfill; elements of life such as the opposite sex or fractured personal relationships with which they never made peace. However:

All incomplete passages become unfinished business for the next generation.

The next generation must complete unfinished business or it will plague the generation to come. If you are the next generation, you condemn your children either to complete or to suffer with the unfinished business you do not handle now. There is no easy way out.

These "ghosts" from your family of origin will haunt your marriage throughout its passages, but this influence will diminish as the years go by. For this reason, dealing with the multigenerational issues will be a task of most passages. That past—our forebears, our childhood, our family of origin, our previous traumas—is sometimes expressed in a set of symbolic statements. As we step up to the altar to speak our "I do's" before God and the world, our hearts speak one or more of these other "I do's" nonverbally.

1. "I DO attribute to you, my new partner, all of the unresolved negative gender stereotypes propagated by my mother and father." Lucky you.

By *propagated* we mean set forth by the parents. Grandparents, aunts, and uncles qualify here too. Negative stereotypes such as "No man can be trusted; they'll all stray on you." "Women have no skill at managing money," and "Men can't be expected to have sensitive feelings." These may all spill over into the marriage.

We recall one couple in their First Passage who, during courtship, were absolutely eloquent in their words of endearment, commitment, and affection. Shortly after the honeymoon, the wife began to notice that, although her husband still displayed interest and affection, he never said, "I love you." Gone were the impassioned declarations. When she drew it from him in a passive way: "Do you love me?" he could say yes. There it ended.

In the rural region where he grew up, men didn't express affection. That wasn't manly. His dad took it a step further. He delighted in teasing Mom and would never say words of affection in front of the kids. The only way Dad related to Mom in front of the kids was derogatory. "How's the old bag today?" Obviously, husbands cannot be tender or endearing.

Interestingly, the woman came to the hospital for tests. She suffered vaginal pain with no discernible physical cause. Doctors referred her for counseling. She was hurt and angry that her supposedly loving husband would not speak his love. The vaginal pain became an expression of her anger and hurt. Once both of them figured out what the problem was, the dysfunction was resolved. Now he knows it's okay to be tender and endearing in marriage as well as in courtship. And when he starts to slip into the old stereotypes, she's quick to put him back on track.

2. *"I DO set about to continue the unresolved battle of the sexes between Mom and Dad. I do carry the banner for Mom or Dad by reenacting the unfinished battle."*

"I see, now," said another patient we'll call Jerry. "If I had married a love-kitten, instead of Stone-Cold Molly, I wouldn't have been able to keep up the fight." The unresolved battle of the sexes between Mom and Dad continued clear through Jerry's extended family. Aunts and uncles, cousins, siblings all harbored resentments and hostilities against the opposite sex. "It all started back with that women's liberation thing," Grandpa grumped. "Things were okay 'til then." No, things weren't. Jerry had inherited a battle generations old.

Because Dad had a long-standing war to force Mom into sexual compliance and performance, Jerry unconsciously picked a frigid spouse. Jerry and his wife had two new battles to win. Jerry had to recognize that this battle was Dad's all along and hand it back to him; Jerry had to make new decisions for himself. The second battle was his wife's. She had shut down internally. Now she had to go back and explore why.

We suggest that you think about the fights between your parents. Be wary of that old nemesis of denial, the natural response that causes us to minimize painful things in order to survive in a family. Also realize that often we literally can't see the forest for the trees. Everything about our family is familiar. It is family to us. Therefore, we don't tend to see the fallacies in our parents' relationship.

Often the battle of the sexes will be fought on battlefronts that involve authority issues, financial matters, sexual intimacy, and time sharing. Look carefully at the bottom-line cause of friction between your parents. To help patients identify these issues we often suggest that they look at their parents' relationship in five different ways. One of five will reveal a clue about the real issues.

The Known Conflict

For instance, you might have heard Mom complain over and over again that Dad doesn't make enough money or Dad doesn't know how to manage the money he does make. That's the overt conflict. Think about the arguments between your parents and determine the known conflict:

"When my mom and dad argued, it was most frequently about
_____. They also
argued about _____."

The Suspected Conflict

You may have never heard either of your parents talk about this issue or fight about it, but you have a hunch that this problem was there, just below the surface.

Or this suspected conflict may be an underlying layer of the main conflict. For instance, Mom might have continually complained that Dad was a poor breadwinner, but in reality Mom was a compulsive shopper. Dad never confronted her about it, so the real conflict between them was hidden.

"I suspect that an underlying conflict between my parents was

_____."

Underlying Fears

Behind all conflict and all anger is fear. We always ask patients if their parents had any strong fears. For instance, Mom never acknowledged her fear of poverty, but she did talk about the Christmas her only gifts were an orange and an apple and a new pair of shoes because her father was out of work during the Great Depression. Her underlying fear was, "We will never have enough to avoid some financial disaster. We are going to run out of money and lose all we do have."

"I suspect that my mom's underlying fear was _____."
"I suspect that my dad's underlying fear was _____."

Disappointments or Disillusionments

Now ask yourself, "Did either of my parents experience any great disappointments or disillusionments?"

For instance, Mom may never have said so directly, but you came to realize that she doesn't see Dad as "Mr. Right." This doubles the ante for you, if you're a girl, as you try to find "Mr. Right." It also doubles the ante for your husband to always perform as "Mr. Right."

"I suspect that my mom has been disappointed or disillusioned by

_____."

"I suspect that my dad has been disappointed or disillusioned by

_____."

Finally, we suggest that you compare notes with other family members.

Input from Extended Family

Sisters or brothers, aunts or uncles, grandparents. When we counsel patients, we often ask permission to talk to a relative in a special session or by telephone. The phenomenon in family relationships can be illustrated by that old story of five blindfolded people who tried to describe an elephant. One touched the tail and described a hairy ball; another held the ears and described long floppy wings; another felt the tusks and described a hard cylinder. Each person had a piece of the picture, but no one could give a complete description of that elephant. We all see our family of origin with that same narrow perspective.

We suggest that you fill in the missing pieces by talking to someone in your family. Play back the memories of your parents' disagreements together. Then think about their actions. Any signs of war? It's your war as well as your parents' unless you give it back to them.

Concerning Jerry's wife, incidentally, she eventually found out she harbored massive guilt and anger about an abortion forced onto her by her parents. She thought she had put all that behind her, but stuffing it away is not grieving it through. She still occasionally goes back to grieve what her parents did to her and her unborn child.

3. "I DO seek a safety zone in this marriage by selecting a spouse who will not challenge or threaten the area of greatest apparent vulnerability in my parents' marriage."

The power of this "I do" is so great that the person may overselect, making an extremely "safe pick." For example, the daughter of an authoritarian, tyrannical father chose a totally lifeless, passive wimp as a safe pick for marriage. Everyone who met him said, "Huh? Why?" The reason, of course: That partner would not run roughshod over her life. She found, six months into her marriage, that he didn't even run smoothshod over her life. He didn't run at all. Within months she was bored mindless with the guy, left without a spark of romance or sensuality. "It's like being married to a potted plant."

Give these three "I do's" a lot of thought. Discuss them together, and then listen to what each other says.

And if at any time you feel you are in over your head—that you have uncovered something too big and too ugly to handle—do seek professional help.

Each of these choices will affect your marriage in this passage and in others and stunt your opportunity to grow. Only commitment to each other—and to the marriage—makes growth possible.

COMMIT TO GROWTH

Somehow, it seemed that every time Carl and Alan ended up in the same place at the same time, so many other things were going on, they had no time to chat. Today, for once, they could sit and talk. Carl hefted his coffee mug. "More?"

"No, thanks. I, uh, have a question. It's, uh, rather personal."

"Shoot."

"We learned in college that when a marriage partner dies, the survivor tends to romanticize the relationship. He or she paints the picture of the past much rosier than it actually was. I know that Beth Anne and I think everything is terribly romantic. It's a lot of fun. Now I'm scared it's going to wear off. It didn't seem to wear off for you two, though. Beth Anne and Annie both say you and Bess have been perpetual newlyweds your whole marriage. How did you manage?"

Perpetual newlyweds? Hardly. Carl shook his head. "I know for sure, if you leave a marriage to its own devices, you'll drift apart."

"Experts agree with that. So how do you avoid drifting apart?"

Carl pondered the question a few minutes. He sipped his coffee; it was cold. "You start out pretty naive. You commit yourself to marriage not knowing what the blazes you're getting into. No matter what you think it's gonna be—no matter what your dreams are—it turns out to be something different. I guess . . . I guess, you commit yourself to go with the flow, whatever the flow ends up being."

"Commitment to stick with it."

Carl nodded. "And commitment to stick with it *together;* I mean really together. Not just to stay undivorced but to stay truly married." A thought struck him suddenly. "You don't marry a dream or a way of life; you marry a person. The dream might change, the way of life probably will, and the person certainly will. And so will you. We all do. Your commitment is to that person all the while you're both changing."

Alan frowned. "You mean you consciously adapt to each other?"

"I doubt you do it consciously, at least not much. Bess and I got off the track a couple of times. Found ourselves drifting away. The conscious part is seeing what's happening and taking steps to bring yourselves back together.

"You're gonna grow, regardless. So when you see yourself growing apart, sit down and figure out how to grow together."

There are a number of ways to maintain the momentum of growth, and thereby complete the passages. These suggestions are not intended to be a rote list. We offer them as a beginning, a guide to help you think how you might nurture growth in your specific situation.

Commit to Union of Purpose and Action

"Let not the left hand know what the right is doing" may be good alms-giving policy, but it's sure no way to run a marriage. Commit yourselves to make no heavy decisions without consulting one another. Questions of finance, child-raising, lifestyle, major purchases—all pertain to the marriage partners as a unit, not as individuals, for the welfare of the marriage itself depends upon harmony in these (and other!) areas. You are working as a team now; teamwork requires that the members keep in step, each knowing what the other thinks and does.

This is not the surface example sometimes given of wifey getting hubby's approval to buy a new vacuum cleaner. This is husband seeking the wife's counsel, as she does his. Two heads are indeed better than one.

Sharing decision making benefits the marriage, but the very process of making decisions jointly provides a far more important by-product—improved intimacy. As two persons work out complex issues, each learns more about the other—how that person thinks, what matters to that person, what that person needs at the deepest level.

We often suggest that couples consider another essential area of growth in their marriage, spiritual growth, which unites their marriage to the purposes and values of the God of the universe, who first ordained marriage.

Commit to Spiritual Growth

Persons completing this First Passage must trust that God exists beyond their family of origin. "Nonsense!" you fume. "Everyone knows that!" Sure they do, intellectually. But in childhood the heart has other ideas, and those ideas must be put away. The heart and head are often miles apart.

The family of origin provides the original source of security. The spiritual challenge of this First Passage is to rip those deep taproots of security out of the family of origin and plant them in the new union.

Too, Mom and Dad were surrogates for God. In a sense, they *were* God. Now they must be lifted from that pedestal.

We urge you also to combat the youthful tendency toward extremes. At one end there is agnosticism: Is there a God and do I need Him? This doubting, healthy in itself, may be covert. If you've grown up in a strongly religious home, you may feel guilty about doubting or failing to evidence perfect faith. Questioning and doubting is natural among Christian couples. As they hustle to develop a firm union, a career or two, a family, a life, they tend to lose sight of God's role in their lives.

The other extreme is a blind, unthinking, unowned allegiance to the God of your family of origin. What do you believe? Why do you believe it? Is your faith your own, or a cop-out in which you let your family of origin make these decisions for you?

The same couple may vacillate between the two extremes. When agnosticism becomes threatening or frightening or unfulfilling, the couple reverts to the family-of-origin spiritualism, comforting and rote. Back and forth, and back and forth. Neither position is the couple's own.

The newly marrieds cannot know God as profoundly as can older people, but they can separate Him from the past and bring Him into the present and future of their new life together. Prayer to that end avails much. So does study and the inner examination of values. The new attitude toward God is an individual walk, of course, but do it also as a couple. Study together. Pray together. Find fellowship together with believers of like mind. Explore God and His claims together. Identify God with your new family in every arena of your spiritual life.

ANALYSIS: HAVE WE COMPLETED THIS FIRST PASSAGE?

If your marriage is old enough to have done so, how well has it survived this First Passage? Is the passage completed? Check the statements below that apply to you. This is the type of inventory we make as we determine if a couple has completed the First Passage. We invite you to make your own assessment and make any adjustments that seem possible.

1. ____ "I am willing to bend on issues that have popped up regarding the nitty-gritty of married life: who balances the checkbook, who does what cooking, who scrubs the toilet. As evidence of this, I can cite the following example:

   _____."

2. ____ "We have reached agreement, or at least an armistice, on some major control issues. Two specific instances I can point to that demonstrate progress are:

   _____."

3. ____ "I am willing to step out of my old family into this new

one. Evidence that I am maturing into the new life as a marriage partner, or have done so, is:

_____
_____."

4. ____ "I have not come as far out of my family as I would like to, as illustrated by this instance:

_____
_____."

"Three things I can do to reduce family ties are:

_____
_____
_____."

5. ____ "I am willing to open up into intimacy. One recent instance in which I let myself be vulnerable to my mate is:

_____
_____."

"In this last week, my mate and I found time alone together (other than in bed!) ____ times."

6. ____ "I can honestly claim that our sex life is open and honest and enjoyable for both of us, more so than in the beginning. A way in which it is improving is:

_____."

7. ____ "Okay. So I am willing to admit that my romance with a perfect partner is an illusion. As evidence that the statement is true, I offer this incident or point:

_____."

8. ____ "I am willing to pursue romance with my spouse anyway. Three instances lately in which my partner and I made a romantic gesture or pursued some romantic fantasy are:

_____
_____
_____."

FROM LA-LA LAND TO THE REAL WORLD

At about two years of marriage, the observant couple will notice a lot of changes in the relationship, and not all the changes are good. Let's see what happens next.

PART
THREE

The Second Passage:
Realistic Love,
the Third through
the Tenth Years

6

CAN YOU
STAY IN LOVE
WHEN REALITY
SETS IN?

*J*ulia Karris sat in our waiting room with a pencil and a magazine she had purchased at the grocery store. Thoughtfully, she went down through one of those quizzes that promise to reveal to you whether you've got a man to fit your temperament.

Finished at last, she compared her responses with the answers in the box. Then she thumbed on back to the recipe pages, but her heart dwelt on that quiz. According to the magazine, her first husband, Rick, had been absolutely right for her.

Jerry was absolutely wrong!

Taking tests is fun, if no grade point average hangs in the balance. Julia had a problem, though—two, in fact. One, she took the test seriously, and two, she was stuck deep in the Second Passage, tussling with a big dose of realism.

Brian Newman smiles at a memory of a test: "Debi and I tried out a test once that was fun to take. It was supposed to measure your temperament and some other things. In doing so it rated us on extremes: depressed versus lighthearted, self-controlled versus compulsive—that kind of thing. You rate yourself and you rate each other."

Debi nods. "It was a revelation, all right. Brian and I took it while we were both still in school. Brian rated himself high in self-control and rated me impulsive. But I rated us just the opposite; I thought Brian was impulsive and I had the self-control. As we talked about it, we came to realize why we responded that way."

Brian goes on, explaining: "Debi is not obsessive about housework the way I am. She doesn't have to have everything in its place all the time. If it doesn't get done that day, she doesn't fall apart. That was the basis on which I was rating her."

Debi concludes: "But I rated both of us according to our work and school habits. At work I was well organized and disciplined. So I saw myself as self-controlled. Brian was very well organized and self-controlled at home, but I was responding to him according to his school work. He hated some aspects of school. He'd put off papers and projects, neglect study and then have to cram at the end. I considered that impulsive and wasn't looking at his behavior in the home apart from his school career.

"We were answering the questions not about the whole person but about one certain sphere of that person."

A GEM OF MANY FACETS

Everyone knows that human beings are gems of many facets. We operate in a multitude of dimensions; in some of them we shine, in some we don't. Hardly anyone, though, uses that knowledge to understand and adjust to others. Even if men and women were simple, one-dimensional cardboard characters, the kind you used to watch on 1950s television, they would mesh together with difficulty. But they are infinitely complex, and that makes true intimacy infinitely harder, for there is no way any two persons can complement each other completely in every dimension.

And yet, our media have convinced us that persons who are truly in love can move through life together in perfect synchronization. There's that vacuous happily-ever-after promise again.

Can two people learn to walk together without tripping over each other? The first task of this Second Passage in marriage is simple and yet extraordinarily difficult: Hang onto love after reality strikes.

THE FIRST TASK: HANG ON TO LOVE AFTER REALITY STRIKES

A pervasive so-far-so-good feeling helps the couple to hang on to love after reality strikes. "We've made it to this point; we've the impetus to keep going." Lord willing in those first couple of years, the young marrieds (and remember this young-married business applies as much to elderly newlyweds as to teens) have ironed out some of the issues causing conflict. One person or the other has made a love gift, or some compromise in easing tensions, or they decided to make the problem a nonissue. Comfortable adjustment has begun.

Too, life is as active and hectic right now as it's ever going to be. There is a momentum, like a strong tidal current, washing the couple along from day to day. Of course, getting caught in a riptide is no fun. Busy-ness also works to disadvantage.

A lot of things other than busy-ness can mess up the smooth progress of this passage.

What Hinders Completion?

This marriage is no longer new. And yet, neither has it a long history. There is great power in the ability of a common history to unite a people, whether it be nations or a married couple. Add to that the fact that couples in the Second Passage are on the run, pursuing careers, making a living, raising the kids, trying to pay for the house or car or perhaps just the daily food. The very tidal surge that carries them along also washes the gloss off all their dreams.

In order to work now, the marriage requires time and effort, the two commodities in shortest supply during this busiest season of life. Some couples may unconsciously ask themselves, "Is my marriage worth precious time and effort?" It no longer seems to be providing all that the happy couple expected on their wedding day. Quite probably, the career(s) aren't panning out according to the dreams, either. They're growing in directions the couple did not anticipate and perhaps do not want. What about the kids? They aren't as manageable and simple as a parent would like.

Now, too, is the time the partners start taking each other for granted. Add to that complacency the familiarity of sex. No longer is it an exploration. The same old marital partners engage in the same old sexual practices. The gloss, the new, has worn off that aspect as well. Too often, disillusionment replaces the sparkle of Young Love.

Anatomy of the First Task

Hercules, son of Zeus and mortal Greek maiden Alcmene, was tough enough to rip the shoes off a horse. He strangled two snakes while yet an infant, and you know how hard it is to choke a snake. He killed a huge, ferocious lion and thereafter wore its skin. His next labor was to slaughter Hydra.

The monstrous Hydra possessed nine heads. The middle one was immortal, and that's not all. Hercules attacked this man-eater with gusto, but every time he lopped off a head, two sprouted in its place. Try as he would, he could not get a head. He eventually slew the Hydra by burning the heads off one by one. The immortal one he buried beneath a huge boulder. Presumably, somewhere around the Mediterranean, that deathless, disembodied head lies yet beneath the rocks, mumbling unkind epithets about the mighty man.

Sometimes, as reality sinks in and the first blush of true love fades, problems in a marriage seem like that Hydra—but you couldn't feel less like Hercules. Master one little difficulty and two bigger ones pop up. Strive with all your might and the monster looms larger than before. Try as you will, you cannot get ahead.

That mythical Hydra is a marriage eater and the "seven-year itch" no myth. Statistically, the highest divorce rate hovers somewhere in this second passage of marriage. All too often, no one sees it coming. In our practice, we frequently talk to friends and relatives of the divorcees. Over and over these people, the people theoretically closest to the divorcing partners, sit in shocked surprise. "What went wrong?" they moan. "Those two seemed so happy."

The Hydra can be bested at this crucial time in a marriage, but it must be slain the way Hercules managed it: Burn off one head at a time.

The major heads of our marriage Hydra are Doubt, Polarization, and Boredom, most of which enter marriage during the Second Passage.

Doubt

Julia giggled self-consciously. "I don't really believe this pop psychology stuff in the magazines, but . . ."

But.

"But this silly little quiz thing confirms doubts I've harbored for a long time. I realize I'm romanticizing my former marriage with Rick; ten years later, it just doesn't seem quite as bad as it seemed at the time. Know what I mean?"

We certainly do know. We hear this stream of thought constantly from different people.

She went on. "Right now with Jerry I'm feeling the same doubts I did with Rick. 'Did I marry the right person?' That question haunts me. Sometimes the answer inside me is yes, and a lot of times it's no. What do I do?"

Sooner or later, and usually during this crucial second stage, almost everyone doubts that the choice of marriage partners was the right one. We find this doubt to be the biggest factor in Second Passage difficulties. Moreover, this doubt usually follows a predictable progression.

First comes the disillusionment. Julia summed it succinctly: "I want closeness from my marriage. Two people linked together intimately. Not just sex, but sharing intimately in all the other dimensions too. Like . . ." she paused a moment, "like mixing black sand with white sand. The grains are still black and white; they haven't lost their individual color; but they make something new that you can't easily separate—gray sand."

"And you didn't get that in your first marriage," we commented.

"No. Rick took; he didn't give. He wouldn't know what it meant to share. At first, I did get it with Jerry. But now Jerry is so wrapped up in his work that I'm strictly second place. It feels like I'm not a part of his world. We don't share anything significant anymore."

"Is Jerry a part of your working world?"

"No. Not at all. He doesn't think my job as a mid-level manager is much. He doesn't bad-mouth my job, exactly, but he constantly minimizes it. That just drives me right up the wall."

"And you're discouraged, because the kind of marriage you want isn't possible."

Julia sat a moment, frowning. "No." The frown intensified. "I'm discouraged because I can't have that kind of marriage with Rick or Jerry. At the back of my mind, I keep wondering, 'Is there someone out there that I *could* have that kind of marriage with?'"

And Julia has just given voice to the next step in the progression of doubt.

Surely there has to be someone better for me. Our happily-ever-after-ending culture has too deeply instilled in us the concept that every Cinderella is entitled to a Prince Charming and vice versa. When the glass slipper breaks, as break it must, our eyes shift elsewhere.

Julia shook her head. "There isn't anyone else. I've certainly not found someone new. I'm just so afraid I married the wrong person again, and I want to get out while I'm still young enough. Know what I mean?"

Again, Julia's attitude is one we see constantly. Most persons who are restless in their marriage want only to get out of it. Remarriage is usually not a consideration. They feel anxious to clean up the mistake they believe they've made and go on. Go where? They don't know. *Out* is the operative word.

Still, they are not out, not yet.

"You know," Julia continued, "now that I look back on it, we weren't really in love. It was a rebound situation. We didn't marry because we loved each other; we married because we thought we needed marriage."

Like Julia, people who feel restless and frustrated in this passage start going back through the files of their mind, digging out the reasons they should not have married in the first place:

"I was too dumb to know I wasn't in love. I was trying to escape from my parents, but I just didn't know it then."

"He's a nerd. Boring. My friends even told me so. But I blinded myself to it. Now my marriage is so boring I can't stand it. It's been one big, tragic, continuous mistake."

And on and on the rationalizations go.

Polarization

Julia and Jerry typify a basic characteristic of marriage—polarization. As one member becomes more dominant, the other becomes more passive. As one becomes more active, the other becomes ever less active.

"If I don't do it, it won't get done," complains the overworked wife who volunteers at the local senior center, manages all the housework and laundry, and also mows the lawn and keeps the flower beds weeded. And she's right. When she doesn't do all that, it doesn't get done, for her husband has, year by year, slipped into the habit of doing less and less.

"Mom runs the house. She runs Dad, she runs the business, she even tries to run the church. And she's not even a deaconess. She tried to run me, but I finally left home. I don't know why Dad lets her be that way so much."

In part, Dad lets it happen because polarization is such an easy and natural trap to fall into.

The characteristics of a polarized couple are not set in cement. Sometimes the spouses subtly shift roles.

We recently had a case that displayed this polarization. The husband started out as the more dominant one. He made all the decisions. He stood tall. Sort of John Wayne-ish. His wife was ill much of the time. He felt protective; he felt a need to give in to her, so to speak. To cater to her needs. As it worked out with time, she became the dominant one. It was a very gradual reversal, but the polarization was there. Now she runs the show and John Wayne has become a shrinking violet.

Brian Newman admits, "Debi and I must constantly keep an eye on this seesaw of strengths. Every couple must. We don't want this natural tendency to polarize to get so out of hand that one of us becomes miserable. We found that when a relationship polarizes, neither member is happy, not even the dominant one."

In counsel we learned that a lot of Jerry and Julia's arguments centered around parenting techniques. "Jerry draws a hard line, particularly when it comes to spending," Julia explained. "Me, I like to indulge Kinsley a little now and then. To Jerry, a 9:00 P.M. bedtime doesn't mean 9:01. I guess I tend to lean way over the other way."

Newlyweds tend to tread lightly with each other, still uncertain of the parameters, still unfamiliar with the intricacies of this many-faceted partner. But by the Second Passage, as the years together bring growth and familiarity, the partners know enough to complement each other, sometimes too well. As one backs off, the other moves forward. When one leaves some slack, as Jerry did with parenthood duties, the other takes it up.

Classically, as this polarization proceeds, the burdened one—Julia in this case—often becomes resentful, and the untrammeled one—Jerry—fails to notice anything has changed.

Is your own marriage polarized? Almost automatically, we can say yes. Everyone does it to an extent.

Is it *too* polarized? When one spouse is frustrated about it, yes. In the "John Wayne" example, not just Dad but the whole family felt frustrated and put off. Think about your own marriage. What are the opportunities for work or play to shift from one spouse's shoulders onto the other's? It's a question to ask yourself now and then throughout your marriage.

How do you see yourself? As aggressive? As passive? How about your mate? We suggest that you and your spouse consider the following polarities. Rate yourselves on the scales (one for the least, ten for the greatest).

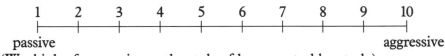

passive   aggressive

(We think of aggressive as the style of how you tackle a task.)

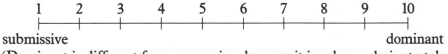

submissive   dominant

(Dominant is different from aggressive, because it involves a desire to take charge of someone else. Do you want your spouse to hear your opinion or does he or she have to agree with you?)

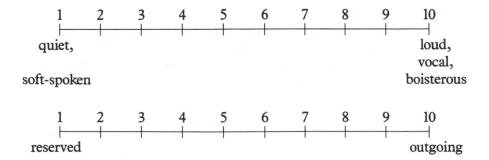

quiet,   loud,

                vocal,

soft-spoken   boisterous

reserved   outgoing

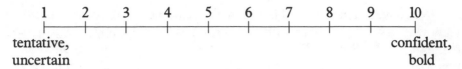

1	2	3	4	5	6	7	8	9	10

tentative,   confident,
uncertain   bold

Now rate your spouse on the same characteristics on the scales below.

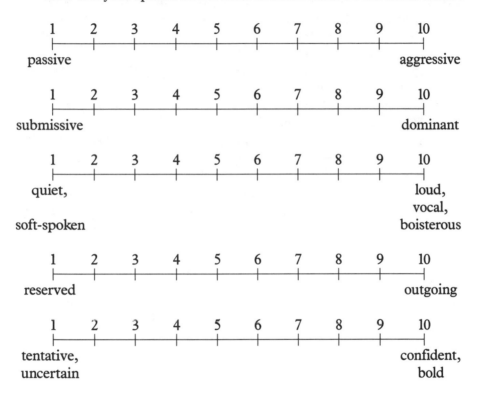

1	2	3	4	5	6	7	8	9	10

passive   aggressive

1	2	3	4	5	6	7	8	9	10

submissive   dominant

1	2	3	4	5	6	7	8	9	10

quiet,   loud,
                    vocal,
soft-spoken   boisterous

1	2	3	4	5	6	7	8	9	10

reserved   outgoing

1	2	3	4	5	6	7	8	9	10

tentative,   confident,
uncertain   bold

Since many of us tend to marry people who are our opposites, don't be surprised if you rate yourself one way and your spouse the other. People who have different characteristics often complement and compensate for one another.

However, this difference becomes negative when you and your spouse become too polarized. The husband, for instance, can become addictively more and more aggressive, and the wife more and more passive.

We suggest that both spouses rate themselves and each other—and then compare their descriptions as they answer three questions.

1. "Do we have a distorted view of each other?"

If each spouse sees the other very differently from the way that person sees himself or herself, then serious distortion is occurring in the relationship. A couple that can't reach consensus as to how they see each other and themselves may need counseling.

2. "How extreme is the polarization between us?"

Obviously if one spouse sees himself as extremely passive and his wife as extremely dominant, the polarization between them might have become destructive to the relationship.

3. "Even though we are different, do we complement each other or compensate for each other?"

In some marriages both spouses will see the husband as "dominant, loud, aggressive, in charge," and both are comfortable with that. The wife may want to be married to a husband who will take charge and she is willing to become more passive.

However, if one or both of the parties expresses strong discomfort with that relationship, then a change needs to be made. The wife may say, "I believe you are basically in charge of this marriage. I've put up with it, but I feel buried, overwhelmed."

We often suggest that a couple talk about the areas that need changing. One wife in our counsel asked her husband, "Do you realize that any time we go out, you always become the center of conversation?" Then she negotiated the following change: "One out of three times, I'd like to see you intentionally withdraw. Give me an opportunity to establish myself in conversation."

Boredom

Complacency, the disease of the Second Passage, is, for all practical purposes, a form of boredom. The new is old, and there is no new new.

Think about the sum of these numbers:

1 woman losing her sense of sexuality as she ages
1 man wondering if he's still got it; after all, sexual expression
    in the marriage has become pretty ho-hum
2 restless people out in the workplace, elbow to elbow with
    other restless men and women
lots of stress at home with the kids
lots of doubts and disillusionments
a dollop of frustration with work, home, everything
The sum = considerable potential for an affair.

Men and women are sexual creatures, mutually and perhaps unconsciously attracted on that basis alone. Physical proximity encourages that sexual attraction, and men and women are working together more and more in nearly every venue. Should a husband or wife, bored, doubting, and anxious in the marriage relationship, find a sympathetic ear of the opposite sex, that attraction multiplies itself.

"Oh, no!" you proclaim. "My husband and I are Christians. We would never consider something like that."

And we reply, "Sadly, that does not guarantee immunity. Christian, Jew, Buddhist—anyone who holds the marriage vow sacred never considers something like that. Yet in our offices we see so many men and women who ended up in something like that anyway."

The seven-year itch.

What is the best calamine to put on it? What's the cure?

SURVIVING REALISM

Combine our cultural desire for a quick fix with the lack of social pressure to remain married, and you would expect a rise in the divorce rate. It would seem that no class or category of person is immune to marriage dissolution. The odds of staying married these days are correspondingly abysmal. How can you beat them?

Knowing the foundational ways in which marriages mature won't guarantee you a long, happy life in union, but it will certainly boost your chances. You can see what is happening and why, and that is the necessary beginning of any solution.

7

HIDDEN AGENDAS: THEIR CAUSE AND CURE

When Rosie and Ralph got married, the whole town talked.

"Whatever made her marry *him?!*"

"I simply don't know what he sees in her."

"Isn't that the strangest couple you've ever met!"

It wasn't exactly the kind of talk that makes a bride proud of her catch.

Rosie's mom, also named Rosie, had actually been a riveter during the second world war. She was never able to live down the good-hearted heckling everyone gave her because of the popular character, "Rosie the Riveter." But she had been an industrious lady who raised her children in spite of the father's constant absences. Now Rosie II shared the same sort of reputation for putting in a hard day's work. At five feet ten inches, Rosie II weighed two hundred pounds, and it was all muscle. She worked as a practical nurse in a nursing home, where raw physical strength served her well.

But Ralph. In Ralph, big, boisterous Rosie II picked not so much a mate as a munchkin. Ralph was five seven and weighed fifty pounds less than Rosie. He was going to school. He was always going to school. At twenty-six, he had still not completed his degree in Asian history and religion. Rosie supported him while he studied. It was easy to see why Ralph married hard-working Rosie—three squares a day and a roof over his head, important considerations for a perpetual student. But why did Rosie marry Ralph?

THE POWER OF THE UNKNOWN

Picture a London-style double-decker bus. Upstairs, a little kid with a steering wheel sits in the front seat, "driving" merrily. As the bus wallows around a tight right turn the child hauls the wheel to the right. The bus rolls into a traffic circle and the child steers straight ahead. They go around the circle anyway. The kid attempts a left turn but the bus angles right. No matter where the child directs the bus, it will respond to the steering of the hidden driver downstairs. That's what hidden agendas and contracts do to a marriage.

All marriages have unwritten secret contracts, hidden agendas. That is exactly why Passage Two is Passage Two.

Hidden agendas, the fine print of the marriage contract which we never read, do not surface as much during the First Passage. The stars in the newlyweds' eyes obscure them even if they do. (This, incidentally, really hobbles premarital counseling. The couple try their best, but eighty percent of the issues they will face later fail to surface before the wedding.) Now, during and following the Second Passage, is when they tend to appear. The hidden contract may lie dormant for years, only to be triggered by some supposedly random event.

The second task of the realistic passage of marriage is to recognize the hidden contracts in your marriage.

THE SECOND TASK: RECOGNIZE THE HIDDEN CONTRACTS IN YOUR MARRIAGE

Rosie got tired of Ralph within a year of the wedding. After all, they had nothing in common. She touted common sense; he dwelt amid dreams and theories. She preferred physical challenges; he played mind games. When they came in for marital counseling, she denied anything could come of it; Ralph was certain counseling could cure the common cold.

Counseling did not cure the common cold, but it certainly revealed important things about their marriage. Rosie and Ralph, like every other couple, entered marriage with two sets of goals, surface reasons and deeper reasons. In counsel, we always work beyond the surface reasons to find what lies underneath.

On the surface, Ralph and Rosie listed these reasons:

1. "I love her. (I love him.)"
2. "She is dependable; a woman should be dependable."

3. "He is interesting; I want intellectual stimulation, a bright partner."
4. "Two can live as cheaply as one."
5. "Neither of us is getting any younger, you know.

Their surface contract, then, ostensibly was to find love before they were too old to enjoy it, and to marry a person with admirable, desired attributes.

The Unspoken Contract

Delving deeply, Dr. Hemfelt uncovered insidious hidden contracts neither person realized existed. Once the core contract was brought into the open, both of them identified feelings and motivations they had never recognized. Like most people, they found that the simple revelation of what lay hidden brings great relief, a feeling of liberation.

Rosie's was, "I will marry someone who needs my support so much that he won't dare go off and leave me." Remember that Rosie's father abandoned his family for long periods.

Ralph's father had never tasted financial success of any sort. He had exerted intense *but unspoken* pressure upon his children, Ralph especially, to become powerful and wealthy. Ralph's father's unfinished business, his hidden agenda: "You will take care of me because I never made it myself." That hidden agenda, like every hidden message from the parents, filtered down intact to the next generation. But Ralph resisted it so bitterly that he still wasn't earning a living at age twenty-six. His contract: "I will so arrange my life that I will never be able to support my father in the style to which he'd like to become accustomed." He married Rosie on that unconscious pretext. While each hidden agenda served its owner, at least in the beginning, both hidden agendas were inimical to the happiness of the spouse. As the marriage matured, the long-range happiness of the couple suffered as well. Friction built rapidly once the first bloom of initial love wore off.

Secret Orders

We have found that most hidden contracts remain submerged during the First Passage of marriage. They usually emerge during the Second Passage or later. As illustration, recall the timeworn plot gimmick of films and novels a generation ago. The battleship commander leaves port under sealed orders. He has no idea where he's taking his fleet until he crosses a certain longitude. Then, in a dramatic moment, he opens his sealed orders and learns for the first time of his destination.

Marriage contracts work just like that. The happy couple go steaming off into the sunset unaware where they're *really* going. Then the sealed orders spring into effect and they find themselves on a totally different course. Apparently God allows a lot of unconscious stuff to remain sealed until the marriage gets rolling. After all, if we saw all the thoughts of our partner's and our own darkest corners of the mind, we would become so disillusioned we'd never get together.

Ralph illustrates another aspect of hidden contracts. Actual response to a contract, and even the contract itself, may be a hundred and eighty degrees off the unspoken word that has come down through the generations.

We ask you to look at speed bumps in your marriage. What blips and jolts have interrupted the smooth flow of that first blush of romance? They quite likely represent hidden contracts surfacing.

Repetition

We have found that spouses burdened by an unwholesome hidden marriage contract don't just fulfill it and get it over with. They act it out over and over again and can't tell you why. The uglier the hidden agenda— that is, the more dysfunctional it is—the more the couple will find themselves locked into repeating it.

So we ask you to examine your marriage, seeking repetitious behavior. If you have ever divorced, look just as closely at the failed marriage also. What keeps happening over and over in your life? Is it healthy for you? For your spouse?

Where do you look for repetition that signals deeper problems?

Your Sexual Life

Do situations or occurrences rob you of satisfaction or orgasm? All couples have their good times and not-so-good times (Woody Allen claimed that even when sex is bad it's good). Rather, look for a frequently recurring problem.

For instance, a husband might realize that whenever he initiates sex, he hears the same refrain from his wife, "That's all you ever think about. That's all you ever value in our relationship." In some marriages the wife may be right: The husband is too aggressive. In others, however, the wife may be repeating an old message that she unconsciously picked up from her parents. Even if the wife does yield to the husband's advances, he may still be frustrated because he constantly feels chastised about his male sexuality.

Your Emotional Life

Do your spouse's actions or attitudes consistently frustrate you? Turn you off? Alienate you? Anger you?

For instance, does your spouse seem to be constantly overreacting to situations? Do you feel as if you are always walking through a mine field, never knowing what will set your spouse off?

List three things that your spouse does that upset you:

1. _____
2. _____
3. _____

Are these things similar in any way (if each of these things is related to your spouse's explosive reactions, that's the pattern)?

"The pattern I see is _____
_____."

The explosive spouse is probably unconsciously responding to a parent who overcontrolled him or her. If your spouse had to claw to hold his or her turf in childhood, that pattern will be repeated in your relationship.

Think about the pattern you identified as we walk through the process of dealing with hidden marriage contracts.

DIGGING UP THOSE BURIED MOTIVES

"It's absolutely hopeless!" Ian, a transplanted Australian, sat in our office scowling. "I suppose it's wrong, but what'll I do? Live in a monastery the rest of my life?"

"I guess I don't blame him, and it hurts me terribly when I find out, but I can't help it." His wife, Rhoda, blonde and doe-eyed, perched elegantly on the edge of the other overstuffed chair. "I have to agree with Ian. It's hopeless. I just can't see any way out. The only reason we're in here is because my parents want us to try counseling before we file for divorce."

"It's merely motions you're going through. Right?"

Rhoda looked at Ian. She appeared almost ready to cry. "I suppose you could say that, yes."

We see this constantly in counsel and in life outside the clinic; people in quiet desperation, devoid of hope. "If your marriage were turned around and the reasons for your problems brought to light, would you make the effort needed to save it?"

Ian shook his head. "I can't see that happening."

"We know that. Would you?"

Ian and Rhoda both pondered the question a moment before responding, weighing the possible consequences—always a good sign. Both were hesitant but both said yes.

We could begin.

What we would do for Rhoda and Ian's marriage, which was very, very sick, are the same things that you can do to improve an already healthy marriage. The principles remain the same; the differences are one of degree.

In clinic work we begin by assuming people in all marriages try to get their needs met, carve out an identity, and establish some sort of lasting security. Their attempts at this may be extremely dysfunctional, damaging to themselves and to the relationship, but the attempts are genuine, nonetheless. When it *really* gets complicated is when each person tries consciously to fulfill these goals in one way, and still pursues the same goals, based on the hidden agendas, in another way at an unconscious level. It's like trying to play chess on two boards at once; you never know where the next piece is coming from.

For example, a man seeks to meet his sexual needs. At the conscious level, he's trying to be a good lover, so that his spouse will respond as a good lover. But his unconscious program is saying, "All women are shrews; don't get too close." He has the best of intentions, but it's not working right because he doesn't know what's going on with that second chessboard.

Examine the Symptoms

Ian came to the United States on a scholarship, studying agriculture at Colorado State. When he left Australia, his mates ragged him good-naturedly about all the sexy, pushy American women he'd have to fend off. Imagine his surprise when he actually met one. She was movie-star pretty, bold and brassy, and promiscuous. Rhoda.

They became sexually involved almost immediately. Charmed by his manners and accent, she married him after a two-month courtship. Two years later, she had shut down sexually altogether and had recently discovered Ian in his third extramarital affair . . . that she knew about. He refused to discuss the possibility of others. The roles had somehow reversed. Prior to marriage he had remained chaste; she flitted about. Now she had turned off to sex even in the marriage bed and he roamed freely.

You can gauge the amount of unfinished business by the amount and intensity of a spouse's hidden contracts. Two people at war, or at quiet war, indicate that major issues were not worked out between the hidden and spoken contracts. We more or less tune out the presenting symptoms—they're only a guide to what's happening underneath—and look for underlying causes. "What are the hidden contracts here that aren't out on the table?" we ask ourselves.

How could a marriage with Ian and Rhoda's shattering sexual problems be mended? We began with an inventory of their parents' and grandparents' possible hidden contracts.

Inventorying Prior Generations

We usually find hidden agendas and time-release capsules in sexual expression, as well as the areas we discussed in Passage One.

Sexual Expression

"Ian," we asked, "if you could put into words your parents' attitudes toward sex, what would they be?"

"Haven't a clue. Never talked to them about it."

"No facts-of-life discussion?"

"Not really. They thought I knew more than I did." He snorted. "So did I."

We asked Ian to assess such things as how he felt as a child when both parents were in the same room: safe? comfortable? on edge? wanting to leave the room? Was there peace or tension? Did the parents fight much? About what? Did Dad go out often or stay out late? How about Mum? How did Mum and Dad respond when a member of the extended family died? How, if at all, did they express grief?

We asked the same sorts of things about the grandparents, both sides, so much as he could remember. He remembered his older cousins discussing openly that his grandfather catted around. At the time, he had no idea what that meant. His father went down to the pub nearly every night, but then most of the men in Blackall did that. His mother liked to read romance novels after the kids went to bed.

His grandfather, a gas station operator, enjoyed moderate financial success, and maintained a steady income even though the farm-based economy of the area fluctuated wildly. Neither parents nor grandparents ever mentioned a word about grief or intimacy.

Rhoda's turn. "Tell us what you remember about your grandparents as a couple."

"Let's see. My mom's mother was the youngest. She stayed home, single, and took care of Great-grandma. She was twenty-six when Great-grandma finally died, and she really cut loose. From sitting at home with a crabby old woman every night, to never coming home at night. Freedom, you know?"

"Then she met and married your grandfather."

"Yeah. When Mom was growing up, Grandma used to mention her past sometimes. It embarrassed Mom to death."

"Embarrassed, or shamed?"

"Shamed would be a better word. Right."

"How did your grandfather respond to that?"

"Don't know. He knew what she was like when he married her. I suppose he made peace with all that."

Rhoda's mom and dad certainly never made peace sexually. Rhoda dredged through her memories, seeking unspoken messages her mother may have delivered. From random comments her mother made just prior to Rhoda's wedding, Rhoda sensed (though it was not said directly) that her mother considered marital sex evil and a burden.

"Reflect on how your parents express feelings toward each other. Do they seem comfortable together? Affectionate?"

Rhoda thought about that a moment. "Civil. Nice to each other. Not what I'd call affectionate." She stared at the wall. Her face softened. "Of course! It was right in front of me all the time. The last five years I was home, they slept in separate bedrooms. They still do. Mom says he tosses and turns too much."

Regarding other aspects of the parents' and grandparents' lives and attitudes, Ian and Rhoda engaged in part guesswork and part detective work. Like figuring out who-done-it in a classic mystery novel, they pieced together fragments of what they knew to make a picture. Ian's father had a master's degree in business, but he never got above clerking, the manager of a small shop in the small town of Blackall. Grandpapa never gave the gas station to him; that went instead to an older brother. Ian's dad was noted for doing everything in a miserly way, even to drinking cheap wine.

"Dad never really achieved any financial security," Ian mused. "Do you suppose I'm trying too hard because of that?"

"The anomaly, if you'd call it that," we agreed, "indicates something going on. That sort of incongruity often tells something."

If, like Ian and Rhoda, you see need for change in the area of sexual expression, you will be tempted to pay attention only to that aspect of your family's past. Go beyond that. Regardless of your speed bumps, explore every area where hidden agendas lurk, including attitudes toward death and good-bye.

Here as well, a dual-answer workbook approach, such as that used in *Getting Ready for Marriage*, can reveal much about your sexual shortcomings and longcomings, as well as those of your parents. Trying to reflect the influences you feel shape your attitudes and pleasures regarding sex, check the statements below that apply to you:

_____ "My parents never discussed sex."

_____ "My spouse and I never discuss sex."

_____ "My family used affection as a reward for good behavior and withheld it for bad behavior."

_____ "A ploy to get the better of my spouse in a fight is to slam the bedroom door. Sex is about the only weapon I have."

_____ "Certain means of sexual expression are taboo to me and I will not let my spouse do them with me."

_____ "If you can't get affection and sex at home, you're sometimes justified in taking an outside lover."

_____ "There were (are) dirty sex secrets in my family."

_____ "I realize now that I might be ashamed of them."[1]

Do you see any relationship between your parents' attitudes and your own from the various statements? As Ian and Rhoda worked all this out they had to keep repeating to themselves, "This is no time for secrets." They were exploring roots, hidden threads, and that meant uncovering some dirt if need be. They reported feeling a mix of titillation and dread as they began honestly to look at their sexual views and mores for the first time.

What Do You Need to Deal With?

So, like Ian, you see abnormality, something that just doesn't ring right. What do you do about it?

Ian shook his head. "Nah! You got kangaroos in your top paddock. You're saying just 'cause Mum would catch my father in the dunny knocking back Africa Speaks . . ."

We interrupted. "Pardon?"

"Sorry." Ian grinned, but the smile faded quickly. "I think you're crazy. You say just because Mum would now and then find him hiding in the privy out back, sneaking a drink of cheap red wine . . . Africa Speaks is this awful stuff . . . And he didn't have a business head . . . Couldn't make a fair go of it . . . Anyway, I can't see how that's affecting what I do on another continent. I like the ladies because I get nothing at home. Believe me, I didn't get married so I could spend years without . . . you know." He grimaced, shamefaced. "It's Rhoda. Talk to her."

"You're half of the marriage. We'll ask both of you. What can you see that was left undone in your parents' and grandparents' generations? What did they fail to deal with? What need did that leave lacking in you?"

Rhoda and Ian worked on that for a week, sorting out details. The answers they came up with: Guilt. Shame. Failure—business failure and failure to establish comfortable sexual relationships in marriage.

"Comfortable sexual relationship in marriage?" Rhoda shook her head during our next session. "Neither Ian nor I have our act together on that one. But we can't fix the past. We can't go back and change our parents' lives."

"True. Ian, with your background you can appreciate this. Picture a series of corrals or pastures with gates between them."

"Paddocks."

"Right. When all the gates are open you can introduce livestock at one end and run them clear through all the paddocks to the other end."

Ian grinned. "Don't tell me you forgot to close gates when you were little too."

"Ah, so it's personal for you. Good. And that's exactly how you stop the sheep or cattle. Close the gate. The distant paddocks are your ancestors. The third one back there is your grandparents. The one next to you is your parents. You're the paddock right here and beyond you, the gates wide open, is the paddock that will be your children."

"The different generations?"

"Exactly. Now let's say you want to grow flowers in your paddock. Intimacy and romance are often symbolized as flowers."

"Not with sheep running through you won't. They'd eat 'em to the ground." Ian's face lit up. "I see! These problems, this unfinished business you call it, are the sheep. The shame and guilt and failure. They destroy the love."

"Exactly. They roamed from your grandparents' pastures and your parents' to your own. If you don't see them and stop them, and close the gates, they'll continue on to your children's."

Ian nodded. "Tell me how to get them out of my paddock."

"You can't get rid of them if you don't notice they're there. You just did that. Once you've identified them, you can control them. And by grieving them and the damage they did to your parents, your grandparents, and you, you close the gates. In fact, some therapists refer to the process as 'closure.'"

Ian never imagined that his parents' or grandparents' marriages could have any impact on his struggles with Rhoda.

The sheep in your own pastures have caused problems, for others and for you. They may not have been dealt with in prior generations, so it is most appropriate to go ahead and grieve them in this generation. The grieving process, generally well known, is dealt with in detail in other works. In our counseling we try to help patients deal with the losses of their lives by grieving them through.

Learning how to grieve is essential in a fallen world. Grieving losses is important in your journey through the passages of marriage. We showed Ian and Rhoda how to grieve through the issues they discovered in their marriage. Let's work through the process of grief now.

Think of a recent occasion in your marriage when you felt hurt or wronged. If you can, use an incident where the wound is still open. The incident does not specifically have to be between you and your spouse. Perhaps you had to place your aging parent in a retirement home. Identify that incident as IT as we move through the stages of grief.

Shock and Denial

When we asked Ian if he knew his parents' attitudes toward sex, he replied, "Haven't a clue!" Yet with a little probing he could remember that his father went to the pub nearly every night and his grandfather catted around.

Think about the way IT startled you at the very first—the shock and disbelief. "That didn't really happen!" "It can't be!" The shock of your incident might have lasted for a fleeting second or for a longer time. People who hang up right here at the beginning of grief walk about, literally, in a daze that can last for years. And that happens, if the trauma is great or the loss severe. Recognize the shock and denial that comes of learning something unsavory or depressing.

Depression

The word *depress* actually means "to put down." Even though we experience depression as pain, it's really an emotional numbness as the definition suggests. We shut down our feelings. Patients often express depression as the world becoming gray, as if the tube on the color television is broken and you're back to the old black-and-white picture. Everything loses color and vibrancy.

People naturally react to depression as Rhoda did. They try anything to get the color back. Rhoda was actually forcing herself to feel again by acting out sexually. Unconsciously she was saying to herself, *Maybe I can feel love and closeness if I enter into these intimate relationships. Maybe this one will do it.*

Do you feel numb? If so, are you trying to jump start your feelings? Recognize that as part of the depression.

If IT is on the magnitude of a lost business deal, depression is no big deal. But if IT is the parent you put in a home or a move to another state, far away from your family and friends, the depression can last for months or years. Depression is an expected and necessary part of the process. Do you recall the depression that accompanied some other major loss in your life?

Expect depression. This is a heavy load you're dealing with. It will weigh you down. Fear not; the depression is almost always temporary.

Bargaining or Magical Thinking

There is a period when you'll seek some way out. We call it bargaining and magical thinking. You might try to cut a deal with God or another human being, perhaps with your spouse or parents.

"Okay, God," you might say. "Get me out of this depression and I'll tithe twelve percent."

"If only I can justify the loss, I won't have to grieve it. The pain will go away." "If only." "If you will but . . ." What bargains or "if onlys" came to your mind when IT happened?

Rhoda was trying to strike a bargain with God. Even though she thought she believed in premarital sex, she instinctively felt ashamed of her actions (we often find this to be true, by the way). She also carried her mother's shame about Grandma's wild oats. Her bargain with God?

"I'll pay the price. I'll be nonsexual in this marriage for a month or a year or a decade—or the balance of this relationship." Unconsciously she was doing penance or wearing that scarlet letter of Nathaniel Hawthorne's heroine.

Unfortunately it's natural for us to believe in bargaining and magical thinking. Are you promising to do *x*, *y*, or *z* to pay the price for this situation in your life? Eventually you must put the magic and bargaining away. They don't work anyway.

Sadness

Sadness is what most people think of when they think of grieving, but it is only one part—this fourth part—of the process. And you can't experience true grief if you haven't really worked through the earlier steps.

Unfortunately people try to go directly to grieving. In counseling they'll indirectly say to us, "Let me be sad for the next hour and get this out of the way." It's the way of our fast-paced society. Before you can experience true grief, however, you must have overcome your denial and bargaining and your depression. Rhoda had to give herself permission to be angry at Grandma for her childish overreaction to caring for her elderly grandmother; Rhoda had to be angry at her mom for talking about the shame she felt, and Rhoda had to be angry that she grew up in a family where the women were not given a healthy attitude toward sex.

Then Rhoda could get to true grief, crying for all the losses in her grandmother's and mother's lives, the losses in Rhoda's own childhood and her premarital relationships, and those of the last two years in a barren marriage.

Now it's your turn. Recount the sorrow IT generated. Do you remember it? Memories of sorrow fade; it's one of the nicest things about sadness.

Forgiveness and Resolution

Forgiveness, acceptance, and resolution complete the process. Be aware that you cannot reach them either without going through the other stages first. Cheap forgiveness and casual acceptance solve nothing.

Once Rhoda was able to grieve her losses, she was able to forgive her grandmother, her mother, and herself. Counselors sometimes talk about secondary virginity or sexual rebirth. If a person truly forgives herself, then she can feel emotionally and spiritually pure. Virginity is more a state of the heart, we've found, than of the hymen, especially for those who have been sexually abused or who have misused premarital sex.

Just who needs to be forgiven in regard to IT? What is your part in that forgiveness? You must also forgive yourself if that be appropriate, you know. Forgiveness is so important and integral a part of any marriage, we will devote a chapter to it later. For now, determine what forgiveness is necessary regarding IT and detail how you should go about it.

Are other steps necessary before IT is resolved comfortably and satisfactorily? A bandage on a cut finger or a letter to restore a friendship—so many incidents require careful resolution. Mending such bridges always pays immense dividends, to yourself and to others.

Having dealt with past layers of problems by grieving them through, you have another task to complete in regard to them. Use them to ferret out what sort of hidden agenda they might have engendered in you.

After reviewing the history of both Rhoda's and Ian's relatives, we posed this question: "Rhoda, it's safe to assume your mother is acting, probably unconsciously, on her own hidden contract when she seeks a separate bedroom or displays little affection. It's also a safe assumption you picked up some form of that attitude. How might you have translated it into your own hidden contract?"

She didn't come up with the answer immediately. It took time. Eventually, she realized what her innermost self was saying: "I'm ashamed. I'm going to create a sexless marriage."

"Ian? What about you?"

"I suppose," he ventured, "something about 'It's all right to take sex outside marriage.' I grew up hearing the church, and even my mum, saying it's wrong. My mind says it's wrong, but that's not my mind talking, right? I can see now how I got the word from my father and his father, and they never said a thing."

Ian and Rhoda came to understand how each was wrong in the relationship. They asked God and each other for forgiveness. Ian broke off the extramarital sexual relationships and committed to being faithful to Rhoda, no matter what. Rhoda chose not to withhold sex from Ian, and instead to talk to him about her anger and fears. Together, they formed a new hope for their marriage.

A New Reason to Be Married

If the hidden contract, now brought to light, is a problem, how do we write a new one? What do we do when the old reasons to be married have been scrubbed? Ian and Rhoda had to write new contracts, new agendas. Let's consider that next.

8

CAN YOU WRITE
A NEW MARRIAGE
CONTRACT?

*J*oe Jacobs stared glumly at his bridge hand. He had an ace and three low-number cards. Barbara had just bid two spades. Now what was he supposed to do? He was supposed to do something when this situation came up. He couldn't remember.

"What am I doing here?" It burst out of him aloud.

Barbara frowned at him. "You're supposed to be learning how to play bridge, that's what. But you're not trying. You're not concentrating. Don't you want to be a good bridge player?"

Her question cleared Joe's mind. Suddenly he realized what was going on, and what he was going to do about it. "No, Barbara, I don't want to be a good bridge player. I don't want to be a bad bridge player. I don't want to be any kind of bridge player. I don't like the game." He dropped his cards facedown on the table. "You learn bridge. I'm going down to the armory. I'll pick you up afterward." And he left the community building, left Barbara with her bridge lessons and her constant parade of activities.

Driving over to the armory, he tried to sort things out. Barbara knew his AA meetings were Tuesday and Friday. Yet she had scheduled these Tuesday night bridge lessons deliberately; he could see that now; a ploy to draw him away from AA. She was always finding something to do on Fridays too. Or she'd say, "You look too tired tonight. Why don't you just stay home?"

Why was she trying to keep him away from AA? It was she who intervened to get him there in the first place. She was the one who confronted him about his drinking, who fought him just as stubbornly when he resisted stubbornly, who helped him return to a cautious sobriety. She was responsible for his recovery. Why was she trying so hard to sabotage it now?

Joe walked into the AA meeting more than an hour late, but they greeted him heartily anyway. He settled into a folding chair with a happy smile, home at last. "Gentlemen," he announced, "I have just played my last bridge game."

Joe and Barbara's marriage presents an intriguing picture of how powerfully the hidden forces of a secret marriage contract work. Joe puzzled over the surface indications, such as Barbara's peculiar resistance to recovery. AA helped him see what was happening below the surface—that Barbara, accustomed to being in control and handling everything, to fixing things up, was suddenly finding herself with much-reduced responsibility, as Joe took over his own life. Barbara was losing power, and that frightened her, particularly because she could not yet trust Joe's competence. But, the third layer down, hidden contracts based on hidden agendas exerted the ultimate influence.

Barbara's father had been an alcoholic. It rather follows that she would marry one; children of alcoholics so often do. In fact, her mother had, for Grandpa Bill "liked his booze." Barbara determined that she would achieve what her mother and grandmother never could; straighten out her man. With the help of Dr. Robert Hemfelt and the clinic, she arranged an intervention in which Joe was confronted by the severity of his drinking problem. As part of the recovery, Brian Newman counseled Barbara and Joe regarding marital health, and Robert treated Joe's alcoholism in group therapy. It worked. For six months now, Joe had kept his sobriety.

Trouble began, though, from the day Joe began to recover. Barbara repeatedly phoned Brian, giving advice, telling him what to do in the counseling sessions. In essence, she was trying to exert control, to shape Joe in the mold of her choosing, to be a cotherapist because she knew Joe best. When Brian confronted her with her unseen agenda, she canceled therapy and tried to talk Joe out of going. Barbara accused Joe and Brian of causing unnecessary conflict. She claimed therapy was making things worse. But poor Joe could see he was becoming better, feeling stronger, getting back in touch with sexuality, growing spiritually. What was this message from Barbara that their marriage was getting worse?

The below-the-surface forces are familiar to anyone who knows about codependency. As long as Joe was drinking, Barbara controlled everything. When Joe came back to life, requesting and enjoying sex more, expecting a say-so in finances, resuming an active role as husband, Barbara had to share control. It was healthy for Joe to share responsibility, but it was threatening for her.

Deeper, darker forces worked here, however. Barbara struggled with two hidden contracts working at cross purposes. First, try as she might, Mom never did succeed in fixing Dad, so Barbara had to try to fix her husband. At the same time, a second agenda competed with the first: A woman's single most important, significant, and noble role is to hang in there in the face of adversity. Take care of the dysfunctional spouse.

It would seem Barbara couldn't have them both. So long as Joe was sick, though, the contracts were compatible, the operative word in the first contract being: *try* to fix. Also, they fit in with Barbara's past; this was how she grew up. Ah, but once Joe made his U-turn, the first contract negated past history and the second contract couldn't exist at all. Barbara no longer had to take care of a dysfunctional spouse. Down deep, where her conscious thoughts never ventured, Barbara felt disloyal to Mom, because the only role Mom ever modeled was of the stoic, the long-sufferer. The bottom line was: Without a sick Joe to take care of, neither Barbara nor her marriage had any purpose. And that, unconscious though it was, frightened her to distraction.

Barbara's contracts, which were so interwoven with Joe's alcoholism, had been negated. She needed to get a new one if her marriage and her life were to have purpose. The third task of the realistic passage of marriage is to write a new marriage contract.

THE THIRD TASK: WRITE A NEW MARRIAGE CONTRACT

In order to build a relevant contract, the couple must identify the sore spots they will have to attend.

Even in the healthiest marriage there come times, usually during the shift from one passage to the next, when a new contract becomes necessary. As unions mature, we all need new reasons to remain married. Also, the times themselves change, altering spouses' roles in society and in the home. Taken step by step, writing a new contract is not difficult, but it should be painstaking.

Review the Existing Contracts

You already laid important groundwork when you inventoried your parents' and grandparents' marital contracts and agendas. We now see how the past wields its weight. The phenomenon involved is called "splitting off."

In psychology jargon, you address each aspect of yourself by either owning it—accepting it and dealing with it—or splitting it off. Picture a family as magnets lying on a table, the big magnets being the parents, the little ones the kids. On the table we dump a spoonful of iron filings labeled, let's say, sexuality. Normally, everyone has some. But the two big magnets for some reason refuse to own their sexuality (sexuality is a common factor in owning and splitting off). They reverse their polarity. Split off from where they ought to go, the filings leap like wild cards elsewhere onto other magnets where they do not belong.

Normally, if a major area of feeling or personality is split off, it goes into the next generation's marriage as hidden agendas. That marriage will either mimic or amplify it, cure or compensate, or rebel against it . . . and eventually, pass it on. In Rhoda's case, her grandmother's sexual excess generated shame in her mother. Promiscuity and shame came together in Rhoda's "I will have a sexless marriage." It did not surprise us to learn that Rhoda's two brothers both suffered sexual dysfunctions that neither ever discussed. All the children of the parents' union will feel the effect in some way or other, whether there is one child or a dozen.

Good news! We have learned that families communicate across the generations in remarkable ways, transcending time and place. If Grandma and/or Mom change, the daughter benefits. A full cure does not come down from above that way, for the daughter still has a lifetime of unspoken messages to deal with and she must take responsibility for her own marriage. But any improvement in the parents' lives, however belated, will help her. Neither is geography a barrier. If something major shifts in the family dynamics, even if the parents live in New Jersey and the children are scattered through four western states, the shift will be felt.

As a first step to writing a new contract, then, you will want to identify all the old ones—yours and those of the past, stated and unstated. Normally we ask each marital partner to work independently at this, then compare notes.

For purposes of this book, you already did most of that when you identified hidden agendas influencing your marriage.

DRAFTING THE NEW CONTRACT

Those hidden contract items become the basis for establishing new contract items, in part. Your new contract will adjust or reverse the dysfunctional items. It will also cover items beyond the hidden agendas. It should prevent future problems if possible as well as solve past difficulties. We're now ready to write exciting new reasons to be married.

"I'm afraid," Ian admitted, "we ran into problems because my hidden contract said sex is all right outside marriage. Now I'm replacing it with 'Sex must stay inside the marriage.' I don't think I can carry it out. Especially if Rhoda can't come around to—you know."

"Do you think," we asked, "that every person who commits adultery has a hidden contract telling him or her it's all right?"

Ian shrugged. "Beats me. Do they?"

"No. Hidden contracts do not control a hundred percent of anyone's actions. A person with a healthy unspoken contract may well fall to temptation, especially if the tempter's contract is a powerful one. And the reverse is true. You can easily fall to temptation, and you must guard against that carefully. But you're no different from everyone else. We all are tempted by wrong, regardless of the contract—sex, dishonesty, every kind of wrong."

"I see." Ian smiled. "The contract just makes it lots, lots easier."

Exactly.

Our clients first sketched the broad parameters of their contract. The basics. We suggest you do so also.

A Statement of Commitment

Determined to be honest, Barbara, the alcoholic's wife, wrote down, "I am committed. I thought about leaving, but I will not consider that again for at least a year."

You must be honest also.

It is valuable to *state some affirmation about each other and the marriage.* Joe wrote, "Barbara brought me back from the dead, literally, and I won't abandon her. I'll put her and our marriage first."

Make certain in all this that you've established the underlying agenda upon which you will base your new contract.

Take a moment now to write your statement of commitment.

_____

_____

_____

Before you write your new contract, let's look at some common dysfunctional contracts we've seen in couples, so you can avoid them.

Major Mutual Contract Issues

Consider these common contracts in two ways: 1) Do any sound like something that could be controlling your marital behavior? 2) Just for practice, how would you write a new contract to counteract each of these, laying the foundation for a healthier union? Notice how detailed you can get.

"My spouse is an emotional punching bag through which I release anger toward other people (or, sometimes, even expunge my parents' anger toward others)."

"I picked my spouse just to prove my parents were right—or wrong—about the opposite sex, another race, a different class."

"I picked a wounded bird to rescue because he/she needs me and won't fly away; in that way I can fix what went wrong a generation ago, and besides, with all the emotional hassle, I won't have to become vulnerable with true intimacy."

"My spouse is an extreme opposite of one of my parents, so I will not have to suffer the way I did when I lived with that parent."

"I need to be punished because I have lots of family-based shame to be paid for, so I picked an abusive spouse."

Those are perhaps the commonest; the list goes on. List two of the old contracts in your own marriage:

1. _____
   _____
2. _____
   _____

Now write a new contract for each of these old agendas:

1. _____
   _____
2. _____
   _____

Now down to the nitty-gritty. Having sketched the broad strokes of a solid contract, get specific about the details. Your new agreement, your revised agenda, should both repeat what is best about your existing contract and also be the antithesis of whatever was dysfunctional about the old one.

Spiritual Matters

There is a difference of opinion in the Christian church between the liberals and conservatives. Unfortunately, that opinion extended right to Louie Ajanian's hearth. His wife, Marj, was conservative; he, liberal. She would argue for as long as it took to get him to accept an inerrant Scripture. He refused to argue. She wanted to keep the faith simple. He liked lots of liturgy and vestments and furbelows. She claimed she would have nailed ninety-five theses to his bedroom door, had she been able to find the hammer.

As they plowed through their Second Passage of marriage, Lou and Marj had to establish two sets of balances. When feelings and faith wax hot, the spouses may find themselves in a battle to pull the other person into a certain interpretation. That was happening to Lou and Marj, as much as Lou would allow. Therefore, they first had to find common ground. This common foundation permits a common spiritual bond that can stand against the differences. Along with union, the Ajanians must have autonomy in their faith. They must each find God as individuals and as a couple. They sought balance between divergent views, based on that common ground, and balance between serving God as an individual and as a team.

This was no small thing for the Ajanians, who shared much common ground—the saving work of Jesus Christ being the solid base. It can be a formidable barrier to a couple holding contradictory or mutually exclusive views of God. A good place to deal with divergent views is right in the contract.

Ideally, both mates will develop the ability to see that different views exist. Trying to understand them may be frightening. "How does my faith coexist with others?" If that overwhelms the inquirer (or causes intolerable tension between the spouses), the inquirer may either move toward disillusionment—"There must not be a true God"—or toward rigidity. Rigidity is blind, unthinking adherence to either the faith of the family of origin or a totally new cultic belief. This Second Passage is a very common time when couples gravitate toward cults.

Dr. Hemfelt recalls a couple who very nearly divorced over just such a situation. They had been married six years. During the third or fourth year, the husband began reading materials by a fringe cult that ties politics to faith. He stopped paying taxes and became militant in his views. "Enough!" cried his frustrated wife, the member of a traditional church. Dr. Hemfelt sorted out that the man had grown up in a spiritual vacuum. At first he was going to blindly adopt his wife's faith. But the cult materials that crossed his path seemed to have the absolute answers he wanted. Her faith did not.

Dr. Hemfelt's course in this case was to help both partners clarify and crystallize what they believed and what they wanted in terms of spirituality. Once they established personal views of God, they could find common ground.

When writing your new contract, you'll want to address the particulars of your own spiritual life.

Sexual Matters

If you want to minimize sexual difficulties and differences, resolve your other control issues in your contract—time, money, and all—for they will spill over into your bedroom. As we saw before, sexual dysfunction may be a symbolic battle reflecting deeper control battles. Of course, each blames the other. So very often we receive a case wherein the wife, unable to reach orgasm, blames him for being too insensitive, as he blames her for being too uptight, and they're actually fighting over other issues.

Sexual difficulties, therefore, exist on two levels: as a reflection of other control battles, and as battles in their own right. To address this, we urge a two-pronged attack, and it can be written right into the new contract. First, the couple needs to be aware of the other control issues and talk them through prior to writing them out. Second, they need to compromise on the sexual differences themselves.

The bedroom door swings both ways. As other issues enter, so can compromise in the bedroom exit to smooth the way in other areas. As Dr. Hemfelt says, "What goes on in the living room has dramatic impact on what happens in the bedroom, and what happens in the bedroom can aggravate or alleviate what goes on in the living room."

Fidelity Matters

This Second Passage is a time of high vulnerability for an affair (so for that matter is the Fourth Passage). In the Second Passage, an affair usually represents a flight away from intimacy. Here is the poor married man or woman, struggling with control issues, financial and career pressures, kids, and, in some, a fear of true intimacy. An affair offers an easy pseudo-intimacy; intimacy with no strings. The new love approves of the harried married person and accepts him or her without conditions. No one worries about who takes out the garbage or who handles finances. Control issues aren't a problem. Persons involved in an affair need not deal with boredom and everyday minor crises. That's the hard work of marriage. Yet these issues create a special, rich kind of intimacy.

Wise marital contractors therefore write a pledge of fidelity into their promises. Will that thwart the chances of an affair? Of course not. But it reduces them by putting in visible, solid, immutable writing the couple's promise to each other. It reminds, it encourages, it supports.

We suggest each spouse write a contract independently, working out his and her new agenda and tasks. The first drafts may be similar for both or quite different. What one sees as a big-ticket item may not be significant to the other. One might want better financial boundaries while the other places better team parenting as the top priority.

Write down whatever you think it takes to move along through the passage and meet the needs of both of you.

Once the contracts are drafted we ask the couples to enter the negotiation phase, which like any arbitration involves some give and take.

Give and Take

Ian: "I need sexual fulfillment."

Rhoda: "Be specific."

Ian: "Intimacy several times a week. No nervousness, no embarrassment. Openness. Some experimentation."

Rhoda: "I can't offer all that—at least not yet. I request in my contract aloneness at least three nights a week and a date night at least once a week, something romantic."

Ian pondered all this a while. "Are we really serious about this contract business? Like a union? You know, unions are the thing in Australia. Everything's union, union contract. Are we doing that here? Like negotiating?"

"Yeah, I guess so."

"And it's going to be binding?"

"I suppose it has to be if it's going to work at all."

Ian nodded, delighted. He wrote down each very specific request on two slips of paper. He gave her hers and kept his. "When unions bargain, they trade off, this concession for that. Now how shall we trade?"

Rhoda was not a born negotiator. She was afraid to give and hesitant to get, lest her hopes be crushed if the promises were broken. She caught on, though, in a hurry. They traded slips and clung to slips and revised slips. In the end they each wrote a contract, which was in effect a binding promise to the other, based on the slips they held at the finish. The contract would be good for one calendar year, at which time negotiations would reopen. Ian wasn't a union man for nothing.

Give and take in open negotiation is an excellent way to work around strongly differing agendas. Parenting, for example, rarely means the same thing to both spouses. Your spouse thinks if you don't tightly discipline a child there will be hell to pay; you tend to feel a little coddling doesn't hurt. You're on different agendas. Best to make some adjustments. And you don't have to have kids yet. Differing agendas are best negotiated even before the first child arrives (or puppy—some people practice on puppies! The Hemfelts did.). Marriages tend to fall apart when the kids come because of the confusing agendas. It helps immensely to have some good strong shoring in place before the storm strikes.

THE GOALS OF CONTRACTS

The bottom line of your marriage contract is the bottom line of any of Ian's union contracts—two entities helping each other succeed and move forward. The antithesis of dysfunction, in marriage as in anything else, is mutual aid, as each helps the other satisfy needs and complete the necessary tasks of each passage.

It is not a goal of the new contract that all parties agree on the same agenda. You may well reach the decision that you have different agendas and different priorities. Matching or meshing diverse agendas in which all parties prosper is just as fine as identical agendas, and perhaps even better.

Be aware that not all meshing agendas are wholesome.

These two agendas, for instance, fit:

He: I believe all women should be submissive.

She: I believe all men should be dictatorial.

But no one's going to grow in that relationship. The love, then the respect, and eventually perhaps even the marriage itself, will die.

An example in our counsel recently illustrates unwholesome meshing of agendas. A husband wanted to carve out a vocational identity for himself and the wife declared a contract in which security was the top priority. Those two agendas could mesh nicely, as he built the security of a strong presence on the job. But they became antagonistic, for he spent long hours on overtime and she languished, uncertain of his love. Her concept of security was emotional; his, monetary.

One result of clear communication and honest contract negotiation is improved intimacy. You know each other better, understand each other better, appreciate each other better. You can better grasp what makes your marriage tick. You can see harmful influences and work out ways together to combat them. You can see the healthy, positive influences and rejoice in them. Just the act of building a mutually advantageous contract can bind you together more securely.

This concept of contract writing is not a quick fix for anything. You have to do the homework first, all of it. If you haven't dug out hidden agendas, the surface patch-up will surely fail.

Robert Hemfelt dealt recently with a couple with perfectly coordinated hidden agendas. Both said, "I'm marrying you so I can have a sparring partner." Unfortunately, a serious case of denial kicked in and neither would accept what their hidden agendas really were. The agendas remained hidden. Any new contract they negotiated set them up to fail because the underlying agreement made fighting inevitable. With new contracts they simply found different things to fight about.

WHEN ONE SIDE REFUSES

Joe did a reverse intervention on Barbara to get her back into counsel (this, incidentally, is a very common situation).

An intervention is not a bright, snappy silver bullet to cure whatever motivational problem a loved one may have. It's a painful, carefully orchestrated, serious tool, not to be taken lightly. In this case, Joe and Brian gathered friends and associates who understood the importance of AA and were seeing troubling mood changes in Barbara. Several had passed through that same crisis themselves. A boss, the children—had Barbara any of those, they would logically have been included. They were coached so as to convey their concern in loving ways. At the appointed time, they arrived at Joe and Barbara's, sat down in the living room, and one by one voiced to Barbara their worries and cares about her loss of happiness. They enumerated very specific instances which indicated the unhealthy changes they saw in her behavior. Together they urged her into counsel, not for Joe's sake but for her own.

But what if Barbara had refused?

In so many marriages, one partner focuses on change and improvement but the other has no interest or may even sabotage it, desperately afraid of change. Then what?

It is *not* true that a marriage can't change for the better unless both spouses buy into the change.

Because we already know quite a bit about Joe and Barbara and their interior motivations, let's use them in a hypothetical case. Let's pretend Barbara backed off and clung to her old dysfunctional attitudes. She would tend the wounded bird whether he wanted tending or not. She would continue trying to fix what her mother and grandmother could not, even if it already fixed itself. She would not give up control (this is not so hypothetical after all; frequently, spouses in our counsel flatly refuse to cooperate).

In that case, Joe would draw up a new contract stating "How I am choosing to be in this marriage." This automatically cancels the dysfunctional contract between Barbara and him. So, as Joe persists in his new sobriety and comes to better understand the nature of his addiction and his recovery, he can change their relationship—*to an extent*—by abandoning the dysfunctional contract.

Invitation to the Dance

Let's illustrate that in a different light through a woman we'll call Katherine. Because of that tendency to polarization we've discussed, Katherine took on more and more jobs in her marriage that, to an increasing extent, didn't get done if she left them to her husband, Glen. Eventually she was handling the checkbook, the income tax, the mortgage payments, social scheduling, and all medical and legal appointments—not to mention mowing the lawn. Glen didn't deliberately avoid those things; he simply didn't get around to them. Angry and frustrated, she turned to a reliable friend, a friend who didn't seem to have that problem, for advice.

The friend suggested that Katherine consider a stalemate. Katherine mulled that advice carefully. It seemed sound. She acted. "I created a crisis," she later explained. "No, that's not quite it. I let the crisis happen. First I decided what I absolutely wanted to get done. That was appointments involving the kids, income tax, and the mortgage payment. I made certain those things were kept current.

"I told Glen I was handing the rest back to him. Instead of watching sports on TV all night, he could balance the checkbook and some of those things. 'I will no longer do them,' I said. He shrugged it off; I don't think he thought I was serious.

"Chaos. I mean, there was chaos. The checkbook was a mess. He got billed for a dental appointment he made and forgot. He showed up twenty-four hours late to his boss's hot tub party. The lawn grew so high we kept losing the dog. I stood firm. 'You take some of the responsibility in this outfit,' I told him. 'It's supposed to be a two-person operation.'

"Eventually, it was. I think the turning point was when the bank called him at work and threatened to repossess his pickup truck if he didn't pay up by the close of that day. He delivered the check in person."

Katherine smiles now. "But I was tearing my hair out by then. It was a learning experience for me too. Now I know that even when only one person forges a new contract, and enforces it, it saps the strength of the old one."

Katherine invited her partner back into the dance. In essence she was doing what AlAnon and other codependency groups have long advocated: Quit enabling. When one person decides not to enable, the other must change. Even if the other party doesn't buy into the new arrangement, crisis develops, and that crisis will force the other party to address the dysfunctional contract.

Ian would have explained it another way. "You're talking about a contract walkout. Union and management are forced to negotiate. The union or

The Renewed Marriage Contract

1. Statement of affirmation; at least one attribute each person admires and appreciates in the other

2. Statement of extent of commitment to the marriage

3. Promise of fidelity

4. Statement of faith, embracing:
   a. Each person's individual statement of faith
   b. Clearly stated common ground
   c. Statement of tolerance (and limits of tolerance)

5. Statement of recognition of old, dysfunctional hidden agendas

6. Declaration of new agendas to redress dysfunctions

7. Sexual contract, including:
   a. Recognition of difficulties or shortcomings in present sexual relations
   b. Steps to improve relations and/or explore new techniques
   c. Details of frequency if frequency is an issue

8. Review of items in first contract, with updates and revisions as necessary

9. Details of everyday life (request for romantic nights out) established through give-and-take (be specific)

company may walk out of contract negotiation if they don't see progress. That's not walking out of the company. The person is not walking out of the marriage, right? Just the situation. When you're on strike, mate, something's got to give!''

Strike the Band

Unfortunately, we find strikes happening in marriages all the time, often at the subconscious level, down on the level of those hidden agendas. They are not engaged for constructive purposes, such as the strike Katherine used to her advantage, and if they go unrecognized, they may last the balance of the marriage.

A very common one we find is the woman who goes on strike sexually. "I'm cooking for you and doing your laundry. But no eroticism." A common way for the husband to go on strike is to stop participating in family affairs. "I'm the breadwinner, and I'm still here," but not at the Little League game, the family picnic, or whatever. Usually if one or the other party is on strike, it has something to do with unresolved, unfinished anger.

Katherine's strike was born of anger, but her strike was not an end in itself, and certainly not intended to punish Glen for wrongs real or imaginary. Her goal was healthy change. A strike without such a goal is futile and destructive.

The final task of Realistic Love is to adapt to the changes that occur when little people enter your family. Kids certainly change the marriage. If you're a parent you know the all-time world-class stressor: the kids. Let's look at what kids are bound to do, particularly in this stage of marriage.

9

CAN YOU CHILDPROOF YOUR MARRIAGE?

*A*rnold." He grimaced. "They went and named me Arnold. You know, the only way you can go through school as an Arnold is if your last name's Schwarzenegger. Even my name works against me."

In our office, frail, slim, balding Arnold sat in his chair in a knot. Not only were his legs crossed but the toe of one foot wound around behind the other leg—a double cross. His crossed arms tightly guarded his heart. Arnold was not a happy man.

"Tell us about your first wife," we asked.

"What's to tell? We were married nine years. Then things turned against me. I was a pastor. I guess she got tired of playing second fiddle to the entire congregation. She left."

"Children?"

"Three. She has custody. Except holidays."

"Let's talk about your chil—"

"And my birthday."

"Beg your pardon?"

"My birthday. The kids get to visit on my birthday. Also on Martin Luther King Day." He shifted in his chair and retied his knots.

We nodded. "How old are your—"

"And Columbus Day. Some schools get out on the Monday when the banks close, and some celebrate the actual day, October 12. No uniformity.

So I got it in writing that the kids visit on the legal holiday, whenever that falls. I work in a bank, you see—I had to resign my pastorate during the divorce—and I wanted the guarantee that I have the day off when the kids are here."

"What do you do in the bank?"

"Advise churches and other nonprofit organizations about investments. I'm considered very good at it. Our bank has seen a 27 percent increase in investment accounts in the last year, and nearly all are with nonprofit institutions. Special rules, you know. It's not your usual investment strategy."

"Your experience as a pastor must be invaluable in that line of work."

"Exactly!" And Arnold launched into a detailed explanation of IRS rulings, and the difference between Fanny Maes and Ginny Maes. We drew him back to the subject of his children, learning eventually that they were aged eight, six, and four.

He seemed to loosen a little, and his face sagged, sadder. "There was a lot of financial pressure when I was pastoring. And time pressures. Demands. Kids take so much time. And confusion. The house was always in an uproar, and a pastor lives in a fishbowl. You know that. Appearances. What will the neighbors think? Kids give nosy neighbors a lot to think about."

He grimaced again. "Ironic. It's all against me. Each year the kids get older, they cost more. More money. More time. Now that I'm making a better-than-decent living at an eight-hour-a-day job, I don't have the kids anymore."

Kids—and the lack of kids if they've always been a part of your dreams for your family—raise the stress level of any marriage. The last task in the Second Passage of marriage is to childproof your marriage.

THE FOURTH TASK: CHILDPROOF YOUR MARRIAGE

"It's a dangerous myth" says Debi Newman, "that having a baby will help save a marriage. They add enormous stress."

Remember our formula:

$$1 \text{ person} + 1 \text{ person} = \text{conflict.}$$

You can see that adding another member promises friction by multiplying the possible combinations. Mom mothers, but at times she also fathers. Dad fathers, but occasionally must assume the mother role. And then there is each adult's individual private life—work, the world outside the home—and their life as a sexually united couple.

Tossing one child into the pot multiplies the opportunities for friction exponentially, and most families have more than one child, all interacting in a multitude of roles. That's more chances to disagree, more power struggles, more differences of taste and preferences, both within and between the generations. Children present many more needs than do adults; needs to be emotionally nurtured on the road to adulthood (and that's not just a pat on the head in passing. Kids have intense needs that must be met immediately).

Kids introduce another hidden negative element, too: From the parents' viewpoint, they provide more opportunity to fail. The woman with low self-esteem, the man who is unsure of himself, not only faces the possibility of being considered a bad spouse but a bad parent as well. And those two occupations are pursuits the world thinks ought to come naturally.

Brian and Debi Newman comment on that. "Over and over in counsel we see parents react out of a fear of failure. But they don't actually acknowledge that fear of failure. Thus they don't realize the grip it has on them."

"We've all felt the pull to give in to our children's temper tantrums in the store, just to keep people from staring and wondering what kind of parents we are," says Debi Newman. "A more extreme example is the mother who was overweight as a teenager. She may now fear that her child will become overweight and experience the same rejection she experienced in childhood. When she sees her three-year-old daughter enjoying food and eating healthily, the mother may panic and try to take away the food, not realizing the power plays or feelings she may be creating in her daughter."

Still More Pressure

This multiplicity of personalities, with all their frictions and quirks, is the least of it. As Arnold realized, children apply financial pressures from conception on. No parent needs to be told the bewildering variety of ways kids cost money, and non-parents don't want to know.

Children do not sit quietly in a corner. They get involved in activities—sports, clubs, myriad activities to crunch the already-busy parents' time and energy.

In the course of these activities, children meet other adults. As a necessary part of growing up, the kids forge strong personal relationships with some of them. When these relationships reach worshipful proportions, and there is a brief, normal period in every child's life when just such a relationship happens, the parents often feel jealous or threatened. Because it sneaks in, unexpected, unprepared-for, the jealousy causes all the more friction and damage.

THE SHIFTING SANDS OF PARENTHOOD

As rapidly as a newborn child changes, the parents change also. And the maturation is quite as predictable and certain in the parent as in the child. The maturation can be broken down into five stages, which obviously do not parallel the marriage passages we're talking about. We will discuss two of these stages—the period of surprise (the first child) and the period of drifting (school-age children) in this passage of marriage. Then look at the other three stages—the stage of turmoil (adolescent children), the stage of renewal or death of relationship (the empty nest), and the stage of joy (grandchildren) in later passages.

THE PERIOD OF SURPRISE—THE FIRST CHILD

The surprise factor, summarized, is the way that third little person multiplies the happiness and the stress of all the family's interrelationships.

Julia Karris gave voice to one element of surprise. "I baby-sat when I was a kid. But then I went home. Even with brothers and sisters, I never realized how a baby ties you down. Every moment it's either with you, or you've arranged for it to be with someone. There's no off-time, no time to walk away from it."

Carl Warden shook his head over the memories of another element of surprise. "I remember our first one. Annie was actually an easy kid as babies go. Still, parenthood was nothing like what I expected. I don't know what I expected, but this sure wasn't it. And I didn't get the worst of it. Annie was two years old when I got home from overseas. Bess took the brunt of it.

"I mean, here's this tiny person all over the house, babbling, insisting you listen to her, play with her, read to her. Tugging on your pants leg. Fussing.

"But the biggest surprise were the power struggles. A child three feet high can't read or write or mow the lawn, and you get into this powerful contest of wills. And Bess and I would get into power struggles, too, over Annie. I don't know how parents ever get past that first one."

Power struggles—that old question, "Who's in control here?" now rephrased to "Who's in control of this child?"—can indeed unravel the marriage fabric, but they also offer the potential to improve intimacy. Power struggles are, in effect, a form of conflict and can be dealt with as the parents would deal with other conflicts. Negotiation between the parents reveals the parents' thoughts and preferences to each other. As the problem is ironed out, each gets to know the other a little better.

One solid principle for keeping kids from damaging the marital bond is for spouses to agree upon their philosophy of child-raising before the fact, not after the kids come along and generate a crisis. The parents should agree in advance on a united front. If that sounds like a war strategy, it is. Kids will divide you if they can, to gain their own ends.

In counseling we again suggest that couples review the parenting they observed in their family of origin. Take a moment to think about how your parents' actions affect your attitudes toward raising children by checking the statements below that apply to you:

_____ "In my family children were encouraged to voice their opinions concerning family decisions."

_____ "In my family children were given an allowance tied to their chores."

_____ "In my family everyone ate something different at mealtimes."

_____ "In my family sons were treated differently than daughters."

_____ "In my family both my mom and dad would try to attend my sports, school, and church functions."

_____ "My father (or mother) didn't pay much attention to me."

_____ "In my family the father was the person who disciplined the children."

_____ "In my family it was okay to spank the children."

_____ "My parents would get angry and slap the children."[1]

Now take a look at your own beliefs about child raising:

_____ "I believe children need to learn how to manage money as they grow up."

_____ "I believe that it is all right for children to talk back to their parents."

_____ "I believe that both father and mother should be involved in the daily care of the children."

_____ "I believe that it is important for children to be involved in extra activities, like dancing, sports, piano lessons."

_____ "How children behave and their manners are very important to me."

_____ "I believe that both parents should discipline the kids."

_____ "I plan to spank our children as a way of discipline."

_____ "I want our family to hold and hug each other."[2]

Compare your answers to this second set of statements with the first set of statements. Which of your attitudes about child rearing has been influenced by your parents? Is that influence good or bad? Now discuss these issues with your spouse. Once you have talked through your thoughts about child rearing and how they have been influenced, for better or for worse, by your parents, we suggest that the two of you enter into a verbal or written covenant concerning child rearing. You can use this second set of statements as a guideline for this covenant.

Remember, however: the family is not a democracy. It is critical that the parents be parents and let the children be children. In counsel we find two situations that usually begin right in this first period of parenthood, and either can irreversibly damage both the marriage and the children.

Fear of Rejection

We are constantly amazed and dismayed at how deeply some parents fear their kids will cease to like them. One of our clients, Amy Marchand, tells her story:

"I suppose every mother worries that maybe her kid will turn out hating her. Look at how children scream and holler when you want them to do something they don't want to. Or tell them no.

"When my little Pete yelled 'Mommy, I hate you!' one day, I think that's what really got me. Pete wanted to play in the mud around the storage shed we were building out back. It was nap time and I didn't want him to get dirty. He threw a fit when I tried to drag him inside, and then he said that.

"I'm ashamed to admit it now, but then I guess I was just shocked. I turned him loose and he ran back to the mud hole. It wasn't long before all he had to do was screech once and we'd give in, both my husband and I. And the more we let him have his way, the more we tried to please him, the worse he got."

We asked Amy this question: "If you were to crack down and enforce a reasonable discipline, do you think he'd hate you?"

She replied, "Yes. He's too used to having his own way."

"Does he really love you now?"

"No."

"Then what will you lose?"

Emotional Incest

When children come into a marriage from prior marriages, the conflict shoots up even higher. Joel and Carolyn found that out the hard way.

Carolyn sat in our office on the verge of tears. "Joel is wonderful. I realize a bride who's only been married eight months is going to say that, but he really is. He's so—so mellow. My former husband, Ralph, was verbally abusive. Extremely so. Our daughter Michelle grew up in a constant state of terror."

Even though Carolyn had only been married eight months she was already in the Second Passage of marriage, since this was a second marriage and she and her husband had children from a previous marriage. Her problems were not as unique as she thought.

"How old is Michelle now?" we asked.

"Almost fourteen. I met Joel at Michelle's sixth-grade open house. His Janna was in the same class. Michelle seemed thrilled that Janna's dad and me were getting together. Michelle was our biggest booster."

"But when you married, her attitude changed."

"Did it ever. There's a lot of jealousy. Joel's kids are jealous because they can't live with him, and they make life miserable every time we have them. Okay. I can see that. But Michelle's got it made. Her natural father yelled at her and put her down all the time. Joel doesn't do any of that. She *wanted* us to make a family. And now . . . "

It's a pattern we see so often. "How is she acting out?"

"Big mouth, talking back. Boys. It's the boys that worry me most."

"Other than Michelle, everything's going all right?"

Carolyn brightened. "Before I ever met Joel, I had already worked through most of the issues associated with the first marriage in counseling—both Michelle and I. We pretty much got our heads on straight, finally. And Joel and I appreciate each other more than most couples do because we've both been around the block. We really got a good thing going, with work."

So what could go wrong? We talked to Carolyn's daughter, Michelle. In the years of living alone with her mother, Michelle had learned to depend upon Mom. She thereby felt safe as never before. Mom supported her. Mom wouldn't let her down. Unfortunately, Mom developed almost exactly the same dependency upon her daughter. Mom needed Michelle for affirmation. She needed Michelle to pick up the slack when life and work got too much. Michelle became confidante, a job she was too young and ill-equipped to handle. When the child nurtures the parent, as Michelle nurtured her mom, we call it emotional incest, as you remember.

We are seeing that emotional incest, the transfer of intimacy from spouse to child, is the single most damaging thing that kids bring to a marriage; and it's not their fault. Kids must be allowed to be kids, without the responsibility and onus of assuming quasi-parental roles.

Kids can also raise the chaos level in a marriage when the couple seems unable to have children.

Pressure When the Nest Stays Empty

Many women, because of long years on the Pill or an abortion in their past, have trouble conceiving and carrying a child to term. Some suffer miscarriage for physiological reasons. This puts another kind of stress on the marriage.

Mary Alice Minirth knows that stress too well. "Our first pregnancy and miscarriage, I didn't know happened. Frank was in his third year of medical school," she recalls. "I was teaching in an inner-city ghetto. I thought my period was messed up from the stress. Not long after that Frank was diagnosed with diabetes, and his future has always been uncertain. My father had cancer. It was the lowest I've ever been."

"We tried again. I suffered three miscarriages in two and a half years. I was trying to teach in that stress situation, and I felt hopeless. Everyone else was having kids. After a miscarriage, I'd get on the elevator to go home and see a mother with a baby in her arms. I'd get in the car and just boo-hoo.

"Some doctors and friends advised us to hang it up. Quit trying. They'd say 'Aw, move on. It's over.' But it's a severe loss."

Frank agrees. "Miscarriage is much more of an issue than most people will admit. It's a severe loss, and you have to go through the stages of grief. A husband must be supportive of his wife. He has to try to understand her emotions because he probably has them also. It's an insight into his own feelings. He may not realize how much it's affecting him. It is. Men tend to lack a keen awareness of their own emotions. It's not that they're not emotional; it's just that, in general, men are not as acutely aware of their feelings as women. Also, talk about the losses. Listening and being listened to is the strongest medicine."

Grieving the Loss

A friend of ours miscarried because she didn't understand how certain chemicals could affect the unborn child's health. "I was two months pregnant when it happened," she said. "Dumb old us, we didn't know that some kinds of paint fumes can induce spontaneous abortion. We were refinishing some furniture, and I got sick from it and miscarried." She stared at her hands in her lap. "I always wonder what the baby would have been like."

"When did this happen?" we asked.

Her eyes brimmed with tears. "Twenty-five years ago."

The loss of an unborn child requires a special kind of grieving, because there is that huge dollop of the unknown. What would that child have been like? Who would the little one have become? To the husband even more so than the wife, that little one is nothing more than a theory, a loss described without ever being seen or touched. Parents of unborn children add those other factors in as they work through their grief.

The first step of the grief process, you'll recall, is *shock and denial.* Mary Alice received a particularly hard jolt when she learned that her "abnormal period" and its consequences was the loss of her first pregnancy. The jolt can be even more severe for a couple who learns of the pregnancy, anticipates the new arrival, and then watches the dream shatter, as the Minirths did during the next three pregnancies.

Feelings run deep and are painful. Anger is entirely appropriate. Never let someone try to talk you out of an emotional response with, "It's only a tadpole at that stage," or "It's not the end of the world" (for this moment, it is), or the cruelest of all, "You (will) have other children. It's not so bad." It is so bad! A death is a death.

The second step is *depression.* Mary Alice Minirth recalls, "I felt hopeless about my past, present, and future. I was almost clinically depressed. I wanted to sleep a lot." This step may be complicated by physiological factors. A woman's hormones alter during pregnancy, and with them her emotional state and balance. Should you lose a child, your body's hormones are thrown for a loop. The physical condition can cause depression apart from the depression of the grieving process. If depression becomes exceedingly severe or lingers far too long (months and months), seek medical help. But do expect depression. It's normal.

The third step, *bargaining,* must not be confused with the advice to never give up hope, and certainly not with prayer. "Lord, please give me a child" is not the same as "Lord, if you just give me a child, I'll _____ in return." Bargaining and magical thinking are part of grieving and should be temporary in nature. Guard, though, against letting one of your bargains or magical thoughts turn into a plan of action. Magic won't help you.

The next step is *sadness.* Losing an unborn child is so sad. Again, you may receive sincere but wrong advice, particularly if your sadness shows clearly or persists a while. Besides, you're overcoming the medical effects of the loss, just as would a woman who gave birth. That makes it all the harder. It is natural and necessary to feel great sadness, let no one tell you otherwise.

The final phase of grieving, *forgiveness and resolution,* brings a measure of peace, but they do not close the book or erase memories. Whom would you forgive? In the case of the woman above, she had to forgive her and her husband's ignorance which led to the circumstance. It was not a deliberate act, but it required forgiveness *for the woman's sake.* If a person was instrumental in causing the miscarriage, such as a reckless driver responsible for an accident in which the unborn baby died, that person must be forgiven— again, *for the couple's sake*. Not forgotten. Not let off the hook. But forgiven.

Resolution is the healthy outcome of the grieving process. Part of the resolution to Frank and Mary Alice's losses was developing a plan of action. "Frank knew how sad and depressed I was," Mary Alice says, "so one day he sat me down and said that, with God's help, we would have a child. 'We will do everything we can—including going to an adoption agency—and then we will leave the rest up to God.'"

Six months later, when Mary Alice became pregnant again, they regrouped. "Frank's plan was for me to stay on the sofa all nine months if I had to. I organized drawers to keep busy. I read the whole Living Bible. It's the last time I did any embroidery."

At three months the Minirths were able to hear the baby's heartbeat. The next two months—the times when Mary Alice had miscarried before— went by without incident. At five months Mary Alice was able to buy maternity clothes for the first time. Everything went well until the thirty-second week of pregnancy when the doctor said that Mary Alice was showing signs of premature labor.

Mary Alice Minirth spent the last six weeks of that fourth pregnancy in the hospital. "It was a frightening time, because I imagined that every little pain would lead to stronger labor pains and to a premature baby. And all along, I feared that the baby would not be healthy. After six weeks, the labor pains seemed to stop."[3] Yet eight and a half months had finally gone by and the baby could arrive any time.

Two weeks later Rachel Marie Minirth was born, a healthy, seven-pound, eleven-ounce, bright-eyed baby. Frank and Mary Alice Minirth had been married seven years. They named their little girl Rachel because of the verse in Genesis that says, "Jacob served seven years for Rachel, and they seemed but a few days to him, because of the love he had for her."[4] Both Frank and Mary Alice felt that God had worked out His plan for their lives in His own way and His own timing.

"We lost one other baby after Rachel," Mary Alice says. "It was right after we moved here. It was excruciating, too, because it went on for three weeks. Lose it or save it? We lost it. But God had given us Rachel, so there was hope. Frank had his career, a new life to look forward to, a new practice. We had a new home and we had company all summer, too, which kept me busy. Old friends. It kept me going after the miscarriage.

"I think I had to fight self-pity most. We had so much, yet I didn't see it. You're blinded to what you have when you're in despair over what you don't have. I kept showing myself I had friends, and I had one child coming into her twos, and we had a worthy goal in life. God was opening up things for Frank.

"By the time our second one was born healthy, my father's cancer was arrested. He lived a full and happy life for many more years."

Today the Minirths have four girls: Rachel, age 16; Renee, age 13; Carrie, age 10; and Alicia, age 1. During this latest pregnancy, as with the others, Mary Alice spent months resting on the couch and Frank suspended any travel outside of Dallas so he could support her and help with the older girls.

Together the Minirths grieved the loss of four unborn babies and together they share the joy of their four lovely daughters, who are now in those years we call, "the period of drifting."

THE PERIOD OF DRIFTING—SCHOOL-AGE KIDS

We call this a period of drifting for several reasons. For one, it seems the family members are each cast adrift, going separate ways, aimlessly. For all the churning activity, you see very little real progress day to day. In fact, with school-age kids, how do you measure progress, if any?

Also, the family itself tends to drift. Pressed severely by all the issues school-age kids dump into the family stew, parents have little time for work, for play, for each other—even for the kids. It just didn't seem this hectic a generation ago.

Schedule Clutter

"Here in Dallas it's achieve, achieve, achieve," observes Mary Alice Minirth. "Overscheduling, both kids and adults."

How do busy parents avoid neglecting the kids' interests?

"Frank is careful about that," says Mary Alice. "The kids' school holidays are already X-ed off his schedule for next year. Renee's school play, for instance. All that. I try to be there all the time, and he's there most of the time. He went with Renee on her wilderness trip, canoeing, and camping. He takes each of them on a trip to Arkansas at least once a year and they get to take another friend and her dad.

"He's a workaholic at play too. He works at playing with the kids, and he loves it. They share hobbies—horseback riding, camping, the outdoors.

"But it's hectic. Last week a policeman called to tell us the horses had gotten out. So Frank was out chasing four horses, with the policeman helping. At the same time a litter of kittens was being born in the barn. Renee came screaming up to the house each time a new one appeared. It was an unusual morning.

"We had no vacation at all for the first seven or eight years. Business or some seminar always involved travel. Then it dawned on Frank that it was time to do something besides work. We vacation regularly now. We still talk about Hawaii—how the flowers smelled, how the pineapple tasted. But mostly we go to Arkansas. The kids like that."

Stability Flutter

What children need most of all, though, at any age but particularly during the school years, is a stable family life. Unfortunately, as the kids get wrapped up in school with all their needs and demands, and the parents struggle with work demands, stability tends to flutter.

Family stability is no stronger, no less fluttery than the stability of the marriage itself. Parents who would give their children the best possible schooling, then, would make the marriage their first priority.

There is a retirement benefit to this. Someday your link to the past, your parents, will pass on. Your link to the future, your children, will fledge. In your house will be you and your mate, your marriage the only commitment designed to last a lifetime. It behooves you to keep it strong now, as insurance toward the future.

Both partners must be involved in this complex process of child-raising. It's not just Mom's duty. A child's concepts of God are shaped by the earthly father. In fact, there are far more Bible verses addressing fathers than mothers.

We've long known that the child blossoms when the father loves the mother. How can the children learn to express love in a family situation? Include them when picking out Mommy's Valentine gift. Might they plan a special Mother's Day or Father's Day dinner . . . and then help buy the groceries? Encourage them to make place cards for Sunday lunch. Let them help choose the Christmas tree. Children learn love and family unity best by being part of the loving family unit.

"One of the best ways to stop the drifting and make time for each other," says Susan Hemfelt, "is simply to put the children to bed at a decent hour. You'd be amazed how many people don't. The kids, especially little ones, need the sleep. And you and your mate need the time for each other."

That brings up the lock on the bedroom door. Nothing cools ardor faster than a little voice at the door, a child who was supposed to go to sleep and for some reason has risen to haunt you. "*Little* voice?!" A friend of ours laughed. "When the kids were small we laid down the law: Once you're in bed you stay there. No problem. It was when they were grown and coming home from dates or college at all hours that we got the bolt for the bedroom door. If you think a little voice wrecks the romantic mood, try 'Hi, Dad! I'm home! Don't bother to get up; I'll find something to eat in the fridge.' "

If you have school-age children, ask yourself, "Where can we carve out some blocks (possibly small blocks, but blocks nonetheless) of time to nurture our union?"

ONWARD, EVER ONWARD

As the children grow, the marriage continues its inexorable changes, from reality into comfort. You are slipping into the next passage much as you would slip into a comfy, familiar pair of old house slippers. If that's not poles apart from the romance with which your union started, what is? It's worth considering in detail, this Third Passage, for it will shape what is to come and can renew that which passed.

But to get there, you must have completed the Second Passage. Check the statements below that apply to you. Again we invite you to make your own assessment and make any adjustments that seem possible.

HOW WELL HAVE I COMPLETED
THE SECOND PASSAGE?

1. ____ "Having shared a number of years of marriage together, I can honestly look at my spouse and say, 'You're someone special. I like you. I still find a fascination with the mystery of who you are. I'm still in love with you.' "

2. ____ "I can think of three specific features, characteristics, or attributes of my spouse that I still cherish at the end of Passage Two." *(For example:*
   - *"You have a clever and spontaneous sense of humor that always keeps our relationship fresh."*
   - *"You have deep spiritual values, which have helped sustain us in the most difficult times."*
   - *"You have a sexy body; after ten years of marriage I still catch myself watching you walk across the room.")*

   _____

   _____

   _____

3. ____ "I have seen you in the illusion of courtship. I have seen you in the difficult moments of stark reality. I have come to appreciate the reality of you in mature love, as much or

more as in early love. Specifically, I appreciate the following strengths you have demonstrated in our most challenging crisis."

_____

_____

_____

_____

4. _____ "I appreciate the boundaries we have established with our children. We have reached that special balance between union and separateness in both our individual and couple relationships with each child."

5. _____ "No child in our family feels excluded or favored, and no child has been moved into the position of ally or surrogate with one parent against (or in place of) the other parent."

6. _____ "If children have not entered or remained in this marriage, due to choice, infertility, miscarriage, or premature death, we have both grieved this void."

7. _____ "I now recognize that I entered this marriage with a number of unrealistic expectations of you and these expectations were the hidden agendas in my emotional marriage contract. I acknowledge the following hidden contracts, both toxic and benign, that I brought into our marriage union."

_____

_____

_____

_____

8. _____ "I am willing to surrender and release the toxic contracts that I imposed on both of us. I do this without a sense of unnecessary shame because I realize I was doing the best I knew how in our early years. However, I also realize the enormous damage these toxic contracts have inflicted on you and me. I am actively seeking to suspend and revoke the following toxic contracts."

_____

_____

_____

9. _____ "Having revoked or amended the toxic contracts that originally brought me to you, I now commit to remarry you and to draft a radically new contract for our union.

The following is a list of new fresh ways I seek to be your partner."

     Mentally _____

     Emotionally _____

     Physically _____

     Socially _____

     Spiritually _____

PART
FOUR

The Third Passage:
Comfortable Love,
the Eleventh through
the Twenty-fifth Years

10

CAN YOU MAINTAIN INDIVIDUAL IDENTITY WITHIN YOUR MARRIAGE?

*A*nd they all lived happily ever after.' Now go to bed." James Jorgensen closed the book and tapped five-year-old Jamie on the head. He looked at eight-year-old Lynnette on his other side. "You too."

Jamie wiggled down off the sofa. "Is Mommy coming home tonight?"

"I don't know. She'll come wake you up and say good night, if she does. Brush your teeth well."

"Don't forget to kiss me and tickle my nose. You forgot that last night."

"I'll try."

Jamie hustled away upstairs.

Lynnette sat, still staring at the book. "Is Joci gonna die?"

"Modern medicine performs all kinds of miracles. I sure hope they can help her. We'll pray hard that the Lord's will be done and He'll be merciful."

"She's only two."

What could he say? James said nothing.

Lynnette slid to the edge and stood up. "They don't really live happily ever after, do they?" She slogged upstairs like an old woman.

James watched her go. The worst thing about little Joci Jorgensen's cancer was not all the time his wife, Lonna, spent at the hospital with her. It wasn't the pain of being unable to help your helpless little girl. It certainly wasn't the financial burden of trying to cover what insurance did not. The worst thing was the way it robbed an eight-year-old of her innocence about the world.

James received the call at ten. He asked Lonna's mother to stay with the children and joined his wife at the hospital for their last sorrowful vigil. It ended at 3:00 A.M.

The doctor looked nearly as haggard as Lonna did. "There was nothing we could do," he said. "We tried, but the bone marrow transplant didn't take."

MY SPOUSE IS LIKE AN OLD SHOE . . .

Five years ago. Joci died five years ago today. By closing his eyes, James could see every picture of the tiny girl in their old photo album. There weren't that many. The third baby is photographed a small fraction as much as the first two.

He sipped his breakfast coffee. "I wonder what she'd be like today."

Across the table, Lonna glanced at him. "Happy. She had such a charming personality. I think she would have kept it."

James smiled sadly. Curious, the way he and Lonna did that. Their thoughts seemed so often on the same wavelength. He didn't have to mention he was thinking about Joci. The anniversary date, a glance—that was enough.

. . . Comfortable, but Wearing Out

On the fifth anniversary of their daughter's death, James and Lonna demonstrated the best and the worst of this Third Passage. They knew each other so well they didn't have to explain their thoughts to each other. In fact, James and Lonna both did that a lot, as if they could read each other's minds. Too, they shared the trauma, literally, that sometimes comes with raising children. Five years did not obliterate the loss of their two year old.

However, as couples build a history together, they may become so melded that their individuality suffers. They may become codependent upon each other. In the beginning, a couple's task is to forge a marital identity out of two diverse personalities. By this stage, the task is nearly the reverse: to maintain an individual identity along with the marriage identity.

THE FIRST TASK: MAINTAIN AN INDIVIDUAL IDENTITY ALONG WITH THE MARRIAGE IDENTITY

Many couples feel as Louie Ajanian did when he told us, "My first wife was like an old piece of clothing. And I was the same for her. You don't have any reason to throw it away, but you're getting kind of tired of it.

"It's become a part of you, and you identify with it and you love it. Still, you start feeling ho-hum, and maybe even a little bitter."

Intimacy vs. Codependency

Codependency is an irrational, slavish, and ultimately damaging dependence upon persons, things, or actions. The term arose years ago as Alcoholics Anonymous began its amazing success story. Persons dependent upon alcohol or other drugs would do well with recovery, returning to near normalcy. But their families would fall apart. Their families were *co*dependent upon their addictions, just as adversely affected, just as unable to relate comfortably in situations where addiction was not a factor.

The concept of codependency today has expanded far beyond that original definition. It now means that, whatever the reason, two people have become so completely enmeshed that their personal identities are damaged or reduced. Each spouse's identity derives from the partner, not from the self.

Exaggerated Dependence

Unexpected things happen to a marriage when codependency comes into play. Picture the spectrum of possibilities as a wheel, as in the figure below. At the top lies wholesome interdependence. Should the couple drift down the wheel counterclockwise, one starts to lean excessively upon the other. They become dependent upon each other. As they proceed on down the wheel toward the bottom, it may appear that one leans more than the other, but in reality, deep down, both lean together.

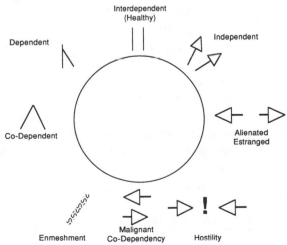

Relationship Wheel

At the bottom, malignantly codependent, these two have become so enmeshed that their individual identities are hard to sort out. Not even they themselves can do it. Sameness and dull complacency result.

We invite you to go down through this series of reflective statements to see if your marriage is hampered by exaggerated dependence. Do you find yourself in any of them?

_____ "I am constantly trying to please and win the favor of my spouse, even if that means burying my own feelings or compromising my own values, beliefs, and attitudes."

_____ "I push for my spouse to always agree with me." (Be honest; the push for agreement or conformity can be overt or very subtle but nonetheless powerful.)

_____ "My mood swings (up and down) are tied directly to those of my spouse."

_____ "Our sexual sharing has become routine and overly predictable." (Has it become so routine and devoid of excitement that your sex relationship has diminished or faded to nonexistence?)

_____ "Either I or my spouse has come to function as a chronic therapist or counselor (rescuer) to the other."

_____ "One of us has assumed a chronic sick role (physically, mentally, or emotionally) which requires the constant attention or intervention from the spouse."

_____ "I have placed my spouse on an unrealistic pedestal."

_____ "My spouse has placed me on such a pedestal."

_____ "I experience withdrawal symptoms when I am out of the presence of my spouse." (If there are brief separations due to work, travel, or such, do you feel a vague anxiety about these times of separation? Have you placed unreasonable demands on your spouse to curtail outside activities as a means of trying to ease that anxiety?)

_____ "I experience unreasonable fears about the status of my spouse's romantic and sexual fidelity."

_____ "I have gradually become a clone of my spouse." (Do you sometimes wonder whether you even know your own thoughts, opinions, values, and feelings apart from those you mimic and mirror in each other?)

_____ "The prospect of a life apart from my spouse (such as a circumstance of premature death) overwhelms me with feelings of terror and insecurity."

If you discover yourself checking several of the statements, consider it an indication that, for you, codependent tendencies may be reaching a problem level.

Yet exaggerated dependence is only half the picture. Let's look at that diagram of the relationship wheel again and see the other side of a marriage that's gone out of whack.

Exaggerated Independence

When the couple drifts clockwise down the wheel, their interests begin to diverge. That in itself isn't too bad. But the momentum, unchecked, carries that divergence to extreme. Estranged, the marriage partners have almost nothing in common except irritation and friction. Brought to its full course, this estrangement becomes constant hostility, or periods of extreme hostility interspersed with periods of extreme "lovey-dovey" closeness. Both the intense closeness and the howling fights are the fruits of codependency and can occur on the same branch, to the confusion of friends and family.

Have you and your spouse begun to drift down that wheel from exaggerated independence to dangerous enmeshment? Check the statements below to see if they reflect your relationship:

_____ "One of us has begun to be constantly critical of the other. This person views the other through a magnifying glass that highlights every flaw and imperfection."

_____ "I have begun to think to myself, 'I don't seem to be able to do anything right in this marriage.' "

_____ "Our marriage has reached a point of mutual impasse over a major issue, like deciding on a unifying team approach to parenting the children."

_____ "I find myself living in a state of constant tension and agitation in this marriage. The moments of peace seem to be only a temporary and fleeting truce before the next inevitable eruption of conflict."

_____ "One or both of us has begun to recruit the children, extended family members, or even mutual friends to take sides with us, enlisting them in these seemingly never-ending disputes."

Does each of you have a long list of accumulated resentments about real or imagined emotional hurts experienced at the hands of your spouse in the previous passages? Are these lists held up against each other as weapons of conflict? Are the two of you well accustomed to playing the mutual blame game ("If only you had not . . . " "If only you would . . . ")?

_____ "Our lives (activities, interests, pursuits) have begun to move in widely divergent directions."

_____ "I have secretly questioned why I'm staying in this relationship."

_____ "I (or my spouse) periodically threaten divorce."

_____ "One or both of us has quietly resigned from the sexual intimacy of this marriage." (Don't limit the meaning to the physical act here. The physical act without intimacy or fulfillment counts as a resignation.)

_____ "Romantic affairs outside our marriage have scarred its intimacy."

We posed these questions to a couple in our marital counsel, Dave and Genie. Reflecting upon the questions, they perceived that they were drifting down the wheel clockwise to exaggerated independence. Dave came to us because his second marriage was fast headed down the same road his first marriage had taken, with disaster at its end. Dave left the ministry after six years' service for the Lord because his wife divorced him. Three years later he returned to the pastorate and subsequently remarried. Eight years later his new wife, Genie, began to nag him with the same complaint his first wife did: "The people in the church always come before your family. You're never here to help me with the kids. In fact, they hardly know what you look like anymore. And I'm beginning to resent spending my every minute with them." Dave was hearing the same tape he had heard in his first marriage. "Women are all alike," he fumed. "Bah!" Dave didn't realize he was the one who had slipped back into his old patterns of workaholism.

We had to help Dave see that his marriage had become that comfortable old garment, present but unnoticed, taken for granted. Again, as in his first union, Dave had made the third leg of the stool—the church he pastored—the most important leg. Dave had to participate in the marriage more; he had become so meshed in his work that it absorbed most of his time and energy.

Genie had her share of the problem too. Genie and Dave had two children of their own. Lyndon, seven, was what they call hyperactive. Not naughty, just constantly busy. He wanted to build a tree house but Genie didn't let him after he fell out of the tree the third time. Lyndon's teacher said Genie ought to have him seen by a doctor familiar with Attention Deficit Syndrome, whatever that was, because he was disruptive. But where was Genie going to find time to take Lyndon into town for that stuff when she had to look after both kids and manage the house and their financial affairs without any help from Dave? The children were becoming more a burden than a joy to her.

We had to help Genie develop her own interests, her own identity, again. She needed to see herself as someone besides a mother and pastor's wife. We helped her shore up her leg of the stool.

REBUILD YOUR PERSONAL IDENTITY

Genie was savvy enough to realize that resentment bears no good fruit. It changes nothing. It poisons only the waters of the person whom it fills. Unwilling to let her resentment grow, and not quite ready to lock the kids in a closet for the next ten years, she chose the third option—carve out a bit of time and effort for herself. We helped her sit down and write out a plan.

Look at the Whole Picture

Genie's plan, subdivided, got the kids through high school and listed the graduation dates. She listed emancipation dates: when each child got a driver's license and no longer had to be chauffeured. Suddenly she could see the light at the end of the tunnel. This hectic child care schedule wouldn't last forever. It only seemed that way.

She listed projects she wanted to complete or begin, projects having nothing to do with kids or Dave or the pastorate. She wanted to finish the afghan she started in sewing class in high school, when they learned to crochet. She wanted to make a really nice nativity set, all handmade with stiffened draped fabrics and porcelain faces and hands; she'd saved all the patterns and instructions she found four years ago.

Finally, she began a calendar of hope, a grid covering the next sixteen years. On it she planned what she would do for herself, year by year, as the kids grew up, and the ages they would be when she did these things.

Don't Neglect Yourself

As for the present, Genie could afford a baby-sitter three hours a week. Then, happily, eagerly, she began creating her nativity set, a few hours at a time. A whole delicious block of free time just for her. No kids, no telephone, no bother.

She spent time also simply dealing with the resentment. She had eventually to make peace with the burden of responsibility for the children.

Because of her light-at-the-end-of-the-tunnel list, she could manage that well enough.

She deliberately made peace with the sacrifices she had to make for the kids. They were inevitable. She grieved losses and steeled herself for the future. Sacrificial living wasn't over yet. In fact, it would probably never end completely.

Genie probably never noticed, but her expanded interests brightened her outlook and even, to an extent, her personality. Dave noticed the change, although he took a long time realizing that some stiff brocade and a few porcelain heads would make a difference.

What are some things you've dreamed of doing?

_____

_____

_____

What on this list must wait until the kids are grown?

_____

_____

What might you do now? If there's nothing here you could do for yourself now, can you think of something else that you could use as time to yourself?

_____

_____

Genie resented the fact that Dave was so busy caring for the parishioners of his church and slighted his parental duties. She did not learn until they entered counsel that Dave resented the time and attention she lavished on the kids instead of him. He felt not so much jealous as neglected.

Genie's full identity had become enmeshed in motherhood and preacher's-wife-hood. There was too little Genie left for happiness. With cases like Genie, we might invite both spouses to draw a series of pie charts to show where they think their time goes. Then we ask that they draw charts to show where they would like the time to go. From there we help them restructure their boundaries, priorities, and schedules to come closer to the dream. This helps both the workaholic and the overloaded mother. Or, they might list the things that take their time, with the most time-consuming items first. The physical ink-on-paper list also helps them to literally see the problem. Rearranging the list is then another visual aid to solving priority and boundary problems. Genie had to re-forge her self, reestablishing her own identity apart from all the demands and circumstances around her. Dave had to recast his identity as a husband and father.

When we work with a couple who cannot bond or are too enmeshed, we ask them to do physical, task-oriented exercises. For example, we had a husband in Passage Three who was tyrannical. He wasn't abusive, but he always had to have his wife with him at home. On the rare occasion he went out of town, she had to call in, or he'd call her. It wasn't romantic jealousy. He trusted her fidelity. It was the sense that "I have to be together with this person." To him, it was not okay for her to be alone. So we gave them a mountain climbing assignment. Rock climbing. They loved it. It was so challenging it developed a strong teamwork bonding, and the husband could begin to give his wife more autonomy. And she found she could demand it more. He could let go on control issues because they could trust the bond better.

That may sound like a contradiction in terms, and it is. It's a paradox in a way, but it's how the emotions work. The deeper and more solid the bond between man and wife, the more they can let each other go—not impose restrictive control or codependent attention.

If the bond is deep, you can let go on the surface, like the man just described. In war, for instance, men who go through battle together never forget the names and faces of people they fought with. Challenge, especially physical challenge, forges bonds.

HEALTHY INTERDEPENDENCE

The object, of course, is to stay balanced up near the top of the relationship wheel. As Frank Minirth explains it, "The goal in marriage is a healthy interdependence. A great mistake is when one partner tries to feel all the feelings (or do everything) in the marriage. Those persons feel everything so intensely, they cannot live without the other person. This leaves the other person feeling inferior. The other extreme is also a mistake, and we see it frequently in the clinic. That's when the person shuts down and lets the spouse do all the feeling (or do everything). God doesn't want you turning everything over to another person.

"We're not saying dependency is bad. Healthy dependency is excellent. Be dependent on God, on friends; that's okay in itself. You have to watch out for the danger of codependency. And incidentally, divorce never cures codependency. The problem lies below the level of the marriage, deep inside the individual."

To use the three-legged stool principle, think that a solid stool requires three sound, sturdy legs; not one or two strong ones with one or two spindly ones.

Maintaining personal identity by avoiding the codependency drift is only one of the tasks this Third Passage requires. To prevent yourself from becoming stuck in the third passage, you must consider others too. One of them is saying good-bye to the past, never an easy thing to do.

THE SECOND TASK:
SAY THE FINAL GOOD-BYES

There it is again. Saying good-bye. Haven't you done that enough? Only by saying good-bye to one thing can you embrace another. You must put down the pen in your hand if you wish to pick up the pencil. That is what good-bye is about. For every good-bye there is a hello.

Two important good-byes remain, and you just about have to reach this stage in life before you can do it well. Deep within each human heart lurks the yearning that somewhere, someone is waiting to step in and direct you in all the right moves. You want a god to take over. And because the human heart feels the tangible and the real so much more easily than the intangible, you substitute your parents as God. Why, it took you over a decade as you were growing up just to realize that your parents weren't perfect. The ancient childhood dream of perfect parents acting with godlike wisdom lingers on, and for good reason.

Parents provide an important safety girdle while the kids are growing up. That buffer against life is hard to shed. A healthy friendship in which the parent is no longer a primary authority figure is not the same as the original parent-child relationship. Delightful and rewarding as the new friendship may be, the past must be grieved and put behind.

If Your Parents Are Not Available

Let us first assume that your parents are either deceased or physically unavailable for some reason. Perhaps a parent, suffering from Alzheimer's or a stroke, or some similar problem, can no longer make coherent contact with you. If you are an adoptee, you may not know who they are. In that case, you have two sets of parents to say good-bye to, your biological parents and your adoptive parents. Write each deceased or unavailable parent a letter, or record a cassette tape.

- Tell of some high points of your memories with them, acknowledging the huge part they played in your life.
- Tell of some values of theirs that you've adopted as your own, thus acknowledging their leadership in your life.
- Tell them of your love as a child to a parent, identifying the emotional bond.

- Forgive them their failures and imperfections. As humans they are bound to have them. Be as specific as you can.
- Say good-bye to the person you have just summarized. Say the words aloud. Write them down. Look at them.

Picture the person in your mind. If, as with an unknown biological parent, you have no visual memories, set your mind on any of the guess-work pictures you formed through your life of what they might have been like. In that case you are saying good-bye to your perception of them as much as they themselves.

Lay your hands flat on the letter, touching it, claiming it in lieu of the person, and pray to God on that person's behalf. Give thanks for that parent's influence in your life (bad influences are never entirely negative; the most destructive influence still shapes you in some positive way as well).

Now, finally, picture in your mind's eye waving good-bye to that person and walking away.

If Your Parents Are Available

If your parent(s) is living and available, go through this same exercise, right up to the final picture of your walking away. But you do not just walk away from your living parents. Neither are they likely to understand should you step up to them and say "good-bye." So in your mind's eye, now, turn around. Picture yourself walking back to them. Place them on equal footing with any other valued companion. "Hello, friend."

It may take awhile, if you are in frequent contact with your parents, to get your heart to accept the good-bye. Remember that changing our words and actions can change our feelings. In word and deed treat your parents with no less respect, no less love, but as friends, not demi-gods.

Failing to say good-bye to your parents with your heart as well as mind is a sure way to get stuck in the passage. As Susan Hemfelt says, "You can't get anywhere focusing on the now and the past. You have to focus on the now and the future."

This passage, then, brackets the age when you can put the childhood dream behind you. No white knight, no perfect parent, not even God, will make your choices for you and clear your path. By now you can also grasp one other good-bye: There is no security here on earth.

One of our friends and her husband began to invest in the stock market during this Third Passage of life. They were preparing for the future—for the education of their children and their eventual retirement.

Our friend began watching the stock market. Each day she would turn to the financial section of the newspaper to read the report of their stocks. Were they up an eighth? Down a half? In the next year their stocks went up a few times, and down even more frequently.

"I can remember when it hit me," this friend recalls. "I was driving to the grocery store after reading the morning paper. All of a sudden the obvious struck me: None of those stocks were safe. There was nowhere we could put our money and know without doubt it would be there for us. No savings and loan association. No bank. No investment was really secure. There was no guarantee of anything for tomorrow. Whatever we had and whatever we did, we had it and did it by the grace of God."

Your security blanket—whatever your security symbols are—has worn threadbare. Here now, at last, it rips asunder. A key factor in this middle passage is your realization that no one human being has ultimate power.

For help in time of strife, pain, and chaos, people in the Alcoholics Anonymous recovery program call upon a higher power of their understanding. At the Minirth-Meier Clinic, and in our own lives, we take that two steps further. We identify the higher power as the God of Abraham, Isaac, and Jacob, the Father and His Son Jesus Christ. And we don't wait for recovery to make Him the third leg of our marriage.

The solid marriages, the stable relationships, all establish God as the third leg early on. This does not mean that if you have not and you've already been married many years, it is too late. It is never too late. But why procrastinate on a good thing if you have not made that choice yet?

We do not mean giving lip service to God or tossing in the saying of grace at meals or church attendance or Bible reading. Each of those things in its place is very important. But none of them alone make God the center of your life and marriage. Those things proceed out of your relationship with the living God.

Once we became God's, we took one more step. We let God guide what we do, through His Word and occasionally through His direct intervention. He is the CEO of our marriages and our lives. We deliberately ask Him to become the third leg of our marriage stool, the pillar of our union.

Susan Hemfelt points out, "Ultimately, we have to look to God for healing and strength, not to each other. Only God knows us well enough to keep us growing in sync with Him."

That is the pillar that forms the only lasting mainstay of marriage.

11

CAN YOU RESIST THE NOW-OR-NEVER SYNDROME?

*I*lona Guthrie couldn't remember exactly. Perhaps it was the day Reede forgot to fasten the tailgate when he was hauling the kids' 4-H sheep in the pick-up truck, and all nine ewes jumped out and ran through Mrs. Ware's flower beds, and then Mrs. Ware's dog chased after them clear around her house and on the second time around they ran over Mrs. Ware. Or maybe it was the time Reede installed the drip irrigation system in the front yard himself, instead of hiring professionals, and they turned it on but nothing happened, and two hours later they got this frantic call from Harry next door that the flood in his basement was a foot deep and rising. No matter. Whatever the exact occasion, there was a day, a moment, when Ilona fell out of love with Reede.

The Guthries, married fifteen years, had three children between the ages of five and twelve, the two boys and the kindergarten-aged girl. The oldest, Wayne, was a good kid, but too smart. He was in all these sports and clubs after school, and Ilona spent half her day in the car fetching him to and from it all. Jeffrey, the next son, would end up in jail if Ilona didn't kill him first. Boy, that kid could pull some lulus!

Little Marcy, though. There was Ilona's saving grace, her little daughter. Marcy was so cute, and very mature for her age. Ilona could depend on Marcy to tell her if the boys were getting into something bad, and Marcy always brought Ilona a smile, usually when she needed one most, and Marcy would never be the do-nothing Reede turned out to be.

Ilona had thought of divorce. She felt it was either "now-or-never." After all she was thirty-three, and she wasn't sure she'd have much of a chance to remarry if she didn't do something *now*. Still the kids needed a family to be in, and what would she gain by a divorce? Reede would still be Reede, an irritating pain in the posterior, whether she was with him or not, and he was, after all, the children's father. Besides, he managed to hold down a job, though not a prestigious one, and it paid pretty good since he got in-service pay increases. Shucks, he'd been doing the same job their whole marriage: driving a truck. No promotions, no managing something. Just driving. Hmmph.

The Guthries farmed on the side, mostly so the kids could have their pony and their 4-H projects. Four-H made a big impact on them.

On Mrs. Ware too.

DISENCHANTED

When Ilona Guthrie first married Reede she was as much in love as any eighteen-year-old, and more than most. Of course, at twenty she didn't see all the flaws that, through time, forced upon her a disenchantment. Ilona did not consider marriage counseling because Reede was the problem, and he would never change. That was just the way Reede was.

Ilona illustrates perfectly the malaise into which a marriage can sink during this Third Passage. Fortunately, Ilona also illustrates how you can turn a faded marriage around, for she did just that. The third task of this passage is to overcome the now-or-never syndrome, the disillusionment that is frequent during this passage and is compounded by the fear, "It's now or never. I've got to get out of this marriage so I can build another life."

THE THIRD TASK: OVERCOME THE NOW-OR-NEVER SYNDROME

Considerable temptation looms in this Third Passage. Temptations to quit trying and just get a divorce; to seek with someone else what you feel is lacking in your marriage (understanding, affection, whatever); to marry your job because on the job you get all sorts of positive strokes and at home you get nagged.

If you've been married ten years or longer, weigh your marriage as you consider these points. If you've been married less than ten years, these may give you insight into the future. Wouldn't it be lovely to be prepared for disillusionment? Forewarned is forearmed.

Ilona overcame the now-or-never syndrome by learning to accept the losses that she saw in her marriage, many of which were inevitable in any marriage.

The Illusion of a Perfect Mate

Think for the moment about your mate. Irritations. Good points. Lousy habits. Shortfalls. Strong points.

Debi Newman explains the importance of keeping a balance as you perform this first part of taking stock. "As you think about your mate, get your anger and hate out in the open where you can see it. We often ask our patients to write out the negative aspects of their mate's personality."

We suggest that you name three right now:

1. _____
2. _____
3. _____

What on this list *really* pushes your button? What disturbs you most? Frequently what seems to be a very disturbing factor to one spouse may actually be a mirror of some sort of unresolved pain in his or her family of origin. It's not that the factor isn't there. It usually is. But the spouse is overreacting to it. Might that be the case with any of the aspects you've listed above? How might one or more of them mirror problems in your childhood family?

We treated one couple, Bernie and Beverly Engle, in which the wife was deeply concerned about her husband's ability to manage money. It had not been an issue during their first two passages; there had not been enough money to manage as they were starting out. Now, in their Third Passage, they were beginning to plan for their future, to look closely at the mortgage, to consider the kids' college funds and their own retirement. Beverly's concerns escalated.

Actually, Bernie was not too bad. Though no wizard, he did all right with their conservative investments. But that wasn't good enough for her. As Beverly explored her family of origin, she discovered that her grandfather had lost a sizable family fortune in the Depression. That wound, untreated, had been handed down through her father to her. As she grieved it, and discussed it with her parents, the excessive demands she made on her husband to be the perfect financial manager moderated.

Expectations are not the only factors. Obviously you can't have a strong marriage if you don't respect your spouse. Ilona had a hard, hard time coming to grips with Reede's weaknesses, just as all couples do. We even admit to having that problem ourselves.

"Frank is obsessively goal-oriented—he's a workaholic, but he's not super-organized in some other ways," says Mary Alice Minirth. "Strong points and weak points. I did pray a long time ago that I wouldn't marry someone who just comes home and reads the paper. I'd much rather be married to him than a lazy person. He cares. He cares deeply, which is characteristic of workaholics."

Think about what Mary Alice said. She found the secret: She appreciates that the weaknesses are responsible for the strengths, and therefore that both strengths and weaknesses together contribute to the excellent man he is. Not just the strengths—the weaknesses as well.

Ilona looked at Reede's strengths, and she didn't mind admitting she had to really dig to root them out. He was steady; the same job all those years, faithful to her from the start. He never once changed a diaper (all three kids), but he was always there to help them with their pony or their 4-H projects. He was just as free with his time helping their friends at their behest, and the local 4-H chapter depended upon him heavily, for many of the kids' parents didn't have the time, let alone a stake pickup truck.

Now bring out in the open a few of the positive things about your spouse.

1. _____
2. _____
3. _____

We call these two exercises a positive-negative appraisal. Strangely, the better you are able to be honest about your spouse's flaws and grieve them, the better able you will be to enjoy your spouse's positive qualities. That's why we ask our patients to clarify the positives and negatives.

Now what do you actually do with these lists you've written and insights you've made? We suggest several things.

One constructive use is to make the lists the basis for mutual improvement in weak areas. Sit down together, never in the heat of anger or debate but during some peaceful time and open negotiations. Beverly Engle tackled the issue while she and her husband relaxed in their hot tub late one night.

First, explain to your spouse what you see as some major deficiencies of your own. Not only are you opening dialogue, you're opening it in a nonthreatening or nonpersonal way. You're discussing deficiencies in general, not just your spouse's.

Next, identify the realistic areas of concern you have about your spouse's attitudes, positions, or performance. Don't dump the whole list on the poor person at once. One topic is sufficient at a time. In Beverly's case, it would be her concern about their long-range financial picture and who would paint it.

Third, having thought it out thoroughly beforehand, acknowledge your own contribution to the degree of your concern. In this woman's case, her family's old, unspoken, long-standing fears about financial safety colored her own attitude.

Fourth, ask for constructive changes in your spouse. No demands, no whining, no hostility, no threats. The spouse is free to grant the request or not. Beverly asked that the two of them review the financial records quarterly. Bernie then would either agree, refuse, or modify the request. "How about once a year instead?" Bernie queried.

Fifth, and this is the most important step, both parties affirm the positive qualities they see in each other. This is that list of positives you made. "Don't be so fed up with negatives," Debi Newman warns, "that you fail to bring out the good qualities of your spouse." For instance, Beverly Engle expressed her appreciation that her man, whether financial whiz or nincompoop, was a constant and loving mate, dependable, possessing strong spiritual roots.

Regardless the outcome of your session, employ one sixth and final step. Use humor and grief to make peace with reality, particularly with chronic stuck areas that don't seem to change. The wife must grieve the scars her family carried for three generations. They will always be there to some degree. Probably Bernie will never be quite the whiz she'd prefer. Humor will salve the hurt. It will help her deal with that realization that life isn't perfect.

There are other ways, too, to use the lists. One is to monitor the weaknesses. Too often, they become addictive or codependent behaviors. The whole family system, then, begins to rotate around that behavior, allowing for it, catering to it, avoiding it, working around it. The classic case is the alcohol dependency of one family member around which all the rest of the family tiptoe. Look down the list again. Any chance those weaknesses can escalate into something that hurts the family system?

Lastly, and most important of all, we urge that you, as we do constantly, give thanks for your spouse and for the positive traits you see. Then grieve through and forgive the negative aspects.

"Grief is not a once-and-done action," explains Robert Hemfelt. "Sometimes you have to go back and grieve through something again and again. The actual importance of a loss has nothing to do with it, either. It's the relative importance, the importance of that loss to you personally, that determines how much healthful grieving will occur. One person may lose a beloved five-thousand-dollar purebred show dog and his neighbor loses a beloved pound mutt. Both losses are extremely heavy. The key is 'beloved,' not monetary value."

One of the big blahs of the Third Passage exists in the bedroom. The bedroom, as you know, mirrors the living room. Spiffing one up helps the other, and when one gets dull the other does too. Ilona Guthrie had to grieve the losses in her sexual relationship with Reede.

The Illusion of Perfect Sex and Romance

"My sex life?" Ilona smirked. "It was a big yawn. A yawn of boredom and a yawn of pure exhaustion."

By the Third Passage, sexual partners are usually pretty well settled into a deep rut of routines and patterns. Predictable.

Even unpredictability can be predictable. In our counsel of a woman with other problems, we learned that every couple of years her husband threatened to quit his job, put everything behind him, and go to Australia and raise sheep. The first time or two she found his threats very frightening. Eventually, she could see it coming. She came to know it was just his way of blowing off steam. He wasn't *really* going to pack the whole family off to the outback.

Like that woman, we all come to know our mates' daily, monthly, multi-yearly cycles. The routine permeates all the other areas of our lives and spills into the bedroom.

A goal of this Third Passage, then, is to combat apathy. We encourage weekly dates to get away from the house and kids. This can be a time for the couple to take retreats—marriage enrichment weekends or a cruise together. Get grandparents to stay with the kids for a week. Rekindle and make fresh the sensuality in marriage.

A comfort/discomfort paradox exists here too. It's responsible in large part for the middle-age crazies you sometimes see. Emotionally and perhaps hormonally, love has wound down somewhat. The husband and wife have settled in comfortably enough. That is, they're established, and that comfort gives them the time to examine their discomforts. People in the First and Second Passages gloss over the discomforts as they try to carve out an identity as a couple and start the family, get the career rolling, and bond together. Those are enormous distractors, leaving scant time and energy to focus on: "Is this the ultimate dream of my heart?" They match their romantic fantasy against reality and find reality sadly discomforting.

The problem multiplies when it appears that other people in other couplings appear to be living out their fantasies. "They're getting it all and I'm cheated."

Dreams are lovely. They're wonderful human drivers. But they must be balanced with the reality. No human being can provide the ultimate romantic union. This is the passage when couples finally get around to making peace with the disparity between fantasy and reality, the dream and the day-to-day.

What to do about it? Hold onto the dreams as a goal toward which to work. At the same time grieve to the point of acceptance that you won't meet them perfectly. Avoid the even more dangerous illusion that if your spouse will never complete your fantasy someone else might. It is just that. An illusion. It gets you stuck back in that First Passage, and the first is by no means the most satisfying and enriching.

Sensuality takes a beating in this passage, too, and must be grieved like any other loss. Major time and energy distractions, from the kids, schedules, and careers, put sex on a back burner—or take it off the stove altogether.

"Doctor, it feels like just pure survival. We're so harried, we collapse in bed exhausted, get up the next morning, and start it all over." Over and over, we hear that in counsel and among our friends. For them, at best, sex becomes a hurried release of sexual urges. At worst, the couples here begin long periods of sexual abstinence because of the sheer exhaustion.

How much time do you and your spouse spend *each week* in sexually oriented intimacy (that is, not the intimacy of talking together at breakfast—only that intimacy which surrounds the sexual union)? Can that time be measured with:

_____ a stopwatch?
_____ the bedroom alarm clock?
_____ a calendar?

Once you have made peace with these losses, you can turn your energies to building a better marriage during this Third Passage. One way will be to build your spouse. You've been working on a new you. Now you can take definite steps to provide your new you with a new mate.

Build Up Your Spouse

Many psychologists believe that negative, tearing-down, derogatory messages are so powerful, so toxic, they can overpower positive messages by a ratio of three or four to one. One negative comment can shoot down the good effects of three or four positive ones. To keep things in balance between the negatives and positives, the positives must outnumber the negative comments by at least three to one. People don't realize that. And yet, what do you remember when someone evaluates your performance? All the plaudits, or the one little negative thing the critic came up with?

We are not suggesting that you lie. The husband is a good financial provider. The wife is a devoted mother. Whatever. But it must be true.

Ilona Guthrie was coming from behind in this area of building up her mate, way behind. She carried little or no respect at all for her bumbling husband. She had soured so much that in her eyes he had no valid position. Once she realized that, she saw also how she had to quit carping and start encouraging him; the way things were going so far was certain to lead to disaster.

He was getting all kinds of good strokes from the outside world. People left cookies for him when he delivered goods near Christmas time. The 4-H leaders praised him to the skies. The church deacons spoke highly of him. At home, Ilona crabbed about his slipshod ways or ignored him altogether. Hardly a buildup. She made a conscious, determined decision to start accepting Reede unconditionally. Warts and all. Okay, so some of the stuff he did irritated her to no end. She would accept it. It was him.

She would forgive him, daily if need be, for the things he neglected or did wrong. And she would forgive herself when she let some irritation get to her. She had to learn to laugh off some of it.

At her Bible study group Ilona and her friends studied the ideal woman of Proverbs 31. "She does him good and not ill all her days." Here was a busy woman who put her husband's best interests first. Ilona always put the kids first. Indeed, she took care to encourage the children, but she never bothered to encourage Reede; she hadn't noticed that before.

How do you encourage your man without sounding insincere? Ilona started out small. In her Bible study group, during their praise session at the beginning of each meeting, she praised the Lord for something positive about Reede. Thus emboldened, she could work her way up to praising Reede to his face. Pretty soon she was praising him in front of the kids. That had never happened before. Did he soak it up? Like a dog laps water.

Ilona made another list. At least twice a week she'd find occasion to do several things. She would definitely do something for Reede. Do what? Something; let the moment decide. She would bite her tongue when she started to say something disparaging and try to break herself of that habit. And she would gouge out a little time to devote just to Reede, like she did for the kids and herself.

Finally, she determined to settle in for the long haul. This would be no instant zap cure, no course of antibiotics and *presto!* the infection's gone. It would take time—the rest of the marriage, quite probably. She prepared herself for that. But then, marriage is a lifelong job.

With no retirement plan.

SERENDIPITY

Ilona couldn't remember exactly. Perhaps it was the morning Wayne's best friend Andy discovered his lamb had gotten hung up in barbed wire and ripped open its leg, and Reede literally picked the squirming sheep up, lifting all four feet up off the ground, and held it at an angle so Andy could carefully cut and unwind the wire. Loading and unloading a truck all day sure does make a body strong. Or maybe it was when Old Nasty Craig, the crotchety geezer who ran the mini-mart on the corner by Shaw's, deliberately shortchanged Jeffrey, saying the kid gave him a one when it was a ten. Ilona wasn't getting anywhere arguing with him because she *knew* it was a ten, and instead of waiting out in the car the way he always did, Reede came inside and took Ilona's part and in no uncertain way made an honest man of Old Nasty. Or possibly it was when, on their fourteenth anniversary, Reede took her out to dinner and bought her flowers and said, "I don't understand the change, but it's wonderful. I love you, Ilona."

No matter. Whatever the exact occasion, there was a day, a moment, when Ilona Guthrie fell back in love with Reede.

12

CAN YOU TRULY FORGIVE?

I forgive you for running over my goldfish in the driveway yesterday." Kinsley Karris stood in the middle of the kitchen floor.

"Thank you, Kins." Julia Karris hugged her fourteen-year-old stepdaughter. Kinsley ran off upstairs.

By the kitchen sink, Jerry gaped. "What?"

"I think it's wonderful!" Julia crossed to him. "That was the first time—the very first time—Kinsley has ever said 'I forgive you' since I've known her."

"But . . . ?"

"Jerry, forgiveness is an essential part of living well. And it has to be learned; it's not natural. It doesn't just come."

"Okay. But, uh, a goldfish . . . ?"

"Oh. Well," said Julia with a wave of the hand, "what happened there is obvious."

Jerry stood blinking. He never did find out.

THE NEED TO FORGIVE

Who are the people who say, "I'll never forgive"; "It's too great; I cannot forgive that"? They are the ones with ulcers, with high blood pressure, with tense relationships. Failure to forgive is poor physiology as well as poor theology (the Lord's Prayer specifically says, "Forgive us our tres-passes as we forgive those who trespass against us"). It is also very poor psychology.

To not forgive is to do one's self in.

The Results of Anger

The opposites of forgiveness are resentment and anger. Anger and re-sentment, though, are secondary. Beneath them lies hurt—pain and the fear of pain.

See a child run carelessly into the street. The distraught parent yanks the child back to the sidewalk and scolds him angrily. Why angrily? Noth-ing happened; nothing was lost. Fear of the pain of loss, fear of what could have happened triggered that anger. In a marriage also, anger and resent-ment are born of either being hurt or the fear of being hurt.

The bugaboo here is that anger and resentment quench intimacy. If you fear being hurt by this person, you cannot feel comfortable close to this person. The fear and anger have nothing to do with the spouse.

One of our patients told us, "My mom was sick a lot while I was grow-ing up. She couldn't care well for her children or participate in their raising the way most mothers did. I got tired of Mom being ill. I came to resent it, and got angry. In my marriage, when my wife was ill, I found myself mini-mizing her illness and getting angry about it. It was a holdover from my youth, unresolved anger, something I had to work through."

We can build another formula from this:

$$\text{unresolved anger} = \text{bitterness.}$$

Put another way:

$$\text{anger turned sour} = \text{bitterness.}$$

Bitterness quickly and coldly quenches love and intimacy. The final fruit is hatred.

Every married couple must, therefore, master the ability to forgive, especially since forgiveness is an essential part of the grieving process. It's a skill that must be practiced daily, for man and wife are constantly exposed to little hurts and major problems.

The Sources of Anger

"Where does your anger come from?" we ask each couple we counsel. "What is its source?"

"From him!" she always insists.

"From her!" he always responds.

It is amazing how often those answers are false. But the truth lies hidden, covered by layers of denial and ignorance. Are any of the following factors sources of your anger?

The In-laws

"Yeah!" laughs Jerry Karris. "You bet. Big source of friction." Jerry may be right, but he's not right in the way he thinks he is.

"Julia worked a long time dealing with her family-of-origin issues," we told Jerry. "How about you?"

"Some. Yeah."

"And you found out there were some serious lacks in your childhood; things you needed that didn't happen as you were growing up."

"For sure."

"So, in the dream-quest for perfect parents, you thought your in-laws, Mr. and Mrs. Marsh, would be all the things your own parents were not. And when the Marshes fell short, you projected all that loss onto them."

"Nah. I don't think so."

We weren't asking Jerry; we were telling him. But we didn't say that. Instead, we worked with him until he himself realized that was what he had done.

Anyone not dealing with family-of-origin issues (that is, unfinished business, lack of nurturing and such) is going to have in-law trouble. If there are issues between your mom and dad, you might just transfer those issues, thinking your brand new parents will make up for all you lacked in the past. This is a big reason there are so many in-law jokes. Ninety percent of it is projection. Jerry's problem was not his in-laws, but his denial, projecting problems with his parents onto the luckless Marshes.

It works the other way too. In-laws who didn't resolve their own issues often transfer them onto the kids. How do you know it's happening? If you suffer chronic, constant anger, resentment, and tension with your in-laws, rest assured projection is involved. That's how to recognize it.

The Irritations of Life

When you stub your toe on the coffee table and accidentally break the breakfast egg onto the burner and that acrid smoke curls up and . . . well, you have no one to blame but yourself. And that is exactly whom you should forgive. Forgiving oneself is just as important as forgiving others.

Hidden Agendas

We have discussed before what intense sources of anger hidden agendas can be. You may have to dig deep to find them, and you may have to change your attitudes and methods if forgiveness in your family of origin was inadequate.

Look into your own past, into your childhood. How was forgiveness practiced and carried out in your family of origin? Ask yourself two questions:

1. "Who was expected to ask for forgiveness for transgressions in your family?"
   _____ Father only as head of the house
   _____ Mother only
   _____ Only children who did something wrong—never grown-ups
   _____ Whoever did the deed that needed to be forgiven
   _____ Whoever was supposed to do the forgiving
   _____ Any of the above
   _____ Nobody. We never thought about forgiveness.
2. "What was our family's attitude toward forgiveness?"
   _____ Everyone was required to forget about an accident or transgression, at least on the surface, once it was forgiven.
   _____ The family never talked about forgiveness or what it means to forgive.
   _____ Someone in the family used this phrase at least once: "I can never forgive _____ (whoever) for _____ (some transgression)."
   _____ The family talked about issues that required forgiveness and tried to resolve them.

Based on what you see in your family of origin, identify two things or patterns you want to see continue in your own family:

1. _____
2. _____

Now identify at least two things you ought to change:

1. _____
2. _____

What anger in your life might possibly point to hidden agendas and family-of-origin habits?

"In some families," Brian Newman says, "after blowups, everyone drifts off. Then they return slowly into good graces again until the next blowup. 'I'm talking to you again,' means 'I forgive you.' But the forgiveness isn't actually done or spoken. Putting it behind is not forgiving, per se. Calming down is not dealing with it. We must be willing to go back, address, and resolve the issues, or they'll just keep reappearing."

"Persons with low expectations and passive personalities tend to adjust to the dominant person in the family," Debi explains. "When the dominant one does something wrong, the more passive members are expected to forgive and forget without mentioning it. We see this especially in dynamics between parents and children, but also between dominant and passive spouses.

"What's sauce for the goose is sauce for the gander; the trick is to recognize what's happening. Both the dominant and the passive personalities must seek forgiveness. Probably what attracted these two to each other was the unchangeable characters. We're not saying to put aside dominance or passivity here. We're saying both persons must change somewhat, move away from this polar teeter-totter, closer to the center."

Your Spouse

Person + person = conflict. It's unavoidable.

The Expected Response

Expected by whom? By God. When Peter asked how many times one ought to forgive, Jesus answered, seventy times seven, meaning in the vernacular of that day not so much four hundred ninety times as an endless number of times. Even taken literally, we're talking daily forgiveness here. That whole passage, Matthew 18:21–35, is most instructive regarding God's attitude toward forgiveness.

WHAT FORGIVENESS IS AND IS NOT

Julia Karris shook her head. "No. Even if I did forgive, I couldn't forget."

" 'Forgive and forget' may be a catchphrase," we reply, "but forgiving is not forgetting. Forgiveness does not mean no memories. It means we choose not to go through life bitter." You can accept the forgivee's mistakes, choose to forgive, and still find yourself talking about what happened.

Nor should forgiveness be instantaneous. Somehow, the forgiver has the idea that once forgiveness has occurred, all those angry, hurt feelings will melt away. Then the forgiver feels guilty, for that very rarely happens. Forgiveness is not a once-and-done bandage over the wound.

You are commanded to forgive. That means you are not supposed to wait for your feelings. It's a considered decision. It is not a single act but a process. Compare forgiveness with salvation. You come to know, which is a cognitive decision with or without emotions. As you learn more, it then becomes a felt thing. Ultimately, it becomes part of you. This is a part of what Paul talks about when he urges us to the renewal of our minds in Romans 12:2.

Forgiving, however, is easier said than done. That's why learning how to truly forgive is the fourth task of this passage of marriage.

THE FOURTH TASK: PRACTICE TRUE FORGIVENESS

"How to forgive? Easy," said Jerry Karris. "You stand in the person's face and say, 'I forgive you.'"

Would that it were so simple. Strong, healthful, effective forgiveness requires six steps.

First, Acknowledge and Admit Your Hurts

"That's quick to do," said Jerry. "Julia's always on my case for something. And her lovemaking's sort of mechanical, you know? Our marriage is on a downhill skid, and she's not trying to make it good again."

"Very well. List all the items—every annoyance and error. Write it in the form of a letter, if you wish, although your mate is not to know about it. Articulate your feelings and thoughts. Some of our clients tape record the letter or dictate it. The whole idea is to help identify the hurt and pain in life. When you have a clear picture of exactly what should be forgiven, grieve the pain they caused, then burn the letter, the paper."

"You're kidding! Burn the paper? Don't show it to her?"

"That will come later. You're inventorying what has not yet been forgiven."

"Yes, but burn it?"

"Look at what you've done to God and He forgave you. Our debt to God is infinitely greater than anything your spouse could do. Your bill to God is paid."

"Well, yeah, but . . . "

The six of us are all firmly convinced, based on our faith and our experience, that only a solid relationship with God provides the freedom to forgive. Put differently, no true forgiveness occurs without a relationship with God because apart from God there is no real understanding of forgiveness.

Second, Commit to Forgiveness

"If I weren't committed to it, I wouldn't try," you insist.

"We mean, settling in for the long haul," we reply.

Forgiveness doesn't erase the past or the effects of the past. Forgiveness must be maintained against the intrusions of the past, and that requires commitment.

Also, you cannot focus on your feelings or you'll never forgive. You can't wait to feel better about it or to somehow feel forgiving because with every hour you wait, bitterness is festering.

Consider Randi and James. Both of them came out of conservative church backgrounds; both knew from childhood that premarital sex was sinful. But they were young and in love and this was Today. Everyone's doing it Today. So did they. Unfortunately, years into their marriage, Randi still had not forgiven James for coercing her into premarital sexual activity. Her smoldering resentment ate into their intimacy, into their sexual enjoyment, into the delicate fabric of their marriage. We could counsel Randi in how to forgive, using these six steps. We could encourage her to grieve the losses her resentment caused. But she had to commit to obeying Christ's wishes regarding forgiveness that lasts. In the process, both Randi and James had to take responsibility for that premarital sex.

Third, Be Prepared to Yield

And again we say, forgiving does not mean forgetting. But it does mean yielding your right to retribution, and that is not an easy thing to do. When you are hurt, you want to lash back. How hard it is to deliberately choose not to demand that right! Moreover, it's not something you do grudgingly. You must voluntarily turn over to God your rights of retaliation. "Vengeance is mine," saith the Lord. In part, that's because He's so much better at it than you could ever hope to be.

We are not talking here about legal actions and contexts. For your own health and peace of mind you must forgive your ex-spouse; it's what God wants of you. But that does not mean you excuse that ex-spouse from child support or other appropriate legal obligations. The crime victim is called upon to forgive the criminal, but certainly not by withdrawing testimony or charges to stymie justice.

Because you are forgiving the person, not the act, this statement does not bear weight: "I can't condone an act like that. Forgiving means putting my stamp of approval on an unforgivable act. It makes that person look all right, and he/she is *not* all right!" Do you see the difference between condoning a possibly unforgivable act, perhaps a heinous, damaging, vicious act, and forgiving the person? Do you see the difference between the sin and the sinner? That is the difference you must make as you forgive and forgive again.

It takes strength and humility to relinquish the right of retribution, and to expose our own hurt. Too much hate gets in the way. Frankly, true, complete forgiveness is not possible in human strength. We have learned from long experience that you cannot wait for the hurt to subside; you cannot wait until a feeling of forgiveness nudges into your heart and mind. It never will. The hurt will fester. You must accept God's help by asking His help. Call on His strength added to yours. And don't wait for a nice warm feeling.

Attitudes are adjustable. At any given moment, with help from the Holy Spirit, a person can say "God, I want to initiate a spirit of forgiveness, now." And it does not depend on the other person.

You see, at the bottom of it, this all is intended for the forgiver's benefit, not the forgivee's. Whether or not you consciously relinquish rights of vengeance and retribution does not depend on the sinner's state of mind. He or she may or may not seem repentant. He/she may not feel sorry or even admit to the transgression. Forgiveness is *your* thing, the action taken on *your* part. Their actions and reactions are up to them.

If you ever doubt that you need to overcome your anger and forgive someone who has hurt you, think about these physical problems that commonly attend unforgiveness. We won't go into forty pages of medical explanation here, but put simply and basically, anger works damage in five areas.

Anger suppresses the immune system. Angry persons are more prone to bacterial and viral infections. The immune system is closely and exquisitely attuned to the body's chemistry. Chemical cues alert the immune system, so to speak, and trigger immune responses. Anything altering body chemistry therefore alters the immune system, usually in negative ways, and the specific chemical changes induced by anger reduce natural resistance to disease.

Anger alters neurotransmitters in the brain. Neurotransmitters are chemicals that help the nerves pass information among themselves. When certain of these brain substances decrease, depression results. When they increase, we see what can be called a manic condition. Altering certain others causes psychotic reactions and sometimes obsessive worry. The effects vary in different people, buy they're there. One chemical we know of affects the anxiety response. In summary, anything altering these naturally produced substances profoundly affects the emotions. And when the emotions are shifted chemically, people cannot just talk themselves out of a mood. They're locked into it until the chemistry is adjusted back to normal.

Anger affects the autonomic nervous system. This is the system which stress triggers into action. The system extends to every part of the body; thus, every part of the body is affected when the system overloads. Something, somewhere, eventually gives. Colitis is one of the common results.

Anger is linked to heart disease. You've heard of the Type A personality. This is the person quick to anger, time oriented, on the go. Statistically, Type A's suffer more cardiac problems and die younger.

Anger affects the hormone system. Your hypothalamus is a tiny blob at the base of your brain, hid by another blob, your pituitary gland. The hypothalamus controls your pituitary which in turn controls all the hormones your other endocrine glands produce. Get the hypothalamus out of whack and secondary endocrine and hormonal disorders result. Anger affects the hypothalamus.

Most medical practitioners agree that in our modern society, up to 50 percent of physical disorders are significantly if not primarily stress related. Anger, resentment, and fear are powerful stressors. But what is most important, they can be reduced or eliminated through forgiveness. (We recommend the book *Worry-Free Living* for a more detailed discussion of the effects of anger and other stressors.)

One final thing you must give up as a function of forgiving: "I relinquish my bitterness that you did this to me." That, too, is terribly hard to do. But it's necessary. When you deliberately put the bitterness aside, you put the issue to rest.

Fourth, Be Open to Relationship

Because forgiveness erases nothing, it is so often hard to warm up again to the person near and dear who wronged you. Forgiveness definitely means choosing not to carry a grudge. The memories remain to be worked through. Remember that the memories live in both partners. You must have time to work through your own attitudes, and you must give the person you've forgiven time and space to work through his or her hurts also.

Eleven years into their marriage, Jeff cheated on his wife Joyce with a brief fling. With difficulty, Joyce forgave him. But in a sense she held a grudge against Jeff for coming back into the marriage after so painful a transgression. Jeff had been dealing with his conscience for several months before Joyce discovered what he'd done. He had that much time to process the pain and forgive himself. Joyce was starting from day one. She needed several months longer to deal with the issue; Jeff could not expect her to be where he was in the process.

Joyce, though, could not leave it alone. Although she technically forgave Jeff, she kept punishing him by constantly bringing it up, making sure he knew he wasn't trusted, making snide comments. Here was Jeff, a better husband than he had ever been before and determined to be faithful and loving, and she was treating him worse than she had ever treated him before. She was no longer open to an intimate relationship with him, regardless of what she claimed her feelings were.

It takes a minimum of three months, and usually six months or longer, for persons in a ruptured marriage such as Jeff and Joyce's to get over the emotional pain enough to restore the sexual bond. Even then the pain is not put behind completely. That's just the start of their return to intimacy and trusting. The person who had the affair must be patient. We recommend the book *Broken Vows* by Dr. Les Carter for couples who are struggling with marital infidelity.

There is one important exception to being open to the relationship—when one or the other spouse is blatantly abusive. We never recommend a person return to an abusive relationship until the abuser is well enough on the road to recovery that the person's health and safety are assured.

Fifth, Confess and Confront

Do this only if it feels right for the situation. Randi and James, the young couple who came out of conservative backgrounds, had marital problems because of premarital sex. It was important that they air their feelings and mutual accusations. For others there may be times when it is just not possible to talk to the person face to face. They may be separated geographically, or so alienated there's not a chance the injured person could ever get them aside. Also, certain subjects should not be aired freely.

As a rule of thumb, we recommend that if there are persons whom you've dated, been serious about, perhaps have been very serious about, these are not relationships to discuss with the spouse. Emotional struggles with such relationships are not good topics, either. Share those with a counselor, trusted friend—what some would call a confessor. When a spouse learns of his or her spouse's emotional entanglement with someone, curiosity runs wild. The spouse hungers to know *all* the gory details. What that other person looks like, where he or she lives, what the person's shortcomings are. . . . Satisfying such curiosity is not an adequate reason to discuss and argue a subject.

Spouses entangled in a dangerous emotional situation or full-blown affair must work through it. They must talk about their continued love for their mate. They must grieve giving up the outside relationship. But not with the spouse. The only time an emotionally confused or misdirected person would mention these matters to the spouse would be if that spouse could somehow benefit from knowing the information, for instance, if the spouse suspects something much worse than the actual instance. Perhaps the spouse is reading in some indiscretion that is not really there.

Assume for the moment this is one of those rare cases where benefit would accrue from confession. "How do I tell her?" he asks. We advocate writing a letter. You can write down—and rewrite—precisely what you want, but when you talk, the focus almost always gets shifted. You lose your point or get off on something else. With a letter there is less chance of miscommunication.

Give your spouse that letter when the person doesn't have to be defensive, can read it in a non-threatening atmosphere, has no need to respond immediately. Let the person have all the time needed to reread it, study it, think about it.

This sort of confession obviously involves confrontation. What should you do if your mate denies the source of anger, or refuses to talk about it? That happens so much.

Let's go back to the case of Randi and James, who bought into the lie that premarital sex was okay, and pretend that James absolutely denied that anything was wrong. He categorically refused to consider Randi's anger and resentment. "Just a hysterical woman looking for an excuse to be grouchy," he'd say, and brush it off.

Randi's first step would be acknowledging her anger, to herself as much as anyone. She would write a letter telling about it. She'd pour her heart out (and almost always, when a person does this, that person is shocked by the stabbing intensity of his or her feelings). Then she'd rewrite the letter into something James could read. She would explain how her anger was eating at her. She would tell how she wanted to restore their relationship to one of love and enjoyment.

Now, understand that because forgiveness is based not on the other person's responses but upon one's own needs, Randi would not have had to write those letters in order to forgive. She could have forgiven him already, without all that.

Whether James responded or not, Randi would have done her part by forgiving him. She was sincere in her efforts. If James still failed to acknowledge a problem, it would become his problem, not hers.

At times it's impossible to talk to the offender because that person is dead or out of contact. Perhaps you are divorced and didn't work through forgiveness with your ex until now. You're carrying unresolved anger. That anger affects how open you are to intimacy with others, for unresolved issues—and anger is only one of many—close a person off to other intimacy. When contact is impossible, it especially behooves you to sit down and work through the issues by recognizing your anger, grieving the losses, and forgiving.

Sixth, Put It Behind

We talked about forgiving and forgetting being two different things. You've forgiven. Now, if possible, forget. If that's not possible, don't blame yourself. Scripture says that God literally forgets our sins and transgressions once we've sought out His forgiveness. But there are only two verities in the world: 1) there is a God, and 2) you are not Him. Human beings, being human, cannot often erase memories. However, if you can do so, by all means do.

BARRIERS TO FORGIVING

"This guy must have been coming down the escalator at a dead run," Julia Karris recalled. "One minute the escalator's clear and the next moment he's slamming into me. Bowled me over, knocked me down the last two steps—I'm just lucky no loose clothing caught in the teeth of the stair as it folded up and went under. He was *so* apologetic. He said he was trying to catch his wife before she left the store—something like that—and wasn't watching where he was going."

"You forgave him?"

"Sure. I've done stuff like that plenty of times. I understood. Forgiving him wasn't difficult at all."

"Perhaps," we suggested, "forgiving was easy because he was a total stranger."

Julia stared at our wall a couple of minutes. "That's true. I never thought of that. If it had been Jerry who knocked me down like that I still wouldn't be speaking to him."

It's So Hard to Forgive Those Closest to You

The people we're most likely to be bitter with, the people who most need to be forgiven, are those closest to us. Husband. Wife. Parents. These are the persons we most need to forgive, for if we don't, we can't hope to work through the passages of marriage. And yet, they are the persons, of all people in the world, we find hardest to honestly forgive.

Julia saw her own weakness in that stranger, and recognized that she quite as easily could have been the one knocking someone else down. Had it been Jerry, she would only have condemned his carelessness. There's a clue here, you see: If you can remember that no one is perfect—not your mate, not your parents, certainly not yourself—you will enjoy greater freedom to forgive.

There is, however, one person even more difficult to forgive than spouses or parents, the person closest to you—yourself. In this case, your self-talk gets in the way. You become angry with yourself, castigating yourself about how stupid you are, what others must think about you. If you are typical of people we know and counsel (and we ourselves), you are much harder on yourself than you would be on someone else. You wouldn't talk to another person the way you self-talk. You certainly wouldn't think that aloud to your best friend. Watch, therefore, for lack of forgiveness toward yourself. Talk to yourself as you would to a treasured friend, forgive your own mistakes, and move on.

And then there's God. When have you forgiven God lately?

"Now you really are kidding!" Julia exclaimed. "God is perfect. He doesn't do anything to be forgiven for."

"True in theory," we reply, "but the heart doesn't deal in theories."

In reality, persons often hold a grudge against God because, being human, they lack the intelligence and foresight to understand why God did a particular thing. It seems so useless. So senseless. So damaging. Why did so-and-so die or I get sick or that tragedy come to pass? Try as you might, you can see only a tiny smattering of what He has in mind. This is a poor comparison because God is so far above us, but think how often a small child cannot perceive what you do or feel because he simply doesn't have the ability to understand.

In forgiving God, then, we end up not forgiving Him for His shortcomings but for ours. Again, forgiveness benefits the forgiver infinitely more than the forgivee. If you feel a need to forgive God for His inscrutability, by all means do so.

FALSE FORGIVING

"Families who stuff away problems and frictions without dealing with them," Brian Newman says, "are meting out false forgiveness. The issues aren't brought out; the forgiveness is never spoken."

False, too, is the temptation to say "I forgive you" as cheap words to get the argument ended or to gloss over painful or difficult issues. Those simple words must be said with meaning for forgiveness to be real.

Often in counsel we see codependents attempt false forgiveness.

Afraid they'll be rejected if they rock the boat, they'll say anything, then stuff their true feelings away inside. You can stuff just so many feelings into a pained heart before something explodes. Stored emotions become bitterness. They will come out as passive aggression, as depression, as anxiety, as physical symptoms. True forgiveness requires that you acknowledge the pain that person's act has caused your heart, but in so doing you commence the healing process.

We often find false forgiveness cropping up in First Passage marriages. The relationship is not fully in place, and both persons lack the security of knowing each other well. In that First Passage, too, both are convinced that if we're truly in love, we shouldn't have to forgive anything. Or, we shouldn't have conflicts! Without fully realizing it, we sweep everything under the carpet. That is the myth of the movie, *Love Story*. We'd like to reverse that myth—"Love means never having to say you're sorry"—to:

True love is constantly having to say you're sorry.

RESULTS OF FORGIVING

Loren and Gayle had been married three years, and they fought constantly. Sometimes she'd walk out. Usually they simply resolved the conflicts by ceasing fighting, often upon the urging of well-meaning friends who wanted to see them stay together. What they were actually doing was putting the issues aside. The issues, you see, were still available, ready to resurface at any time. Loren and Gayle's fighting lost or gained intensity from time to time, but it was always there. Nothing they fought over was resolved. They never examined the issues, and they never ever forgave.

Did Loren and Gayle have a satisfying marriage? They thought so. They didn't like the fighting, but what can you do? Their differences were irreconcilable, and you know what irreconcilable differences can lead to.

Relief came, eventually, when their friends finally got them into counseling. We helped them acknowledge that they were never resolving anything. Putting aside a fight is not dealing with it. In Loren and Gayle's case, healing commenced when they brought the issues out, examined the past to see where they originated, and then forgave each other the hurt and irritation. For six months thereafter, they would drop notes or call, telling in glowing terms about the latest forward step into further intimacy.

An issue forgiven is an issue at rest. The anger may not be resolved and certainly not forgotten. But the issue itself will not be brought up again, having been literally laid aside. Dennis Rainey and others call the stuff you drag out later "bazookas in the closet."

Unresolved anger damages intimacy; forgiveness mends it.

Without forgiveness you will get stuck in a passage. When people mature and change (and when a marriage matures and changes), they inadvertently step on each other's toes. Moreover, married people make mistakes which require forgiveness, sometimes in megadoses. Until the mistakes and issues of one passage are resolved, the couple cannot move on to the greater intimacy and new horizons the next passage introduces.

But there's far more. Forgiveness offers freedom from guilt, resentment, hostility, and bitterness. "I will never allow another person to ruin my life by hating them," said George Washington Carver.

By forgiving, you allow God's love to shine before your spouse. But there's even more.

We cannot have intimacy with God except that He forgave us and thereby broke away the wall of sin between us and Him. Jesus in the fifth chapter of Matthew instructs His followers to leave their gift to God on the altar if they have a point of friction with another. He says to go to that person and deal with the problem; only then is the believer prepared to give a gift to God. By forgiving, you do your part toward laying the problem or point of friction to rest. You thereby prepare yourself to freely enjoy a close relationship with your Lord.

What greater reward can there be?

13

ARE YOU PREPARED FOR THE INEVITABLE LOSSES?

*M*idlife is horrible! It's horrible. Life was going along pretty good, everything going well, kids fine, marriage good . . . I hit midlife, one parent died, aunts and uncles died, my father-in-law died, a child became ill, responsibilities increased. Midlife is tough.

"You change positions. No longer is there anyone to look to. There's no dad there, no mom to take care of you. No one there to wipe away the tears. You can no longer go to your parents. They took care of you, now you're gonna take care of them. In a sense you don't totally lose it all; they are with you in mind and memory, but not in the practical everyday. You move into the final position as the elder, the grown-up, the one to be depended upon, which is frightening; it's a tough transition emotionally. You're not only saying good-bye but taking on roles and responsibilities you never had before or even thought about.

"Fortunately, the body of Christ is broad, and God uses other members of the body to support you, but it's a change in your support base, all the same.

"Young love is great. Your twenties were great as you firmed up your commitments, laid out goals. You decided how your own family would run. The thirties are tremendously productive, high-energy years. Then the forties. You can't see as well, your parents are starting to die, you yourself are slowing down physically. . . . Midlife is tough. In my opinion, maybe one of the worst phases."

Whose opinion? Dr. Frank Minirth's. The man who gave talks on beating the odds—the farm boy who completed medical school, his residency, and seminary; the diabetic who lives his life a day at a time—suddenly found the odds taking a turn against him.

You, too, are fighting the odds by this stage of marriage. So much is at stake, just as your capabilities crest the hill and start their inexorable roll down the sunset side.

CRISIS AND CHANGE

Recall the example of the squirrel up in the decision tree. The tree has so many branches Y-ing off by this stage of the game. Some of the branches the squirrel could scamper out on lead to better branches, more options. Many dead end. Here it is so easy for people swamped by decision-making to simply get stuck at the Y.

Debi points out, "You can't be asking questions about midlife now, and reevaluating. The time for questions is done. You're there. This is now the time of either crisis or growth, a major, major Y in the tree of decisions. Crises will either destroy you or generate new intimacy and growth."

Remember that crisis is not necessarily a burst of anger and panic. Crises can also come and go silently, leaving behind not conflagration but quiet desperation. Dangerous opportunities. The issues of midlife are coming on stronger now, more demanding, more immediate; unless they've been resolved in the past, they're looming much bigger. Divorce is a too-frequent outgrowth of not making it through this difficult midlife passage.

This is a reason there are so many midlife sexual affairs. People can't cope with all the pressing changes, so they try to cope with surface issues. Find someone young, shift attention from the painful realities to a less painful fantasy, renew your own aging body with someone more youthful-looking and attractive. The divorce rate is not necessarily higher at this stage, but many people, miserable with their dead dreams, simply have not bothered with the actual legal steps; they've divorced in spirit though not in fact.

Not all dreams have died. By midlife now you may be living many of your dreams—if not exactly, at least close. This is the passage also where lovers can really start growing. This is where they either renew love or live in the pits. Too often, usually for lack of the effort to change, couples live in the pits unless something jolts them into revitalizing their love.

Working with you are memories and history. You've made it this far, despite some ridiculous escapades. The end is worth shooting for! Perhaps it's even worth shooting for with gusto.

The Differing Ages of the Third Passage

It is worth noting at this point that not everyone saddled with Third Passage problems (and blessed with its joys!) has actually entered this Third Passage chronologically. Some persons, marrying late, telescope the passages, though not by choice. More of life seems to happen to them quicker.

These days, people in their thirties are having babies the same as the twenty year olds. Parents of same-age kids will be a decade apart in age. That's not negative, but it changes the marriage passages picture a bit. These people who are getting a late start will be hit by factors of different passages all at once.

Susan and Robert Hemfelt married when she was twenty-seven and he thirty-two. "If you have later-life babies," Susan explains, "your family will feel more stress. The kids are growing, too young yet to be out on their own—sometimes even too young yet for school. At the same time, your parents are getting sick, possibly dying. The frustration is multiplied when parents and adult children don't live in the same area.

"I have a good friend, a forty-year-old woman with a girl my daughter's age—three. Her aging parents are very sick. She spends her weekends going out to help them; the other siblings share the responsibilities; she doesn't have to shoulder it alone, praise God. Yet she's being torn.

"Older people are also more likely to move through the passages themselves more quickly for several reasons. They want to be at the same place as people who married younger, and they're more mature to start with. They have a strong personal identity. They've been out on their own awhile."

Susan says, "My generation is going through control issues, starting a family, and tackling third-passage issues—all that starting simultaneously. We're not taking the burdens and responsibilities in order. I had my first child at thirty, and then three more, bam bam bam."

Added burdens and responsibilities add up to greater stress. But there's a plus side to starting out later, also. As Susan explains, "If you're older, and more mature, you can handle added pressure better when you get all that at once. I was established in my career when we married, and Robert had his underway also. We had both finished our education and had been out in the world awhile. I had confidence that if I didn't like where life was taking me, I could change it. I couldn't have had that assurance earlier. So I didn't feel trapped. A lot of friends who married young did feel trapped.

"Also, a crisis in your twenties is merely something you roll with in your thirties. You've mellowed out more. You can tap into the experiences of others because you've been around longer and seen more. It's easier to see how others did and did not do things. You're calmer, more resigned. You've seen friends go through it. Maybe what they did didn't work at all . . . or someone did so and so and it worked real well . . ."

And because the older couple is probably more financially secure, they have more and better options open to them. Susan's nanny is an example. Not many young couples can afford that option. Because they were financially well founded, Robert and Susan could.

"I told him," Susan Hemfelt recalls, " 'Robert, I'm going to be a fruit-cake if we don't do something.'

"I was handling a four-year-old, a two-year-old, and the baby. Robert listened. That was Friday. We had a nanny on Monday."

Susan notes that she is better able to handle the stresses of a later marriage because Robert listens to her. (He does not always respond the way she thinks he ought, but he listens. And that in itself is reassuring.) But her recollection brings up another point. Life and marriage are a little different for people who got started late with the process.

All couples in this passage, however, face the realities of middle age, which causes us all to pause and take note of where we are and where we are going. The fifth task of the Third Passage is to accept the losses surfacing now.

THE FIFTH TASK: ACCEPT
THE INEVITABLE LOSSES

Four friends sat around discussing just when they truly realized in their hearts that they weren't young anymore.

"I watched the Mousketeers when I was a real little kid," said one. "Jimmy Dodd. Annette and Tommy and all them. I felt suddenly, terribly old the day I heard two of the Mousketeers had gotten divorces."

"I was going through employment applications," said another. "This one man listed as his birthdate the day I graduated from college. 'The kid can't even get his birthday right,' I mumbled. Then I realized it was correct."

"When the sales clerks come up to you and address you as 'Madam' instead of 'Miss.' "

"When my hairdresser stopped cracking her gum long enough to say, 'When we gonna start rinsing this gray, honey?' "

Good-Bye, Lost Youth

"What has it all been about?" Marj Ajanian pondered that question aloud. "I asked myself that a million times after my kids got bigger. I didn't have any use anymore. Maybe I never did; if I hadn't raised my kids, someone else would have, and maybe better than I did. Then I married Louie, and I had a reason again. And yet, it wasn't a really good reason. A woman's supposed to be more than just a sidekick for a man. Sure, I worked my whole life, but where's something to show for it?"

Men feel the emptiness, too, as they face aging and their waning sexuality. A man wants to be interesting to young women. He innately yearns to charm cookies, not dog biscuits. And we've found that our patients pretty much all are aware of the way modern American culture emphasizes youth over wisdom and blatantly encourages everyone to diligently fight any sign of aging. All that cultural emphasis makes the job of acceptance extremely difficult.

Not long ago a woman named Darla went to a plastic surgeon seeking breast augmentation. She was in her mid-thirties and her breasts sagged. The surgeon suspected hidden motives, anticipated that she would probably be disappointed with the results, and sent her to a psychologist first. Thus did she arrive at our clinic.

At Darla's age, her mother had gained sixty pounds, letting herself go. Dad, disgusted, divorced her when Darla was still a teen. The mother's fear and vulnerability about aging had spilled into Darla, fostering her excessive concern about her physical appearance. Her husband repeatedly reassured her that he loved her as she was and was very cool toward breast surgery. Darla then began to wonder, "If I'm not doing it for my husband or my marriage, why am I doing it?" She went back and grieved the pain of losing Dad. She grieved the inevitable loss of youth.

This time she grieved it all completely. Before, she had hung up in the bargaining stage. Her preoccupation with plastic surgery was her way of bargaining, her way to outmaneuver the clock. She was stuck back in the First Passage, when youth was the key to love, and stuck in the bargaining stage of grief, bargaining her way out of the aging process.

We urged her to celebrate the positives. Her husband wasn't making his emotional and sexual love contingent on some false image. That was important. They were entering financial security for the first time. They knew a lot more about achieving good sex than they did ten years ago. They worked better as a parenting team now. All that went with aging. In the end, she decided to put surgery on the back burner although she didn't abandon the idea completely.

Loss of youth isn't just physical. Susan recalls, "I was twenty-seven when I married, very late getting going with kids and a family. For most of my twenties I was on my own, and I wouldn't give that time up for the world. It gave me wisdom and stability I couldn't have gotten any other way. But I grieve that loss, too—not having kids earlier. I wish I could have done both. So I take care of it, put it behind me by celebrating and grieving, and don't think about it anymore."

Aging affects different aspects. List them. You included the positives, we trust. Rejoice in them. Only the negatives need be grieved and resolved. Your grieving may have to be divided by topics, so to speak. Look at the losses incurred in each aspect. You'll want to meditate upon each of them and deal with them separately.

Good-Bye, Lost Health

Annie Warren Millen, having married off her last nestling Beth Anne, felt at loose ends. As if someone had let all the air out of her tires. Like a stalk of wilted celery. She got a medical examination with all the extras. She got her Pap test and mammogram. There had to be something wrong physically for her to feel so shot down all the time.

Everyone knows you begin to deteriorate physiologically around forty, but no one who has not yet reached that age dares ask just how much.

Apart from all the diseases and disabilities associated with aging (not all of which actually are a function of aging), there's menopause. Women with low self-esteem, women already uncertain of themselves, dread this clear, bold evidence that they're getting old. A few hearty souls, so relieved that the inconvenience is finally over, send out announcements. The attitudes of most women fall somewhere in between. These days, medicine can make subtle adjustments to ease the problems traditionally associated with menopause, from mood swings to osteoporosis.

Indeed, medicine now offers a growing arsenal of tools to deal with the diseases and disabilities of aging. Replacement hips, hearing aids and such can do much toward alleviating problems. We still have our troubles; but it's easier than it used to be.

We counsel every reader regardless of his or her age to stay on top of potential health problems. Keep a lid on them. Many can be minimized or even solved if caught in time. We now have the ability to live longer and more productively. Tap into it.

It is appropriate—in fact, it's essential—that you work through the reality of your fading physical vitality. Working through it involves both accepting it and grieving the losses. You need not succumb and give up. You should not. But neither can you glibly deny what is happening.

Improving your physical health, of course, as well as coming to grips with it, helps your marriage directly. The better you feel about yourself and your marriage, the less likely you will be to get trapped in the passage.

"Your ticker's fine," Annie's doctor announced, "but your female system is going to need attention one of these days. Your frequent and irregular periods are one reason you don't feel great. You're not anemic, technically, but it's pulling your blood count down."

"What do we do about it?"

"Nothing for now. Come back and see me again in six months or a year."

Annie left his office fuming. Easy for a male to say. He didn't have to live with this constant lack of pep or the messy inconvenience of irregular periods. But more than that was bothering her. If she had a broken leg, they'd fix it. If she caught pneumonia, they'd medicate it. But her problems were so vague, her symptoms so diffuse, there was no clear answer, no easy fix. That's the trouble with the results of aging, Annie bemoaned. They're so indefinite.

If you are in this Third Passage of marriage, or have reached that age, you are beginning, like Annie, to feel the effects of all those years of wear and tear on your body. Such losses are properly grieved through, as are any others.

Let us go through the grief process again, from a somewhat different angle. We emphasize it because it is so centrally important to your negotiation of all the passages of marriage.

First, list some physical differences, both positive and negative, between your body today and what it was twenty years ago.

1. _____
2. _____
3. _____

Now list some differences of performance. What is your body less capable of doing now? Is it better at some things than when you were young?

1. _____
2. _____
3. _____

Those items that improved over the years are worthy of celebration. We always encourage patients and friends to celebrate both things that are good and things that could be worse than they are. In fact, that's a good reason to celebrate in any case. Your state could be worse.

Now go through the items of loss one by one. Celebration and grief go hand in hand. Grief is as appropriate now as celebration was. Have you adequately grieved the loss of youthful health? If no such feelings come to mind, perhaps your grieving is not complete.

Can you remember feelings of shock and denial about those items of loss you listed? *(For instance, can you remember the first time you tried to look up a telephone number and had to hold the directory at arm's length to read it?)*

_____

_____

How about anger? Perhaps it was brief; perhaps it hung about your head like a cloud for years. *(Have you felt continual irritation at not being able to read maps, the writing on business cards? The anger at being unable to do something so simple?)*

_____

_____

Depression. Anger turned inward. It may come on you simply as "a bad case of the blahs." Has depression been a part of your response to the ravages of aging? *(Do you feel angry when you can't lift something because you now have a bad back? Does that anger turn to depression?)*

_____

_____

In what ways have you been bargaining with the aging process, stopping it in its tracks so to speak?
_____ Wrinkle cream?
_____ Hair color?
_____ Cosmetic surgery?
_____ Medications and vitamins?
_____ Excessive physical exercise?
(Be honest. And what has it benefited you?)

Can you think of an occasion or occasions when this phase of grief loomed large in your life as the truth of aging forced itself upon you?

_____

_____

After the emotions are cleansed comes resolution, forgiveness, acceptance. The process of physical aging has been programmed into you. Every human being ages similarly though not identically. In fact, the effects of aging are so uniform that we can often guess a person's chronological age within a few years. In short, God built you to grow old. In this fallen world every blessing is sullied, but it is a blessing no less. To accept that God knows what He's doing—yes, even when He came up with this aging business—provides a wonderful freedom from anxiety and despair.

That is our attitude of resolution as we come to terms with God's inevitable process. What is yours?

The final good-bye needs to be said to those dreams you've nourished since childhood, your answer to the question, "What are you going to be when you grow up?"

Good-Bye, Vocational and Financial Dreams

By the Third Passage, most couples must face and accept certain limitations on their financial and vocational achievements. "Is this all there is?" they ask themselves. Or, "Has it been worthwhile?"

Lost dreams forge great bitterness. To paraphrase the words of a retired friend of the Minirths': "When I graduated from high school I was going to change the world. By the time I finished college I hoped to make my mark in America. In graduate school, I thought I might change a little of Arkansas. Now I'd be content to redecorate my office."

Rare is the person who meets or exceeds the dreams of the beginnings of life. All the rest of us mourn shattered hopes. We wanted our kids to be farther above average than they are. We wanted to be higher up the vocational ladder and more elevated in the community than we are. Regrets. Emptiness. Too much of life is gone and not enough has been accomplished. Those are the generalities. For the moment, ponder the specifics of disappointments in your life and of things yet undone. You will, we hope, plan to focus in the long run on the successes.

What is a dream of yours that you fulfilled?

_____

What is a dream as yet unrealized?

_____

Do you still plan to fulfill it? _____ yes _____ no
What is a situation others might consider a dream come true that happened to you although you never anticipated it?

_____

> When you first married, what did you think your income would be
> by now (factoring in inflation)? $_____
> If you haven't yet peaked out, can you achieve that figure?
> _____ yes _____ no

Speaking of things undone, put a magnifying glass to your career or job. Have you advanced as far as you wish? "Job" includes domestic responsibility, the woman or man who stays home with the kids. That person is working just as surely as the office executive, and her job is far less routine and predictable. If you work in a competitive environment, younger hustlers may be out to supplant you. What, if any, writing do you see on the wall?

If you have failed to reach your vocational or financial goals to date, and especially if you've reached them or nearly so, and then slid back because of today's financial climate, there is cause for grief.

First look at the disparities between your hopes and your realizations. Then, following the progression of grief steps outlined earlier, identify the shock and denial (that's important here, the denial). You may be suffering depression right now because of your unresolved hopes and dreams, but that's not the same as a temporary depression induced by the grieving process. (Remember the definition of depression? Anger turned inward.) A caution about the bargaining aspect of grieving: Bounce your plans off someone else, preferably a trusted associate other than your spouse. Remember, bargaining joins with wishful or magical thinking here: "If only I could earn fifty dollars a week extra, I will _____." That might be a sound, reachable goal, or it might be magical thinking. Ask someone practical about the bargains you strike with yourself.

THE WONDER YEARS?

The core of any marriage are the man and wife. But all around that core buzzes a potential problem—the kids. Kids, the marriage's greatest blessing, are also its biggest pain in the patoot. Adolescents, who are building an adult or near-adult identity of their own, pose special problems. Let's examine those now.

14

IS THE ADOLESCENT IN CONTROL, OR ARE YOU AND YOUR SPOUSE?

*H*e was as near perfect as a son gets," moaned May Lucas, "until six months ago. Now he's not worth dirt."

"James is fourteen now?" we asked.

"Almost fifteen. Thinks he's ready to tell the world where to get off. He slops around in those ridiculous clothes all the kids are wearing now. His hair was so pretty when it was cut right, dark and wavy. Not now; not dyed pink, let me tell you."

"How have you and your husband approached the problem so far?" we asked.

"LeRoy comes down hard on him. I don't agree with that at all. I think LeRoy is much too harsh. So I try to soften his hard line the best I can. We argue over it a lot. LeRoy's fed up. Just fed up. He's ready to get the Army to consider drafting fourteen-year-olds. Whatever either one of us does, nothing seems to work."

"Tried bribery, restrictions, groundings, all that?"

"All that. We cut his allowance so many times it looks like cole slaw. I don't know where he's getting his money and that scares me to death."

"Won't he tell you?"

"Tell us? Hah!" May shook her head. "He won't tell us if he's breathing or not. We can't get through to him and he won't talk to us. It's a disaster, Doctor! And I say it again, he was as near perfect as a son gets."

May and her husband were caught in the shifting sands of parenthood; they'd hit the third stage, the period of turmoil, which can be difficult for any parent.

THE PERIOD OF TURMOIL: ADOLESCENCE

Take all the causes of drifting and chaos that school-age youngsters generate and multiply each one. Now multiply the sum of them. Whatever school-age kids do and need, teens do and need more of. Clothes? Supplies? Medical? Transportation? Activities and organized events? Right. Now throw in dating, schmoozing at the mall, physical changes of maturation, awareness of self and of the opposite sex, the need to become independent by slow, painful degrees, increased scholastic pressures, harder moral choices, the plethora of choice in entertainment, activity, friendships, ways to get in trouble, ways to shine. Did we mention conflict and control issues . . . ?

So many crises come at about the time kids enter their teens. Like any other conflicts, they can tear your whole marriage apart. Or your marriage can grow stronger as parents help each other and the kids.

We often receive couples into counseling when their teens get out of hand. May and LeRoy Lucas were typical of such couples: middle class, mainline church, midlife. Because in many ways they illustrate problems posed by emergent teens (although no one's problems are clones of anyone else's), let us follow their progress as they work toward the sixth task of the Comfortable Love passage: Help your adolescent become an individual.

THE SIXTH TASK: HELP YOUR ADOLESCENT BECOME AN INDIVIDUAL

Some say that teens can tear a family apart. That, we have found, is not exactly true. Actually, teens put stress on every family because of the teens' own challenges and tasks. The stress is natural and necessary. The trouble that stress causes was already there, latent. The stress will rip open any unhealed wounds of the parents and reveal any passages left incomplete. Count on it.

Two central themes of growing from preteen to adulthood underlie everything about your teens' development—their behavior, their maturation, their problems, their victories and defeats. The better you, the parent, understand these central themes, the better you can help both your teens and your union.

Individuation and Control

The first of these underlying themes is individuation. The teen must shift his whole being from family member to solo individual, from governed to capable-of-self-government, from child-treated-like-a-child to adult-peer-of-adults. Too often, the social and legal strictures of our culture work against the child's efforts. The child is treated like a little kid one moment and like an adult the next, without rhyme or reason.

The second theme is control. It's the old question, "Who's in control here?" now revised to include the teen. Are the parents in control? Is the teen in control? Or is one parent or the other in control if the teen manages to divide the marriage team?

Resolving control issues seems like a never-ending battle between teens and parents because it is. Teens have to experiment with control issues in order to test their own abilities. The teen says, whether consciously or not, "Can I control my body? Can I control my environment? Can I make and control money?" And the biggest question: "Do I have control over my own life?"

When we explained this to May, she nodded sagely. "I knew that. I mean, if I'd stopped to think about it, I'd know that. The control part, especially."

But therein lies the rub. You will remember that the foundational tasks of Passages One and Three of your marriage involve individuation. Passage One requires that the couple meld their singleness into a team. The Third Passage calls upon each of them to not let individual-ness get lost in the marriage union. And Passage Two deals heavily with control issues.

If either or both parents have not clearly resolved the individuation and control issues of their premarital lives—that is, their families of origin—and of the first three passages of their marriage, they will not be able to parent their teens well now.

As the teens bump into these universal, foundational issues of individuation and control, they need a steady guide, a model. Parents who have not come to terms with those issues cannot provide the guidance. The parents are just as much at sea as the kids. That leaves the kids without an anchor.

As the children work on their own issues of control and individuation, the exuberance of youth sets them to bouncing off the walls, so to speak. That's healthy. But they must have solid walls to bounce off. Those solid walls are the steady parents, the parents who have already dealt with the issues, both personally and as a marriage team. The parents can then set clear boundaries. The children can then test those boundaries and learn about themselves and the world.

Children need to separate from their families and find a niche of their own ("individuate" is the technical term), but they also need to be able to come home, particularly during their late teens and early years of adulthood. We mean emotionally here rather than residentially. A young adult sometimes covets the advice and wisdom of a parent figure, particularly when facing momentous decisions or tragedy. If Mom and Dad are confused or weak about their own values, perhaps even their own individuality, once the teen takes wing, there is little to come back to.

This is true even before teens take wing. Over and over, ideally, the adolescents try on independence like a garment, see what happens, and then come back to reaffirm and reembrace the stronger, more positive values of the parents. If the parents' values aren't solid, the teens find themselves in limbo.

Rarely is all this a conscious realization. "I need you to be a guide, but when I look up I find nothing" is hardly ever a spoken feeling. It lies below the conscious, at the bottom of things, working its influence undetected.

Such an unconscious realization triggers anger in the child, usually, or depression. It also generates a lot of friction. As a tactical maneuver, the adolescent may try (again, unconsciously) to provoke the parent into taking a stand. The child wants a solid wall; instead he's feeling a padded cell. The potential for dangerous escalation then is unlimited. The more the teenager acts out to express all those needs and frustrations and anger, deliberately causing friction and getting into trouble, the more uncertain the parent becomes about his or her own abilities—the wall becomes still less solid, the teen bounces off it still more wildly, trying to find a firm surface. And down and down it spirals, to disaster.

How do you stop the spiral and climb back up? Two things you must do: First, understand yourself and your spouse.

Understand Yourself and Your Spouse

As the teens encounter the issues of individuation and control, their struggles will activate and bring to the surface all the old unresolved tasks and problems in their parents' past.

This is immensely important. At the very time the kids need their parents the most, the parents flounder in the same confusion the kids feel, reliving their own past problems that had never seen solution.

May grew up under an authoritarian father. Too authoritarian, in her opinion. Her LeRoy, praise the Lord, was a gentle, loving man, not the least stern or unyielding. He had one little kink, though; he had to know where she was all the time. *All* the time. Each bedtime, she had to recite a litany of where she would be the next day, and what she would do. The next day he might call during the day to make sure her schedule was in place. When he got home from work he unfailingly asked her where she had gone and what she had done. There was nothing accusing about his concern. He certainly did not suspect infidelity or any manner of dishonesty or cheating. But the pressure was always there; he had to know.

On the surface, May accepted his need to know. He didn't hang out at the bars, he didn't slip around, he didn't smoke or have any bad habits. He provided well for his family. She could forgive him his little peccadillo.

They had never worked it out as a control issue in their Second Passage. They had never mentioned it or discussed it in the First or Third Passages as an invasion of her autonomy. But that was only the surface. Down deep, resentment about being overcontrolled boiled furiously. Now their fourteen-year-old James was fomenting open rebellion. James knew nothing about May's resentment; she herself refused to admit it. Surely there couldn't be any connection. Could there?

There certainly was. As James began maturing into adulthood, the old child roles didn't fit anymore. Almost overnight he began expressing rebellion, and if you asked him why (which we did) he would say he didn't know. It was true; he didn't. James was expressing frustration at his father's iron hand (which had not changed since James was a little kid), but he was also expressing May's unacknowledged frustration. He would miss curfew, neglect chores. As LeRoy exerted more control, dealing out punishment as well as discipline, May became more lenient. Digging beneath the conscious, we revealed that May was enjoying her son's rebellion.

"That's foolishness!" May exploded. "He's driving me crazy. He's got me as scared as a rabbit in a fox den. How could I enjoy that?"

James was living out her rebellion for her; she couldn't do it, so it got passed as unfinished business to him. He was frustrated anyway and chafing at the bit. It fit, in a twisted way, that he could take up her cause with his. Of course, then his behavior became all the more extreme.

True, May never said, "Go ahead and disobey your father" out loud. But she sent him signals so subtle, so covert, not even she noticed them. For example, when LeRoy would deny James his allowance, May would slip him some money.

Although that was the picture we uncovered, simply telling the Lucases what was going on and turning them loose would settle nothing. Head knowledge is not the solution; it is the first step to the solution. The second step is to shore up your marriage.

THE MARRIAGE TEAM

May and LeRoy had to look at their marriage and the way they parented as a team. May protested, "But it's James's rebellion we want to deal with, not something that's gone and done with in our marriage. Our marriage will do fine if James straightens up."

We asked, "Will your marriage survive if James continues as he's going?"

"I don't think so," she replied. "There's too much strain."

"So what we're dealing with here is adolescent rebellion."

"That's right."

"Good," we said. "And that rebellion is damaging the marriage, so we have to shore up the marriage. Then we all agree. Now. The first step you take in changing James's behavior is to mend your own past. There is no quick fix, no other way around it. Shall we begin?"

1. The parents had to go through their own appropriate adolescent rebellion sooner or later—that is, either during their adolescence or now, in counsel. LeRoy had done so. May had not. We will not go into detail here; but in summary, we led May back in memory through her own adolescent years. She had to establish her identity apart from an authoritarian or controlling man. She did that, essentially, by affirming her individuality and giving herself permission to become her own woman.

If you have not dealt with these issues as they pertain to your individuality and your marriage, we urge you to go back through the first three passages in this book or to explore the steps to individuation in *Love Is a Choice: Recovery for Codependent Relationships*. You must cover this essential groundwork before continuing.

2. The parents must have gone through enough adult individuation that they can confidently establish a strong value system of their own. To rephrase it, they must have clear boundaries around themselves, drawing a solid line between right and wrong, good and bad, satisfactory and unsatisfactory. Ethical, moral, religious, legal—values in every arena must be firmly in place. The child may or may not stay inside the lines, but the child *must* know where the lines are.

We find that, like LeRoy and May, parents' reactions to adolescent rebellion fall into one of two categories. Like LeRoy, they may overcompensate, mimicking their parents and quite frequently going to more of an extreme. LeRoy had a strict upbringing, and he tended to overcontrol James.

May illustrated a reaction formation, or inversion reaction. That's psychological language for "I move in the opposite direction of what the original model is inside me." May shifted from the tack of her authoritarian father to become extremely permissive. Her father's boundaries were rigid and narrow; she was incapable of setting any at all.

In Passage Two you looked at your parents' parenting techniques. Most people parent either the way they were parented or in reaction to the way they were parented. For a moment, think about your parents' parenting techniques again. Was there a strong difference in discipline between your mother and father? Extreme differences, such as LeRoy and May showed, indicate something was out of whack. How strongly did they adhere to a clear values system? Whether you accepted those values or not, did you understand what they were?

The next part of looking at your marriage is to look at the way you parent as a couple.

WORK AS BOTH A PARENTING TEAM
AND AS AN INDIVIDUAL PARENT

What makes teen parenting so stressful? . . . other than the teens, that is. Stress comes when parents must present a united front, and yet they must relate to the children in an individual way. That's hard to do because you must keep shifting roles, from parent to peer to parent to peer, sometimes in mid-sentence.

"Explain." May Lucas studied us suspiciously.

"Frankly," we said (in so many words), "you and LeRoy are showing how not to about it. He leans heavily on James; you tip off the other way and treat James leniently. LeRoy cuts his allowance, so you slip him some money to make up for it. You undercut each other."

"But LeRoy's so harsh. You're saying that's best?"

"Actually, either both parents harsh or both parents lenient is a better way than parents differing so widely."

"United front?"

"United front."

"LeRoy would never soften up just 'cause I asked him to."

"Have you two ever discussed it?"

"Argued about it."

And we gave the Lucases an assignment. "Tonight, sit down facing each other. Each of you explain what you don't like about what you yourself are doing."

"Wait. You mean, I tell LeRoy what I think he's doing wrong."

"No, you tell LeRoy what you think you yourself are doing wrong.

Then he tells you what he thinks he himself is doing wrong; he sees himself reacting in anger without thinking, perhaps. Let him tell you. You both know the criticisms you level on each other. You've heard them often enough that you needn't repeat them now."

"That's so true." May nodded sagely.

"You are not confronting each other. You're sharing your mutual problems and feelings of doubt. This more than anything else will remove the spirit of confrontation and replace it with a spirit of cooperation. Because your second assignment, then, will be to agree on firm, solid boundaries. Totally agree. You will have to compromise some, both of you. You'll have to give on some points completely. But when next you face James, you should have a united, unassailable plan for parenting him as a team."

We urge that when it comes to setting bounds for teens, while it's important for both parents to voice their concerns and work to compromise, it is equally important that the teens not overhear or be privy to fights and negotiations. We do not mean that parents should never disagree or fight in front of children. Children need to see and hear that Mom and Dad can disagree and that's natural; the love stands secure. But not when it comes to setting teen boundaries. Model your conflict resolution in other issues.

May snorted. "You don't know our son. He'll think of something that isn't in the plan. Just you watch."

"Then you and your husband meet privately, beyond James's hearing, determine what to do about it, and act on what you decided."

May shook her head. "James's not gonna like this *at* all."

Kids don't—or so they claim. In truth, for their sense of security, for a solid base, teens need desperately to feel that unity. It's emotionally very scary if one parent lays down a rule and the other undercuts, invalidates, or excuses that rule. Even if it's not actually spoken, the child can hear, "We don't know; we haven't reached a decision yet." Teens need black and white, another way of saying clear, vivid lines. The parents' indecision may lead them to extreme acting out—rebellion—trying to force the parents' hand and draw the line.

Brian Newman says, "We all know this, as counselors, but it became vivid to me during one particular counseling session with a sixteen-year-old boy who had suddenly been misbehaving at home.

"Six months before his sudden change, his father had read some parenting material and had decided he was too hard on his son. When the son felt his father holding back discipline, he began to do anything to get his father's attention.

"In one session, the son actually told his father, 'I need to know you will punish me if I do something out of line. If I come home after curfew, you should make me sleep outside. Then I'll learn.'

"I couldn't believe I was hearing this from a sixteen-year-old boy. It was obvious to me that the earlier parenting the father had done gave a great deal of security to this son."

If you have teenaged children, see how well this exercise applies to you. If you do not yet, consider the questions carefully as a foretaste of what you will want to do.

1. Do your teens encounter a united team across all the major boundaries, including (but not limited to):
   _____ Rules of the house (keeping a neat room, picking up clothes and towels, tidying the bathroom)?
   _____ Friends: who visits and when, what behavior is acceptable and what's off limits?
   _____ Curfews?
   _____ Scheduling decisions: who gets the living room to entertain guests; who gets the car (and driver)?
   _____ Work permits and income opportunities?
   _____ The heavy questions: drugs, booze, cigarettes and grass, sexual continence, other moral issues?
   _____ Church attendance?
   _____ School performance standards; a certain grade point average and/or behavioral expectation?

2. Do you and your spouse present an adequate model of shared religious faith and values system?
   _____ Are your basic values (sanctity of life, honesty) in general agreement?
   _____ If there are major differences in your value systems, do your children understand both systems and how they differ?
   _____ Do you adequately model the exercise of religious faith, both individually and as a team? (You do not have to have identical relationships with God; you do have to respect each other's details of belief.)
   _____ When your children look at you and your spouse, do they see responsible adulthood?

3. Do your children know they are in a safe haven?
   _____ If they encounter trouble—the law, an accident, a

       misunderstanding—do they feel secure enough to come to you immediately?

_____ Can they come to you with intimate problems and *know* their problems will reach no other ears but yours?

_____ In the last week have you and your spouse each individually praised your teen about something at least once?

_____ Frequently?

Note in that last survey question how important it is for parents to address their kids individually and as a team. A team is more than twice as protective as an individual. It is a bulwark, a solid front. And yet only an individual can lend an intimate and sympathetic ear. We advocate protection, not overprotection. You do not always feel confident about a situation; think how much more so your teens may feel at sea in a threatening or unusual situation. They need to have back-up; a recourse to fall back upon when everything goes down crooked.

As we counsel teens, over and over and over we hear how agonizing it was when they encountered a problem—pregnancy, drugs, a teacher or other adult making a sexual pass—and they felt they had no one to turn to for advice and protection. One or both parents were not there for them in a protective capacity.

In contrast, one young lady, Allison, told about an incident she experienced soon after she got her driver's license. "We're farm kids; we all live way out. One night about fifteen of us from youth group drove into town. It's almost fifty miles. Jeannie and Amy were with me in Dad's pickup. We sat in the parking lot at the pizza place, listening to the radio and waiting for the rest of the kids to get there. We got out and locked the doors—and there were the keys in the ignition and the radio going!

"The kids right away started thinking up ways out of it. One wanted to break the seal and lift out the back window, and one wanted to take up a collection to pay for a locksmith. They thought I was nuts and even tried to talk me out of it, but I called up Dad right away. I told him what happened. He drove in, fifty miles one way, with another set of keys. We got the truck started okay and ran the battery back up. Afterward, he thanked me for not letting the guys try to break into it; they would have messed up something for sure. And he thanked me for turning to him when I needed help."

Allison's dad did more than just be there for her when she needed him. He praised her for her good judgment by thanking her. This is so important. Teens desperately need affirmation. Their years are plagued by doubts and insecurity. What comes across as cockiness or indifference is actually fear and doubt. Praise should be both spontaneous and planned. Applause and cheers at the basketball game. Telling how well pleased both parents and grandparents are with the progress shown on the child's report card. Praise for personal grooming or attention paid the family pet.

In his autobiography, hockey star Wayne Gretsky tells that his father appeared at a hockey game in which it was anticipated that Wayne would break still another important league record. Wayne did, the game paused, and his father joined the others on the ice to congratulate him.

"Where's your wife?" people asked Walter Gretsky. "Shouldn't his mother be here for this, too?"

"She's at a junior league game cheering his brother on," Walter replied. "'Wayne isn't the only hockey player in this family,' she says."[1]

One or the other of them would be there. Although Wayne was essentially on his own in the big leagues at age fifteen, he knew his parents were behind him, with protection and with praise. And so did his siblings.

May Lucas studied the last question of the previous exercise with a baleful eye. "I wish we could find something to praise James about. The pickings are sure slim in that department."

"Then praise the obvious," we suggested. "Is his physical growth on schedule?"

"Ahead of schedule. He's big for his age."

"Praise his growth. You mentioned you didn't like his hairstyle, but we assume he's very careful in his grooming."

"Oh very! Of course, he's real, *real* careful that all the care doesn't show."

"Of course. How about, 'It must take you half an hour to put that hairdo together. That's a lot of patience.' Or, 'I saw you help Suzie next door. I'm proud of the way you treat women. Real grown up.' Get together with LeRoy and figure ways to express your praise and approval on a planned, regular basis."

"Not lying, but finding things. I see." May sighed. "I didn't get any of that when I was growing up."

"Then it will be especially hard for you. That means none of this will come automatically. It may seem foreign, or even counterproductive. You'll have to force yourselves and practice doing it as individuals and as a team."

Like father, like son. There's a reason for that. As adulthood looms, adolescents even more assiduously blot up their parents' attitudes.

Parents serve as role models for individual taste and appreciation. May and LeRoy illustrate that well. May likes contemporary art. She genuinely appreciates it. LeRoy calls it "acres of blobs"; he's a Frederick Remington-Charlie Russell fan himself. Such diversity is healthy. James sees that divergent tastes can live in harmony. And he sees two parents with a mutually respected appreciation of art.

Parents modeling separate relationships with God may worship together and engage in their own private study—or perhaps even vice versa, worshiping in different churches and studying together. What do the kids learn? "I can't do it for you. I can't do it to you. You have to approach God as an individual." Adolescents have budding spiritual awareness about this time. By example, the parents in essence are giving the kids permission to search for their own relationships with God.

"Do James and LeRoy ever go out and do things together?" we asked May.

"Not lately," she replied. "LeRoy says James has to straighten up before he'll take him anywhere."

We were quick to suggest LeRoy and James spend time together in some enterprise—attend sports events, go to a movie, go fishing, catch the laser light show at the science center. We suggested that May also spend time one-on-one with James. This was not the time to wait until James shaped up, so to speak, or the time to withhold favors as if behavior were a condition of love and affection.

James needed individual friendship with his parents. He needed their assurance that, "You're all right. You make mistakes, but you have value. You'll amount to something." All that is spoken in the simple, "I want you as a friend."

In their one-on-one role with their child, Mom and Dad model their femaleness and maleness. This is woman, infinitely more complex than any stereotype. This is man.

Again, if this was not the pattern in your family of origin, you'll have trouble getting into the swing of treating a teenager more as an emerging peer and friend and less as a child. It's not going to come naturally or spontaneously, but it can be done.

Stop and think for a bit about the male and female roles you grew up with. They weren't seriously contaminated, were they? For example, we counsel families where the woman's only strength, her only ability to manipulate others, lay in being constantly ill and needy. Or the father, a pillar of machismo, never dared demonstrate affection or sorrow. What models did you see in your teen years? Is that what you want your own children to see?

At this time the spouses need each other as a support system, because teens are just plain hard on parents. As teens break away, developing their own identities, the parents have to develop their own identities apart from their kids.

"That's ridiculous!" snorts the adult. "Of course I have my own identity."

"Bravo!" we reply. "But we encounter so many people, friends and clients both, who have invested their whole identity—and their self-esteem—in their kids. It's so easy to do. You want the kids to be like you, or better than you, and the family disintegrates. Parents' self-image must not depend upon their kids being unrebellious, smart, perfect, or whatever, but so many, many do."

"True," you say, "but it's not all the parents, especially when the kids go into high school. I may be a famous leader, politician, author, musician, movie star. But at my kid's school I am ever and anon 'So-and-so's mother.'"

"Isn't that the way it is," we agree. That is why good personal boundaries are needed here. And the spouse helps set them.

A final part of working together as a parenting team is to balance privilege against responsibility.

BALANCE PRIVILEGE AGAINST RESPONSIBILITY

Ruth grew up under circumstances just the opposite of May's. In Ruth's family of origin, chaos reigned. Her father was disabled by illness most of her life, and he simply abrogated his position as head of the house to Mom. His health problems kept Mom preoccupied and the family in turmoil. Now Ruth, near the end of the Third Passage of her marriage, faced the adolescence of her daughters aged twelve and seventeen. Ruth had learned early to be her own parent, to be responsible for herself. Now she was compulsive and over-organized, though not militantly so.

The only way Ruth knew to raise teens was the way she had raised herself. She ran their lives. She was never harsh or dictatorial. She was simply always there to do everything for her daughters. She did a lot of their homework. When the twelve-year-old had a falling out with another girl on her soccer team, Ruth talked to the coach, the other parent, and the other girl herself, mending the rift single-handedly. Her daughter received no experience or responsibility in handling even that casual, temporary conflict.

Although the seventeen-year-old was gifted academically, her teachers noted that she never took the initiative on anything. As long as a teacher or coach guided each step, giving her specific orders, she did very well. On any open-ended project, the child sat paralyzed. When teachers voiced complaints, Ruth went to school and talked to those teachers. Her response was to do everything; "I'll supervise her more closely—make sure she gets it done." The teachers realized they were listening to the problem, not the solution, and sent Ruth to our counsel.

Ruth's parents had never presented a model of how to balance privilege with responsibility. Ruth, on her own early, knew complete privilege and complete responsibility beyond her years. She had to learn that lesson of balance now.

Part of Ruth's solution, therefore, was to back off and give her girls autonomy and freedom, including the most important freedom, the freedom to make mistakes. To help her do something she had never seen done or done herself, we gave Ruth some assignments.

One assignment: she was not to supervise the girls' homework. They were to do it or not on their own. Talk about frightening! Ruth sat wild-eyed and weepy as she told us how her daughters' school grades had fallen precipitously. She realized that some evenings the girls were not studying. They weren't always completing assignments or doing required reading. She very nearly stepped in. It took vigorous confrontation from us and help from her husband. To that point he had been passive, letting the little wife raise the daughters without his interference. The father's passivity was basically a control issue from Passage Two. He invested himself in his job and let that be his sole arena of control. There had been no sharing between Ruth and her husband regarding parenting. They had to learn from the ground up how to be a team.

To begin with, Dad had to step in and tell Ruth, "No. We'll honor what the counselors say and not exert excessive control." As Ruth moved back, her girls gradually assumed some self-responsibility for their schoolwork.

Ruth learned the lesson May and LeRoy came to grasp also: By giving children the freedom to fail, while they are still young and it's safe to do so, that freedom fosters new responsibility rather than breeding irresponsibility.

"James can't handle what I give him now; no way will I give him more freedom and responsibility!" May stormed. As James went through his rebellion, the only response May and LeRoy knew to make was to revoke privileges. Reducing privileges reduced the responsibility to be mature, and that did nothing to bring back into balance that important polarity, "privilege versus responsibility."

In dealing with your child, envision an old-fashioned, two-pan balance beam, the kind of scale blindfolded justice holds aloft. On one side, privilege. In the other pan, responsibility. Add weights to one pan, the other pan requires more weights, too, in order to maintain level balance. "The more I want my child to accept responsibility, the more freedom I must give, appropriately."

You may find this terribly frightening. You must realize that as you grant more freedoms, you are *not* granting license for irresponsibility. You are laying the foundation for greater responsibility.

You must explain clearly and repeatedly about the balance scale. Your child must understand that to receive more freedom means to take on more responsibility. Fortunately, by early teens, kids can grasp concepts of that sort well.

The most frightening arena of responsibility of all: teen sexuality. May turned white just thinking about James acting out in that area as he acted out in others. "The worst thing I could ever find in his wallet would be a condom," she said, "and it would be the best thing I could find."

May was onto something with that comment, although she had to come to terms with it better. You must also take an immense step with your own child; you must accept and endorse your adolescent's emerging sexuality. After all, God put it there. Denying it isn't going to serve any purpose whatsoever. We suggest that you do this in three healthy ways.

First, you must have accepted your own sexuality.

"Well, of course I do. I mean, I've been married so many years that . . . " May looked confused.

"Are you comfortable with your sexuality?" we asked.

She thought about it a while. "Yes. Yes I am."

"Then that hurdle's past." We know of many cases, however, where Mother thinks sex is nothing more than a duty, or Dad feels sex is dirty. Many of us develop sexual taboos from our early experiences or attitudes picked up about sexuality during childhood.

Consider one young woman whose mother sat down with her on her wedding day and gave her a long dissertation on sex (the first and only time she'd ever talked about it). It was a duty, certainly no fun, always suspect as being dirty or crude. The daughter married on schedule and got nearly through her Third Passage before it caught up to her. Sex for her had never been good because of both the overt negative message from Mom and the lifetime of hidden messages that had said the same thing. The daughter's crisis came when her own teen daughter entered puberty. Mom had no way to help her own daughter understand that it's okay to be a woman and engage in marital sex. Mom didn't repeat the overt negative messages she herself had heard, but she sent them implicitly. Her daughter lived out the dark side of those negative messages, promiscuously acting out sexually during her early teens. The daughter was affected because the mother had never made peace with her sexuality.

Second, you must also have completed the sexual dimensions of your prior marriage passages before you can help your children go through this most confusing and frightening physical change of their lives.

How do you and your spouse compare with the guidelines we've discussed in Passages One and Two? If there are problems, the kids will unconsciously pick up on it.

Debi Newman says, "We've seen many sixteen-year-old girls become pregnant outside marriage, just as their mothers became pregnant during their adolescence. It is very important for parents to make peace within themselves about their sexual past. Parents shouldn't feel like they have to tell everything they ever experienced sexually to their children. But if the children know about negative experiences in their parents' pasts, it is important to be open and share what the parents learned.

"Parents need to forgive themselves for their sexual past as a part of nurturing and raising their children. Ultimately, the children are responsible for the choices they make."

Third, the parents must be certain to recognize, acknowledge, and endorse their teens' sexual feelings.

May's eyes got too big to fit in the doorway when we said that. "You can't be serious! James doesn't need one little speck of encouragement to act up. Can you imagine what he'd be doing if I even mentioned something like that? 'Oh boy! Mom says it's okay!' Especially 'cause he only hears what he wants to hear—not what I really say."

We responded, "Pretend you wake up one morning, walk out in the living room and there's an elephant. Full grown elephant. That's impossible! And when everyone else walks around the living room they don't seem to notice it. You think your mind is slipping. How come you're the only one who sees that elephant?"

Teens, boys in particular, wake up one morning with strong sexual feelings and fantasies. This is frightening for a child. Something that suddenly dominates your thoughts—an elephant in your living room—is something no one else will acknowledge. "Am I weird? Doesn't anyone else feel this way? The other guys talk about it all the time, but do they really feel what I feel or are they just saying that stuff to sound good?"

Parents who acknowledge and endorse their children's growing sexual feelings are not endorsing those children to act them out. "Banish those thoughts! Get those feelings out of your body!" does nothing to alter the powerful hormonal surge of adolescence. The thoughts and feelings come to stay.

An appropriate response? "I remember when I was your age. It just about takes you over. It's really hard to keep those feelings in their place until marriage, but it's worth it."

Throughout this chapter we've been talking about shoring up your marriage in relationship to your adolescent. And we've suggested that May and LeRoy Lucas had to take a careful look at their own relationship too. We'll look at the intimacy possible in the comfortable passage of marriage in the next chapter.

15

CAN YOUR SPOUSE FULFILL YOUR NEED FOR INTIMACY?

*C*ream separators? Oh my, do I remember cream separators!" Louie Ajanian's wife, Marj shook her head. "Every farm had one. Big stainless steel unit that stood on legs in the corner of the kitchen. It was basically a couple of steel tanks, one inside the other. Mom made us girls clean it every day. It broke down into half a dozen parts and you had to scrub and bleach each one to prevent contaminating the next milking. No smell of sour milk, of course. Spotless. And change the gauze filter. Just washing the separator took half an hour. Kids these days have no idea what 'thankless task' means.

"The big dairies separate the milk themselves now, with super-duper equipment. They can separate out the butter cream, and make skimmed milk of any weight they want, better than the old farm separators could. I'm glad for the kids' sake that the old separators are about gone."

There may not be many cream separators in farm kitchens anymore, but numerous separators exist in marriage. Quietly and usually unobserved, they skim off the richness, the good stuff, and leave behind a watery substitute for the real thing. Anyone who grew up on fresh whole milk proclaims how pallid 2 percent is.

By the Third Passage (or frequently even before then), serious threats to intimacy abound. At times they cannot be resolved by a few simple changes or even by writing a new contract. They must be ferreted out and reversed, or the marriage partners will find themselves either stranded on base or deliberately walking off the field.

"When love dies," Debi Newman observes, "it is not in the heat of battle. It's when a partner believes the other will never meet the needs for intimacy."

The seventh task of the Third Passage—Comfortable Love—is to maintain an intimate relationship with your spouse.

THE SEVENTH TASK: MAINTAIN AN INTIMATE RELATIONSHIP

"But I don't *need* intimacy. Well, yeah. Sex. But not intimacy, not like you're talking about." Lee Atkins, five years a paramedic for a major ambulance company, sat in our office. His bride of ten years insisted he undergo counseling or they were finished. So here he was. With his track record at age fifty-one, he didn't really expect this marriage to last forever—this was his third—but he really loved the woman.

"But that's not intimacy. I mean, love isn't intimacy, right?"

"Right," we agreed.

"I'm sure some guys need intimacy. And I suppose a little of it's nice. But, well, it's not a requirement for me, like food and water is a requirement. A need. Do you understand what I'm trying to say?"

"We understand clearly. We hear it all the time."

Intimacy is the sharing of the soul—hopes, dreams, fears, shames, joys, sorrows. Intimacy is knowing another person deeply and well and appreciating him anyway. It's an easy, comfortable balance between dependence upon another and independence—the living of one's own life; of aloneness and sharedness; of distance and closeness. We talked about interdependence in Chapter 10; true intimacy is interdependence. Early in this passage the marriage relationship is still swinging between the extremes of dependence and independence. By the end of the Third Passage the fine balance can be achieved. Knowing I have a mate for life, I share all, bare all.

Men and women have two needs in their relationships with others, some teachers claim. They need to impact others' lives and to enjoy a personal, intimate relationship. Men tend more toward the need for impact, and women toward relationships, but that's merely a matter of degree. Both need both. An aside: men and women with heightened needs for relationship are going to find themselves especially vulnerable in the public workplace.

If we would convince Lee Atkins that he, like any other man, actually needs genuine intimacy, we would have to show him the barriers to it which he erected within himself. In our counsel, and also in our own lives, we find many barriers to true intimacy.

Root Causes

What are the down-deep barriers to intimacy? See if any of these root causes are spoiling your relationship.

Motives

Theologians call it the sin root. Greed. Fear. Selfishness. An inability to trust, an inability therefore to give and compromise. I want it my way. And I want it all.

Denial

A friend we'll call Jean defended her marriage proudly and vigorously. "We have just about a perfect marriage going," she said. "We've been together twenty years. That says something."

"That's a lot of joy and sorrow, anger and contentment," we agreed.

"Anger? Oh, no. No sorrow. We never hurt each other. That's what I mean when I say we have this perfect marriage."

By looking only at the positives, many couples deny their true feelings. Two persons in the same bed, under the same roof, can't get by without hurting now and then. Masking feelings, denying the speed bumps, is not true intimacy. They are not sharing.

People who look like a perfect couple to the outside world may well be a perfect couple in the privacy of their lives. But they also might be separated from each other even though they're living together—even though they look so good.

Self-preoccupation

Self-preoccupied? What's that? It is when your interest and attention are focused inwardly, your face turned away from your mate. Depression is an important form of self-preoccupation, very self-centered. Addictions, similarly, turn the person's attention inward. Even if you hate yourself, that's still self-centered. Your attention is on yourself.

Other Preoccupations

"If we had an evening together, it meant the secretaries made a scheduling error," said Jane Fonda, commenting on her divorce from Tom

Hayden. Two busy lives flying in different orbits can wreck intimacy. Your life doesn't have to be as busy as a movie star's either. The common pressures and distractions of modern life suffice.

A formidable barrier looms when both partners work full time outside the home because of financial necessity. When the mother would rather stay home and raise her children herself—or the father, for that matter—tensions rise just over the situation itself. Romance does not comingle with tension.

Think of all the tugs and pulls. The man, and frequently the woman also, is under much pressure to be competitive, to succeed (whatever job success entails). If the man's career has plateaued, shame, feelings of inadequacy, self-hate or self-disappointment all add to the tension—particularly if his wife's career is taking off, as it frequently does once the kids get older. Man and woman both may project such feelings onto each other. With emotion and stress running rampant, the doors open to an extramarital affair.

There's just plain physical weariness. There's the pressure to spend time with the kids, and the load of guilt for not spending enough of it. Neither person has anyone upon which to dump frustrations; neither one wants to hear the other's problems. Brian Newman chuckles. "Debi and I solve the problem of dumping on each other by holing up in opposite ends of the house. When both of us come off a bad day—and that happens frequently—we need the separation. We put off decision-making and even face-to-face contact until we're both settled."

Robert Hemfelt soaks in the hot tub, eating popcorn and watching the news. Susan curls up with country living catalogs and daydreams. Whatever works.

Giving Advice

"But what would my spouse do without my advice?" you protest.

"Depends," we reply. "Did your spouse ask for it, or did you give it unsolicited?" A common example: He shares a problem from work. She volunteers a solution. Her effort comes across as, "You dummy, you couldn't think of this yourself. I have to fix it for you." He was not looking for a solution; he wasn't even complaining, really. He was sharing his problem and his feelings. We find that sometimes this very situation is why one partner stops sharing. Sharing encourages intimacy. Failure to share broadens separation.

Feelings

David and Teresa Ferguson, affiliated with the Minirth-Meier, Wilson and Tunnell Clinic in Austin, have been through the Third and Fourth

Passages. Now they work as a team dealing with troubled marriages. They see three feelings that help intimacy quietly slip away.

The first feeling: "I no longer trust you to prioritize me." "We have found," says Teresa, "that after ten years or more of marriage, the husband's priorities usually are: first, his job/career; second, hobbies, TV, or sports; third, his kids; fourth, his wife; and fifth, God.

"His wife's priorities, though, usually rank: first, her kids; second, her church or civic service or her job; third, her husband; fourth, God; and fifth, her own parents."

She's fourth on his list and he's third on hers. That hurts. And if this priority list is true of your marriage, it is very hard for you to sustain intimacy.

What's an ideal list? The Fergusons suggest: first, God in my life; second, my spouse; third, the kids; fourth, job and church; and fifth, TV, hobbies, or sports. The children are nurtured not so much by Mom and Dad as by the solid union. Putting the marriage ahead of the kids as a priority is actually putting the kids ahead, in the end.

The second feeling that fosters distance is "I no longer feel you care because of unhealed hurts." Picture a cup which holds your feelings. It's finite. It can only hold so much. Once that cup fills, something has to go before other things can enter. The person with untended hurts from childhood, plus an accumulation of hurts from the marriage itself thus far, has no room left for feelings of care, love, joy. They get squeezed out by the mass of pent-up feelings hiding in the cup. The only way to empty the cup of those feelings, and make room for happier feelings, is to grieve and release them through the grieving process we're suggesting throughout this book.

The third feeling stymieing intimacy is "I no longer feel your love since taking has replaced giving." In the Third Passage, the couple have not really cultivated to this point the art of giving to each other. Life has been too cluttered until now, what with career, kids, housing decisions, and all. And, because of accumulated hurts, either partner may fail to recognize when a gift is being given. With the partnership drifting into complacency, much is taken for granted. Each partner thinks the other knows about needs but doesn't care enough to fill them, when in reality, neither partner sees them. Both partners tend to take what they need by manipulating and demanding.

If these to a greater or lesser extent are the deepest underlying attitudes in a marriage, the causes and symptoms become all the more virulent. If you are in the Third Passage, do you see any of these attitudes and feelings in your own outlook? How about your partner's? If you are in the First or Second Passage, can you see seeds of these feelings sprouting?

Symptoms

We look for specific warning signs that repairs are needed, that the passage has become stuck, unable to mature into the next stage of life. Does your marriage suffer from any of these common signs of being caught in this passage of marriage?

Sexual Difficulties

If sex ceases or nearly so at this stage of marriage, it is not the symptom of a bad marriage. It does identify that the couple are stuck, hung up in the passage. Sometimes, it indicates that one or both partners falsely believe that sex tapers off by now (Robert Hemfelt's mother announced to Susan that older people are sexual beings, too; she was in her seventies). Very late in life—beyond the seventies—a couple's love may well transcend the physical, as sexual vigor wanes with age. We're not talking about that here. In this passage, the partners are young enough to comfortably maintain an active and vigorous sex life. If they do not, something wrong is afoot.

We always hesitate to declare a norm regarding frequency of sexual intimacy, unless you call "extreme variation" a norm. When pressed for a very general ballpark figure, we suggest that two or more weeks between episodes of sexual intimacy and intercourse is a bit too long. Assuming good health in both marriage partners and assuming no extenuating circumstances (the birth of a baby within the last six weeks, for example), partners in their forties and fifties are probably getting together sexually a couple of times a week or more, couples in their thirties somewhat oftener.

Trouble signs we look for in counsel are: if sex is less frequent than once a week; if only one partner initiates sex; if one or both partners let go physically—gain weight drastically, get frumpy, neglect hygiene or such. These are usually barometers that the sex life is deteriorating and therefore the partners are moving apart. Something is going wrong with intimacy.

Charles, currently in our counsel, sought help for sexual impotence. His sexual relationship with his wife had never really been strong in their marriage, and she complained of its infrequency. That in itself is a warning sign: one partner or the other believes frequency is too much or not enough. In recent years, however, "infrequent" trickled away into "non-existent" in Charles's case. Not even his wife bothered to try initiating sex anymore. She had been disappointed too many times.

We insert a disclaimer here: Individual physical or psychological issues may cause impotence or drastically reduced activity. Use of various drugs or alcohol, just short of abuse, can greatly reduce libido. Some diseases, such as diabetes, and many kinds of medications (antihistamines, antidepressants, some heart medicines) hamper performance. Ask your doctor about that when receiving a prescription. A death in the family, extreme anxiety—traumatic events also can temporarily cool ardor.

Anger, depression, or fear, which may not be tied to anything in the marriage itself, may generate sexual problems. We know of a man shocked by the sudden loss of his job; things had seemed so secure; the company appeared to be doing well, his job was important . . . and then, out of the blue came the layoff. He'd never been without work in his life before. Devastated, he went through an exasperating six-month period of sexual impotence.

Most frequently, distorted notions or expectations about sex put the clamps on. For instance, when the first baby arrives, Mom or Dad or both gain fifty pounds and let themselves go. Below the conscious level, they could be saying, "Sex in a family is wrong. We're now a family. If I'm too fat to be desirable or sexy, we won't have to worry about it." Another example: A woman enters menopause and she or her husband or both falsely believe her sexuality has ended.

When we examine symptoms we look first at the couple's relationship, which may be hindered by hidden agendas or ghosts from their past, but we also cover all the other possible sources, physical as well as others.

Another persistent warning sign is a preoccupation with affairs, either actual or imaginary. When fantasies constantly invade sex, or if one or both spouses prefers fantasy to actual sex, warning bells ring. Charles's wife fantasized sexual unions with persons she knew and also with film celebrities. "As long as you're not doing it," she commented, "it doesn't matter who you're not doing it with. The sky's the limit." Some fantasizing is healthy for eroticism. To obsess, however, is very dangerous and damaging, for this reason. Moments of ecstasy and orgasm are extremely vulnerable bonding times. The partners imprint on each other, in the classic sense. Each time a partner focuses on a person or fantasy other than the spouse, the fantasizer has destroyed the opportunity for powerful bonding that time. That moment is lost. A couple can get by in Passages One or Two without bonding strongly, but in the Third Passage, with its strong pressure to drift or separate, the couple need this bonding to stay together.

We also consider it a warning sign if couples rely on porn to jump-start their flagging sex life. Reliance on masturbation, either gender, as a substitute for marital sex is understandably a big issue as well.

We look, too, for discouragement. By this Third Passage, men find themselves taking longer to achieve and maintain an erection. They may "fold in the middle." The temptation then is to believe the old days are gone forever and just give up. Women produce less lubricant, making penetration, at least in the first moments, more difficult and uncomfortable.

Charles's medical workup showed no physical problems. The hidden agendas we uncovered were not too far off the reality mark.

There are many "elsewheres." Do you see yourself in any of these?

Power Struggles

You're unconsciously mad at your spouse for getting paunchy and maybe a little overweight, and otherwise showing signs of aging. You therefore withhold sex as a punishment. That's using sex as a power tool. A woman—or man—who feels otherwise powerless in a relationship may feel sex is the only weapon in her or his impoverished arsenal. Power struggles in other areas of life—the kids, the finances, the degree of interaction with in-laws, autonomy and control in the household—slop over into the bedroom.

Financial Struggles

Charles and his wife did not evidence this symptom, but many do. More obvious signs are big debts, bounced checks, bankruptcy. But the signs may be perplexingly subtle. No big warning bells bong with bounced checks or unpaid bills. Most frequently it's simply that they cannot seem to save; they can never get ahead.

Counselors say that the combination house and car payment and all other debts should together total out to less than one-third a couple's take-home pay. Special situations, of course, may well be outside a person's control. In Texas in the eighties, we saw the oil boom collapse. A lot of fortunes caved in with it. However, we also find it a general rule that if a person is prone to repeatedly make speculative deals, that often says something about the person emotionally. In some professions, such as the ministry and teaching, the money simply may not be there.

Several years ago we helped a financier. It turned out that his hidden agenda was, "The only way to prove I love you is to provide handsomely." As a result, he was susceptible to wild investments. He went through several bankruptcies, but he always managed to pull his fortunes back together. In that way he was brilliant. In matters of love, it took us a long time to help him alter his agenda to, "I love you, and I'll do my reasonable best to provide for you." His wife had been on the verge of divorce because she couldn't stand the roller coaster ride. They're humming along at a much more modest financial clip now—no steep hills and deep valleys—and he's loving the new, less-hectic lifestyle so much, he's considering retiring. She's all for it.

Another financial warning sign emerges when two partners do not share financial handling and decision making. This need not be a fifty-fifty thing. But both parties should be fully apprised of the union's finances, both having input into decisions and, ideally, veto power. In distressed marriages, we usually find a significant imbalance in that.

Frequently one partner, usually the husband, deliberately withholds financial information. "If she knows how much we make, she'll just want to spend it." "If she knew the truth, she'd start nagging me to make more." Money and sex are the two big control issues; when they are combined, the mix can be volatile.

Have you ever heard these statements of financial blackmail perpetrated on partners? "If you loved me you'd buy . . . " Or "I'll cut back your allowance." Or the non-breadwinner may say, "I'll spend you into oblivion." Dysfunctional couples may often use money to beat up on each other.

Excessive or Malicious Fighting

Please note: There is nothing wrong with anger and disagreement. In fact, such friction is both necessary and inevitable if persons are to reveal themselves wholly to each other. People in a good marriage fight. *BUT*. When fighting is chronic or becomes physical; when it degenerates to physical, verbal, or emotional violence and abuse; when it spills over into the kids' arena (either a spouse enlists the kids in a gang effort against the marriage partner, or one spouse takes it out on the kids); when major issues are never resolved; when fights span several days or simmer for long periods; when you find yourself fighting just for the sake of winning—the red flags wave.

The subject matter of fights may provide a clue to growing separation. If fighting degenerates into character assassination ("I know you don't love me; you can't love anyone") or taking your partner's comments or actions personally when they weren't meant that way, we look for the deeper problem. When a couple find themselves fighting about who leaves the toothpaste cap off, the fight is never about toothpaste. It's about unresolved issues both are ignoring. Uncapped toothpaste is easy to see, and it's not painful. Deeper issues, hard to see, almost always hurt, so they are avoided.

Dr. Hemfelt dealt with a couple recently whose wife complained, "After I finally pried him off the sofa, he went out and trimmed the shrubbery. He absolutely scalped them!" and she popped photos out of her purse to prove her point. "He did it to get back at me." The shrubbery, of course, was not the issue, and her inappropriate personalization of his actions fit right into the picture. Sometimes it is quite appropriate to see that a partner is getting back in some way. But in many cases, this among them, what the one partner saw as a direct affront was merely the other person's attempt to work off anger in a constructive manner that somehow went awry. The big point is often not the action itself but how the action is perceived.

("Incidentally," says Robert, "Susan claims I scalp our bushes. A real burr job. She doesn't take pictures, but she does express pity for the bushes.")

We find one other aspect of unfair fighting that warns us of serious separation. One or both persons simply bury anger for a long period. The opposite also counts. One or both partners explode instantly. Even more commonly, we see both happening; the person (or persons) stuffs the anger away until finally, an explosion flings it all at the partner at once.

Physical Separation

In a sense, deliberately separating physically is nearly as painful as divorce. We're not talking here about legal separation, but about more subtle splits. Charles's wife did that. She'd go to the next state to visit Mom for a week at a time. Several times a year she'd visit her younger sister for a few days, just to "keep the family bond going." Added up, her little excursions totaled months.

Some separations are necessary, determined by circumstance. Business trips. Illness in the family. Taking the kids to out-of-town events such as contests, medical appointments, athletic games. But when you separate often for reasons other than that, problems surface. Lonely and angry, and with no other way to get Charles's attention, his wife ruptured the fabric of commitment. We cannot be together, so we will not be together.

REPAIR

"There was one nice thing about cream separators," Marj admitted. "Filter dolls. Every farm girl had a fancy look-at-it-but-don't-play-with-it doll decorating her bed. It was dressed in milk filters, hundreds of them stitched together in a big frill with colored ribbons and yarn. Out of misery, beauty."

Out of misery, beauty. Improving intimacy will work wonders for a marriage. Philosophers for centuries have delighted to point out how closely akin are love and hate, as if love and hate were two aspects of the same thing. In a large way they are. To the degree you can love a person, to that degree you can hate him or her.

"I'll sure buy that!" claimed Lee Atkins. "I was so certain my wife and I would be in love forever. We're talking about deep, deep love here. She hired three different lawyers, each one specializing in a different way to milk the ex. She still can't stand the sight of me, and every now and then she'll call me up and say so. Can you believe it?''

We certainly can. Usually, though, the love-hate tug-of-war is not that brutal. In most couples it's more mild-mannered, only occasionally getting out of hand. Love is nurtured when our need for impacting others and for enjoying healing, comforting intimacy is well met. Hate is generated by fear and hurt and also by the fear of being hurt. Needs have not been met; we fear they never will be. If you remember that love and hate, both of them the most impassioned emotional responses a human being makes, spring from the same roots, you can turn hate around to love and separation to intimacy.

In the clinic and in private counsel, our patients consider the symptoms to be the most important; after all, they have to suffer with them. We don't ignore the symptoms, but we go beyond them to explore underlying causes. The causes, then, point the way to possible solutions. Treating the symptoms only does no good; the causes will still be there to prevent treatment from "taking" or generate other symptoms.

MAJOR DAMAGE CONTROL

If you see your marriage in a serious slide toward destruction, you want serious steps to reverse it. Join a couple in our counsel, Rick and Nancy. The process they used employs five steps.

Rick and Nancy, married fourteen years, had daughters aged ten and twelve. They came to us because they could see their marriage and family falling apart and had not the vaguest idea how to snatch happiness out of the brewing disaster.

Their sex life, we learned, was virtually nonexistent. He considered her cold and unresponsive. She called him emotionally distant, sexually exploitative, and mechanical in his lovemaking. They both pursued careers. He tackled his in classic workaholic fashion. She worked as a department store buyer during the day while her girls were in school. We uncovered one of her hidden agendas early: She unconsciously purposed to build enough of a financial cushion that she could leave Rick.

Nancy's father, a dissipated alcoholic, eventually walked away from his family. Rick's father stayed home, but he was hardly closer to his children. Cold and emotionally distant, he pretty much ignored Rick. Both individuals, therefore, dragged a heavy load of baggage from the past.

To help them unload all that baggage and renew their lives with each other, we led them through five steps toward wholeness. You, too, can use those five steps to help a damaged marriage.

1. *"What is the old family-of-origin wound keeping me away from intimacy?"* Rick and Nancy's were obvious—alcoholism, abandonment, distance. You've already explored your own wounds. You, like Rick and Nancy, have to acknowledge them. Rick and Nancy had not, not in Passages One or Two, not recently. Both buried the old pain. That put deep cracks in the foundation of their union. One way they un-buried them was to hear each other's story.

Previously they constantly attacked each other for not sharing, for failing to be part of each other's world.

"He doesn't care about my interests."

"She doesn't listen and doesn't give a hang."

That all stopped as we had each one tell the other what it was like to grow up in that family of origin. They ceased the litany of mutual blame as they heard from each other the pain of growing up. The tone of the session shifted dramatically. Each person felt more sensitive and compassionate. Each became a better listener.

2. *"What are the wounds in my own marriage now that steer me away from intimacy?"* Review the earlier wounds of your own marriage. How did your spouse hurt you? We hope they are not as extreme as Rick and Nancy's. Nancy suffered breast cancer in her mid-thirties. Rick didn't really mean to seem indifferent, but the situation frightened him. He felt confused, uncertain. What should he say, if anything? What should he do? He had no idea how to deal with it all; he ended up simply withdrawing out of fear. Nancy understandably felt abandoned. In our office she talked about the pain of the occasion when she went to be fitted for a prosthesis.

"I begged him to go along," she related. "He sort of waffled. Then he scheduled an out-of-town business trip for that week."

"Some business trips can't be shifted," Rick complained.

"Oh, no! You could call the shots, Rick. You're the manager. It was you. Not circumstance. I was devastated. I don't know how I got through it alone. And believe me, I had to walk that whole road alone."

Rick and Nancy both had to grieve out the fear and anger generated by prior disappointments and letdowns. It was the only way to clear away the wreckage of the past.

You, too, must similarly clear away such wreckage. You will find that some of that painful wreckage is due to false assumptions. And that is the next step.

3. *"What assumptions have I made about how my spouse sees me?"* Nancy assumed, because of his distance and withdrawal, that Rick didn't care. She assumed he was insensitive to pain and to her disfigurement. Maybe he didn't love her as much as she had supposed; maybe he didn't love her at

all. In reality, he was feeling intense fear, not indifference, but culture and his early life with an undemonstrative father had conditioned him to hide it. He had never given himself permission to talk about feelings. If by this Third Passage your needs are not being met, you will start to make negative assumptions about what your spouse feels. Those assumptions, apart from being unjust, destroy intimacy. Sometimes the assumptions are true or at least border on truth. The vast majority are not.

Rick, meanwhile, was assuming that because of Nancy's bout with breast cancer, she was no longer interested in physical love. She took his distance to mean that he no longer found her attractive. Can a vicious cycle of assumptions and counter-assumptions be operating in your marriage? Have you two ever simply sat down and talked about what you feel and what you think each other feels? It comes as a vivid revelation that what you think you know about your spouse simply is not true.

Questions 1, 2, and 3 cleared away inhibitions and false assumptions that keep the healthiest of couples separated. With questions 4 and 5, we piece each other back together.

4. *"What fears and resentments do I harbor that my spouse won't recipro-cate my efforts?"* we ask couples to ask each other. "Would you make the time and effort to step into your spouse's world?"

"Well, sure, I suppose. But you don't understand," Nancy insisted. "He wouldn't return that to me."

"Have you asked him?"

"It's not that easy. You see," Nancy said, "we're so different. He likes action movies; that stupid Chuck Norris type stuff. I like romantic movies. He only likes go-go-go business travel; I want to take a cruise or something else leisurely. He would spend his whole life puttering around on this little farm he owns in East Texas. I like my own backyard here in town, thank you."

Rick picked it up. "Our differences are too extreme to patch. I appre-ciate formal worship. She wants to go to this couples' class. We end up in two cars on Sunday morning. She goes to these self-help lectures all the time. I hate them. Politics; you name it. We're on opposite sides of the fence."

Both persons feared that any effort they made to enter their partner's world would go unreciprocated. This is nothing more than the old primal human fear of abandonment or rejection, concealed in very cloudy dress. Both Rick and Nancy had to ventilate that fear by voicing it. They had to sit down and discuss it back and forth. Once on the table, it can be dealt with.

5. *"What am I willing to give in order to get?"* Liken this final step to a cultural exchange program. We send a student abroad and the host country

sends a student over here. In the process we export Americanism and improved understanding, and bring the customs and traditions of another culture into our home. If a married couple have drifted off into separate worlds, freezing intimacy, they must rejoin, reconnect, reunite. They have to essentially learn a foreign culture—the life of their spouse.

Rick and Nancy sat down for a round of businesslike negotiating. "If you do such and so, I'll do so and so." As cold and mechanistic as it was, it got the attitude of sharing back in place again. As you tackle your give and take, remember that it works only if the other steps are completed first.

You complain, "I shouldn't have to go through mechanical steps to do that." We agree. But many couples need that mechanical bargaining because they have become strangers. They have forgotten how to share. They are suspicious, cautious, uncertain of each other's motives. They must relearn the needs, tastes, interests, and passions of their spouse. It's very much like two people visiting faraway lands and getting to know each other.

Rick and Nancy hit a hard bump in this step. They agreed to work past that fear of rejection. They agreed to step into each other's worlds on a give-and-take basis. That's how Nancy ended up on the East Texas farm over the Memorial Day weekend. She despised bugs. May is a buggy time of year. She didn't like dirt. There she was out there, planting late vegetables and chopping weeds. "If it means so much to you," she said, "I'll try." Neighbors rented the pasture, and their retired plow horse scared her. The old mare weighed in at 1,500 pounds. Their gander chased her.

Back in the peace and orderliness of their suburban home at last, with no geese trying to pinch them, Nancy invited Rick to the last lecture of the series at the local college—"Building Commitment" was its title. Rick declined.

And right there, the whole intimacy-building project went somewhere in a handbasket. Nancy was furious. She went way, way, *way* out of her way for him and he couldn't spend one lousy evening at a lecture she was sure he would find immensely helpful. Her fury wasn't all just anger, you see; it was actually that old nagging fear that he would abandon her in her efforts, fail to join her world, leave her holding the bag. Rick apologized, as soon as his crass error was pointed out to him. They cautiously and reluctantly started over with the fifth step. The second time, it worked.

Sampling each other's world does more than just build intimacy, although that is its primary purpose. Rick and Nancy's diversity was not a barrier in their lives, but a wonderful source of enrichment. By sharing in each other's pleasures they could tap into that enrichment. Your diversity is just as rich.

16

HAVE YOU COMPLETED THE THIRD PASSAGE?

*E*veryone seated at the conference table in the Minirth-Meier Clinic in Richardson, Texas, had been married at least ten years. Many were nearer the twenty mark. Dr. Hemfelt passed around eleven legal-sized pads, one to each person. "I'll give you eight categories," he explained. "For each of them, think about the dreams and expectations you started out with in your marriage. Whether they were exaggerations or illusions you harbored or seem quaint or nonsensical now, write them down. Then write down a brief description of what you see as the reality. How do you view those dreams now? Have you abandoned them? Did you achieve them? Take what time you need."

Robert performs this exercise frequently in group counsel. You can do it yourself at home. Its purpose is to clarify the issues of your marriage and how realistically you see its future. This then becomes a good guide as to how well you are completing this passage. It also provides an insight into what you might want to change in your contract.

BALANCING THE DREAM WITH REALITY

We invite you to explore your past and present and thereby perhaps see your future. We've provided answers we typically hear to prime the pump for you, so to speak, if you feel a bit stuck in places. Try to look at both positives and negatives of your reality.

1. Sexual romance

Write down your dreams below. *("I assumed romance would be similar to what I read in romance novels, continually intense and passionate.")*

_____

_____

_____

Now write a description of your marriage as it is now. *("We have had a good relationship. It fulfills me if I rein in my original dream.")*

_____

_____

_____

2. Finances

Your dreams *("I planned to own my own business by this time.")*:

_____

_____

_____

Now reality *("I'm an area manager for someone else. But at least I have as much financial security as the job permits. And I can go home and leave my job behind. I couldn't do that if I owned the whole shebang.")*:

_____

_____

_____

3. Social prestige

Your aspirations *("I grew up on Bon Aire Drive. My parents were top of the pile. I expected to be there in the new town where we moved.")*:

_____

_____

_____

In reality *("We've never attained social prominence in this new town and with my husband's income we never will. On the other hand, we found a good church. I didn't have that before.")*:

_____

_____

_____

4. Sharing with friends

Your dreams *("I'm gregarious and outgoing by nature, so I pictured my wife and me with a wide circle of ten or fifteen close couples, and we'd entertain every weekend."):*

_____

_____

_____

The reality *("I find it hard to accept that we've got maybe three close couples and one eccentric single. There's not a lot of close sharing, and my wife is the opposite; she doesn't like to entertain. Frankly, I don't see anything positive here."):*

_____

_____

_____

5. *Dream of children*
This category has two parts. One is whether you wanted children and if so, how your reality matches with the dream.
Your dream *("I always wanted to have two children."):*

_____

_____

_____

The reality *("One of four couples struggles with infertility and we're one of them. We've tried everything. My husband is resigned to the fact we won't have biological children, but I'm having trouble with it. So I guess you'd say we're halfway; he's there but I'm not."):*

_____

_____

_____

The second part of this category has to do with how your children are turning out. Does that approach the original dream?
Your dream *("I wanted my children to share my beliefs."):*

_____

_____

_____

Reality *("My kids are their own persons. They have at least temporarily rejected some of my beliefs."):*

_____

_____

_____

6. *Spiritual*
Your dreams *("My family I grew up in was constantly involved in church, all of us. We loved it and it was a vigorous church."):*

_____

_____

_____

The reality *("My husband is a good man and a Christian. He's saved. We go to church every week, but it's not the center of our lives. I had to accept that those growing-up days are probably gone forever and I can't replicate what I grew up in. It's not just my husband. I can't find a church around here as vibrant as my old home church."):*

_____

_____

_____

7. *Miscellaneous dreams*
By miscellaneous we mean that sort of dream—or dreams—that might begin, "Someday I'd like to _____," or "When I'm married I want us to _____ whatever." Dreams that are unique to you and don't fall into any other category.

Your dreams *("I always dreamed I'd somehow be able to enjoy lots of world travel. My parents did that in their younger years, but not after I was born."):*

_____

_____

_____

Good old reality *("I have a good marriage, but our family income is modest to say the least. International travel just is not possible. I had to grieve and accept that. It was hard. What I've done, though: I've replaced that dream with an interest in geography. I teach kids, as a volunteer in our church missions program and a library enrichment program in geography. It's not the same thing, but it's a taste of all those faraway places with strange-sounding names."):*

_____

_____

_____

8. *My spouse in general*
Your dreams *("What can I say? She was going to be built like a* Sports Illustrated *swimsuit model, earn a Ph.D., and cook like Julia Child."):*

_____

_____

_____

Reality *("Would you believe an All American at a junior college and built like a quarterback in* Sports Illustrated? *But man, can she cook! And I love her and she loves me!"):*

_____

_____

_____

_____

Those glaring deficits, where reality comes nowhere near matching your dreams and aspirations, must be grieved through. When your dream and reality match or nearly so, you've ample cause to celebrate. Celebration is the other side of the grief coin and is totally appropriate. If none of your realities come close to fulfilling your original aspirations, look again at that area. Did you set your dreams too high? That, too, should be grieved.

BALANCING IDENTITY AGAINST REALITY

A goal of this passage from the first has been to maintain and develop your own identity, lest your uniqueness be smothered in the comfort and complacency of your marriage. Reworded, you must avoid a codependent relationship with your spouse in which you become either buried in enmeshment or estranged in constant conflict.

Again we offer an exercise to help you think about this. If you have been married more than ten years, weigh your situation with these statements. Do they pertain to you? How well have you established an identity of your own apart from your marital identity?

"I can name three friends with whom I'd like to spend the day. I can trust them with most (but not all) secrets."

1. _____
2. _____
3. _____

"I can picture several things my spouse and I can do together in the next ten years. At least one of those things is more my idea than my spouse's."

1. _____
2. _____
3. _____

"I can list three foods I like better than my spouse does, three foods my spouse enjoys more than I do, and at least one film or television show I've heard of that I think I would enjoy but my spouse probably would not."

"Three foods I like: _____ "

"Three foods my spouse likes: _____ "

"Film or television show I'd like but my spouse would not:

_____ "

This exercise is also a measure of how well you've completed the Third Passage. If you have trouble with more than a couple of the items, you are stuck back in the First and Second Passages where you were trying to meld your personality into your spouse's.

THE NEW CONTRACT

"Why write a new reason to be married now?" scoffs the skeptic. "If I didn't already have a reason, do you think I'd be married this long?"

One of our patients had a reason: She couldn't think of any good excuse to divorce. That was a lousy reason. We've heard other, more valid reasons, like the many Christians who believe the Bible verse, "God hates divorce," and therefore are committed to remain married. We suggest that you carefully consider the covenant agreement between your spouse and yourself. It should be a key part of your renewed contract.

Do you write a new contract at this point because you blew the old one? No. You write a new one because you and your mate have changed so much that your outlook and needs have changed. It is time to rediscover and reaffirm new ways to feel about each other. This is a reflection of new realities as well as old promises. It is not the covenant promise itself but the working guide to that promise.

What might a new (or renewed, if you wish) contract entail? Check the statements that apply to you.

_____ "We renew our original pledge of fidelity."

To guard against the remote chance of straying, as part of your new contract you may want to mutually agree to avoid any and all flirtations, suggestive comments, and careless touching with the opposite sex, tempting situations—in short, any first step down the wrong road. Don't deny the sexual energy between men and women ("Aw, I don't have to worry about that. I'm fat and forty-five") that is always there.

_____ "We each promise to keep the union strong."

We see a lot of ambivalence in this passage. You love and hate the life you have now. In your contract, train that ambivalence into a firm decision to stay with your mate and to love that person. Note those are two different decisions.

_____ "We'll each find a same-sex soul mate."

An executive who found himself in an extramarital affair and was later restored to his wife says: "I would encourage every man to have another man he can look eyeball to eyeball with and talk about tough issues of life; to be accountable to. Every man needs that kind of friend." This should not be a parent or sibling (they're too close, and share too many of your own anomalies). You might want to write a friend into your contract.

_____ "We commit to the spiritual growth possible now."

You are at last capable of putting away the persons (Mom and Dad particularly), things, and institutions that could function as gods in your life and seeking out God Himself in a new dimension. The commitment to spiritual growth means periodically reviewing your life. Are some of those non-gods creeping back into it?

_____ Success on the job?
_____ The biggest (or cleanest) house on the block?
_____ The fastest boat or car?
_____ The highest academic degree?
_____ The brightest, best-behaved children?
_____ The best-looking spouse?
Have you successfully said good-bye to them all?

_____ "We commit to making God the third leg of our marriage."
_____ "We commit to forgiveness."

Don't forget the occasional need to forgive God and to come into a closer relationship with Him.

ENCOMPASS MORE OF GOD

One of the women sitting around that conference table in the Minirth-Meier Clinic, evaluating the Third Passage of their marriage, was Diane.

She did what all those old romance novels and feel-good movies used to tout: She defied her father's wishes to marry the man she loved. Daddy was wealthy. He could not abide a young man who left law school and essentially dropped out of polite society in order to pursue an art career. Despite that Diane's husband carved a successful niche for himself in art circles, relations between Diane and her daddy remained cold and restrained from the engagement right up to his death.

With his passing, during Diane's Third Passage of marriage, she found herself in a profound spiritual crisis. The God of her prior Christian convictions appeared to be far too unfair and vengeful to warrant worship. She dwelt to the point of obsession on the tragedies that struck believers and unbelievers. She could not be reconciled to them. Because her crisis of faith coincided closely with her father's death, her pastoral counselor sent her to us.

To make a long therapy story short, Diane figured out that the death of her father had triggered within her the memories of all that pain she felt when her human father rejected her. She had projected the pain and injustice together upon her heavenly Father. Only after she grieved all that pain and released it, could she come back and embrace her heavenly Father. And embrace Him she did, more profoundly than ever she had known Him before.

Unresolved issues can and do spill over into the Third Passage, or wherever they are triggered by some event. And they can bar union with God just as easily as they bar intimacy with your spouse. If you have trouble reaching new depths of oneness and understanding with God, look to your past for clues. Is something back there damaging your faith now?

Carl Jung believed you do not come to a true mature spiritual acceptance of God until the second half of life. Only now, in this Third Passage, can you get down to the deepest levels of spiritual insight. There are two archaic and distorted views of God you may have to dismiss first. One is the Santa Claus God, who can supply the grocery list of needs you present Him in prayer. The second is the harsh and vengeful Scorekeeper God who's planning to punish you for all those wrongs. Both are supported by selected Scripture verses. Neither represents the true God Scripture.

How much of your past is coloring your view of God now? First, what are your human father's (or adoptive father's) characteristics? *(Loving and supportive, for instance, or demanding and harsh?)*

1. _____

2. _____

3. _____

What are your mother's characteristics? *(Forgiving and understanding of your problems, for instance, or distant and uninterested in your activities?)*

1. _____
2. _____
3. _____

Now what are God's characteristics as you see them? *(Do you see Him as remote and detached, or as a Father who supports you when you're feeling lost or depressed?)*

1. _____
2. _____
3. _____

Compare the lists. Either your parents do indeed reflect the heavenly Father—and some do, because that's what parents are supposed to do according to divine plan—or you are projecting your earthly parents' image upon the heavenly one. Even more likely, you are coloring your view of God in a limited way by your memories of your parents. Give the point as much thought as possible. Lord willing, it will lead to deeper insight.

Those are the big, overriding concepts to consider. Now let's look at the mid-level contract items.

MID-LEVEL ITEMS

Go back to the specifics in that inventory of dreams and realities. Are there dreams still within your reach, perhaps if modified? You're too young to abandon all your dreams. Perhaps by restructuring them somewhat, can you still have a shot at those dreams? What can you improve? Sex? Financial status? How can you go about it? Write that into the contract.

"We can still realize these hopes and dreams:"

_____
_____
_____

"These are some practical ways to reach those goals:"

_____
_____
_____

Some will never be achieved. Things will go wrong. Here is the place to make the commitment to the grief process. "Commit to grief? How dis-

The Renewed Marriage Contract

1. Statement of affirmation; at least one attribute each person admires and appreciates in the other

2. Statement of extent of commitment to the marriage

3. Promise of fidelity

4. Statement of faith, embracing:
   a. Each person's individual statement of faith
   b. Clearly stated common ground
   c. Statement of tolerance (and limits of tolerance)

5. Statement of recognition of old, dysfunctional hidden agendas

6. Declaration of new agendas to redress dysfunctions

7. Sexual contract, including:
   a. Recognition of difficulties or shortcomings in present sexual relations
   b. Steps to improve relations and/or explore new techniques
   c. Details of frequency if frequency is an issue

8. Review of items in first contract, with updates and revisions as necessary

9. Details of everyday life (request for romantic nights out) established through give-and-take (be specific)

mal!" you protest. "Not at all!" we assure you. Healthy grieving will bring peace and ease the pain of disappointment and frustration. Grieving brings you to terms with reality. It is the only way to expunge anger and prevent the inward-turning of anger into depression.

_____"We commit to grieving all losses."

And now to the fine tuning. Remember when you analyzed your mate's positive and negative attributes in Chapter 11? Use that analysis in a mutual promise to work at minimizing the negatives (or irritations) and to affirm and praise the positives *on a regular, frequent basis*. Be specific about needs and preferences in this part.

_____"I commit to affirmation of positive factors in my spouse."
_____"I commit to attention and care toward minimizing the
        negatives."

That contract represents twenty-five years of your life. By now you've probably spent more time with your spouse than with your parents. Your history together will be part of the blessing you take into the next passage of marriage, Renewing Love.

PART
FIVE

*The Fourth Passage:
Renewing Love,
the Twenty-sixth
through the
Thirty-fifth Years*

17

CAN YOU OVERCOME THE SLINGS AND ARROWS OF FORTUNE?

*A*mericans have been sold a bill of goods that everything can be forced into continual perfection. What you want you can have. Whatever the threat of tragedy, you can insure yourself against it, insulate yourself against it. And if by some chance tragedy befalls you, someone else was responsible, so sue them. They loused up your otherwise perfect existence; let them pay.

Unfortunately, real life doesn't work that way.

THE POWER OF IMPERFECTION

The storms of life generate far more than misery and frustration. They trigger very real physiological and psychological changes. You can get sick from too much stress and tragedy in your life, and it is *not* "all in your head." Your body chemistry shifts, causing physical symptoms and lowering your resistance to disease.

So powerful is stress, some researchers have set up a numerical system, assigning stress points for various crises. In one of the most popular of these systems, the top three stressors—divorce and separation, the death of a spouse, the death of a child—are all relational. The bereaved feel a loss of intimacy, a sense of isolation. Marriage provides the best insulation against crisis (married men live significantly longer than do unmarried men), and it creates the most profound stress when it goes wrong.

Retiring, losing your job, going to jail, getting sick, even moving to a new home, all cause stress. Any drastic shift in the status quo upsets more than just your routine. Good changes work as much havoc as bad ones. Winning the lottery is about as bad for you as going bankrupt. Getting married scores stress points. So does parenthood or marrying off a child.

Taken one or two at a time, all these kinks in the plumb line of life cause little more than temporary problems. When several of them befall you at once, the points add up and trouble follows. Their power can overwhelm you.

Not all stressors and crises are recognized as such, at least not at the time they happen. As Mary Alice Minirth points out, "People who came back from World War II shaped the generations that followed. Many of them had the anger and frustration we call Post-Traumatic Stress, though it wasn't recognized then. It shaped how their families were raised. They weren't fathers in our modern sense. Everyone now is into 'Let's be good fathers.' But to that generation, back from war, Father went out and supported the family and that was all. The roles were rigid, and they were stressful.

"The Depression and World War II together fostered a lot of uncontrollable stress, so that everyone felt like a survivor: 'We did our thing and we made it.' That could be a whole book, just on how the thirties and forties shaped us. Because then came the Me generation."

Things that seem simple—"piece of cake!"—produce stress. One of those stressors is nothing less than your movement from passage to passage through your marriage. You can't avoid it. The crises come when the rules of the game shift but the referee doesn't tell you. Spouses' attitudes and priorities must change to fit the changing nature of the marriage, but there's no clear indicator as to how or when. Sometimes the two partners fail to change at the same time. One, still wrapped securely in the First Passage, may be drooling at the thought of romance while the other, having moved on to the passage of reality, is getting a little bored with this whole scene. In short, the abrupt changes that always happen in real life can easily unhorse marriage partners, whether or not those people know the changes are happening.

To an extent, stressors are what you make them. "Oh no!" shrieks the young teen. "I'm doomed!" Her crisis? A pimple just prior to a major date. To her, it's serious. To Dad, it's all a joke . . . until the picture tube blows just as he plans to watch a major sporting event. ("So what?" muses the daughter.) Overreaction and underreaction, like beauty, are in the eye of the beholder. But the crisis exists in any case.

Acne outbreak or plague outbreak, crises must be met one way or another. Actually there is more than one way. Susan Hemfelt points out, "There are three ways to address a problem. The all, the nothing, and the large gray area. Ideally, you tackle every problem with a comprehensive 'all' solution. That's the best solution possible to the problem. The 'nothing' approach is ignoring the problem, or getting stubborn, or going into denial, or maybe taking the wrong tack.

"Then there's the broad gray area that's a bandage for the situation. It's not going to cure anything. You're not actually solving the problem, you're just putting it off temporarily. The problem will show up again, maybe worse next time. But you have to do something immediate, so you put on a bandage. It's not the 'all' solution, but it's not the 'nothing' one, either."

Crises arise in every passage of marriage, of course, but they seem to have more profound implications as you grow older. A crisis you could bounce back from in youth becomes overwhelming in later age. You have little time left of your life to repair some crises—financial setback, personal problems, career difficulties. Therefore, confronting crisis becomes a major task. Handling it well is an important goal.

THE FIRST TASK: COMBAT
THE CRISIS OF THIS PASSAGE

Here's that squirrel on a major limb of the decision tree again. A pine marten comes scrabbling up the trunk in hot pursuit—crisis! Will the squirrel end up as the marten's lunch? The squirrel dashes up the nearest branch, out the closest twig. It hangs, bobbing, on the very end of the branch. With a valiant lunge it leaps five feet to another branch and skitters out a whole different limb system to make its escape.

The squirrel, pressed by circumstance, had little choice. It got away the best it could, not via the preferred escape route but out the quickest, nearest escape route.

Similarly, persons faced with crisis may have precious little choice in how to respond. The choice is made for them by circumstance and their own natures. The squirrel, for example, could not fly away as would a blue jay. Different people respond naturally in different ways (based as much on their hidden agendas as on their natures, incidentally), and the reaction is pretty much automatic. It's the first and quickest thing to do, not necessarily the best.

Some persons slip instantly into denial. This isn't all bad. At times, couples need a measure of temporary denial. For example, we spoke of James and Lonna Jorgensen in Chapter 10, when they lost their daughter to cancer. One of the most severe losses a couple can suffer, the death of a child, crushed James so thoroughly and instantly, he couldn't even call the relatives to tell them. Lonna did the phoning. She made the funeral arrangements. She maintained a stiff upper lip. As James came to terms with their loss, she kept the family going. Six months later she fell apart and James couldn't figure out why. After all, it happened and it was over with. James had worked it through; he was well along with his grieving. He didn't understand that Lonna, having hidden the truth behind a thick layer of denial, was just now beginning to grieve. Denial is a necessary part of the grieving process. Only when it is carried to extreme does it become malignant.

Some persons respond by giving up. "Giving up" means anything from walking away from the problem and going fishing to committing suicide. People without courage to commit suicide may commit passive suicide.

A man we'll call Howard did that. A year after his wife was assaulted and raped while jogging in the park, Howard had gained almost seventy pounds. He smoked a pack of cigarettes a day although he had only taken up smoking six months earlier. Alarmed and exasperated, and dealing with her own problems, his wife gave him an ultimatum: Seek counseling to turn this around, or we're through.

After giving Howard a complete physical workup, we asked him, "We understand one of your wife's complaints is that your sexual relationship has all but disappeared."

He grimaced. "No 'all but' about it. It's gone. I don't blame her. Who wants to make love to a blob like this?"

"To what do you attribute your extreme weight gain?"

"My father was heavy, and my grandfather too. It's in my genes. You hit a magic age and whammy! From weasel to whale."

"Over five pounds a month?"

"It happens."

"Why the smoking? That's another complaint your wife presented to us."

"I don't know. All my brothers do. And I've always felt like I was a smoker. You know how you feel a natural urge for something? I've always felt that."

"And just recently put it into practice."

"I've lost confidence in all that surgeon general stuff. They tell you to take aspirin, and then they say it's bad for you. And they tell you don't eat cholesterol and then they say, well this kind's okay but that kind's not.

They say you can't get AIDS from your doctor and then that dentist . . . you know. It's all a bunch of rot."

"And how often have you been arrested for drunk driving?"

His mouth dropped open. "How did you know that? It wasn't really an arrest; I wasn't driving. I was off on the road shoulder. He couldn't arrest me because he couldn't place me behind the wheel when the car was in motion. He just gave me a lecture and a lot of dirty looks."

Actually, we didn't know about it; although we don't often do so, we were taking a shot in the dark. Driving under the influence of alcohol is a common form of passive suicide, as is taking drugs.

The more we talked, the more we picked up one obvious sign of depression after another—disenchantment, malaise, an I-don't-care attitude, lack of sexual desire, self-hate. Because depression is anger turned inward, we then dug down for reasons behind the anger. The violation of his wife, of course, was the big one, but we found others as well. Latent, the others had created their own silent crises, what Dr. Hemfelt calls a state of quiet desperation. The latest outrage tipped Howard over the edge, from borderline depression into full-blown depression and self-hatred.

Some people respond to crisis by turning to an addiction, either by itself or in conjunction with other responses. People with a history of codependency problems are especially vulnerable to addictions, obsessions, and compulsions.

Some turn against God. "If He really loved me . . . " "It's His fault. He's omnipotent; He could have prevented this."

Some turn against their mates. Many is the case we see of a person in crisis blaming the spouse, fairly or unfairly.

SURVIVING IMPERFECTION

And some, to the enormous benefit of their marriages, turn not against their spouses but toward them. That is the positive way, the method of surmounting crisis that leads to a stronger marriage and healthier relationship.

The Minirths dealt with major losses in the past, and they deal with loss and crisis today. So do the Newmans. So do the Hemfelts. So do you.

Not every crisis resolves itself satisfactorily. Not every squirrel finds an escape route. Let us assume for the balance of this chapter that your marriage has already been damaged by crisis. If it has not (and few have not), you will still find this recovery model useful for ironing out the little wrinkles as well.

For purposes of the exercise, think of a crisis or problem that caused friction recently in your own marriage. It might be that your company has forced you into early retirement or demoted you or downscaled your job. For convenience, let's name that incident "IT." Work through IT along with us as we describe the process we use at the clinic to help patients deal with crises.

This process consists of ten steps, some very brief and others lengthy and difficult. From time to time, you may find yourself recycling through one or more of them as additional issues emerge.

Step 1: Suspend the Blame Cycle.

Dr. Minirth talked at the beginning of this book about a friend who was giving up his wife and kids for a new, romantic, First Passage love. That story, just recently resolved, has a happy ending. Let's see how the satisfactory resolution came about. We will call him John and his wife, Gloria.

You will recall that John was laying all his woes at Gloria's door. It was her fault he was seeking love elsewhere. The man was projecting his own feelings of inadequacy and his genuine shortcomings onto his spouse.

In large part, that is what blame is. The blamer is projecting all his or her own pains and frustrations onto the projection screen of the spouse. It's easy to do and far less painful than admitting pain and frustration. By focusing all that blame on someone else, the blamer escapes the white heat of the spotlight on his or her own actions.

As John did, you must first of all suspend that blame cycle. No longer do you seek in someone else's actions the source of your own misery. Tackling this man's problems in a clinic setting, we asked both John and Gloria to take this first step. Which of them actually should be taking the blame? The wife, of course, would say, "It's his fault! He's the one who wants out." Neither from this point on is assigned blame. Neither.

We've counseled a number of couples who are working through a crisis like the one we suggested to you: the husband's demotion at the age of fifty-five or so. In one instance, the wife's career was just beginning to galvanize as the husband (we'll call him Larry and her Beverly), who had been a research manager, was essentially told by his company, "For the last ten years of your career with us, you will be training field sales representatives about our newest equipment." It was their polite way of saying, "We're really through using you for major work. We're going to keep you on the payroll, even at your present salary, but we're doing it out of obligation, not because we need you."

Beverly had originally gone into real estate as a lark, just to see if she could earn a little money after all those years of staying home with the kids. Now her mounting success had become an issue between them. Blame often surfaces in indirect ways, as it did in this instance. Larry didn't outwardly blame his wife for his demotion, but his hurt turned inward into depression, and that surfaced as anger and a critical attitude. Nothing his wife did was right. He criticized her housekeeping. Her cooking. The hours she devoted to her career, even though he had originally encouraged her to try real estate. Finally, he began to sabotage her work indirectly.

When Beverly wanted to rent some office space outside the home, Larry warned her about the high overhead, about the volatility of real estate. Underneath he was saying, "Are you really sure you can make it? Do you really know how tough it is? Your current success might be just a fluke." Talk about bursting someone's balloon!

In the crisis or problem you put in mind at the beginning of this section, how could you be expressing the blame you feel or how is your spouse expressing it? *(The man who was demoted, for instance, also became more controlling about general household issues, such as finances. Suddenly, he began scrutinizing all his wife's expenses, even though together they were now making more money than ever before.)*

_____

At whose door was the blame laid? _____

Who deserved it? _____ *(The right answer is "Nobody.")*

Step 2: Acknowledge Your Contribution to the Pain.

John had to examine his own actions. How was he hurting his wife? How was he damaging his children? He was certainly not acting in a vacuum. What were his own shortcomings? "None," he said at first. And we invited him to look again.

As you think about that recent incident in your life, you will see that IT affects both partners and probably other people as well.

List two persons hurt by IT and how they were hurt. *(Larry, the executive who was demoted, was hurting his wife by criticizing her and also by sabotaging her effectiveness at work.)*

1. _____

He or she was hurt in this way: _____

2. _____

He or she was hurt in this way: _____

What peripheral damage was done by IT—loss of money, time, effort, prestige? _____

_____

_____

Now the big-ticket question: How much of that pain and loss could have been avoided or minimized had you acted differently?

_____

That's your contribution to the crisis.

Once Larry had acknowledged his contribution to the pain in his marriage, he also had to admit his own fear and vulnerability. Finally, in one session he was able to turn to Beverly and say, "I am afraid. I feel inadequate. I am scared about my long-term ability to provide for our family."

"I" statements, such as these, are not blame statements, which always begin with the word *you*. Instead of the previous blame statements ("Your job is insecure. You are taking too much control of our marriage."), Larry was now owning his pain. "Yes, I have begun to be hypercritical and over-controlling as a way to mask my fear and insecurity." Once he admitted this, his inappropriate actions were no longer necessary.

Step 3: Examine the Status of Your Marriage: Have You Negotiated All the Tasks in Each Passage So Far?

John was not ready to admit that he was hung up in the First Passage, seeking that idealistic love. He certainly denied Dr. Minirth's opinion that if he couldn't make it into Realistic Love with this wife, he'd likely not with the next one either.

Gloria was just as recalcitrant. "I'm not the problem," she insisted. "John is." She had to go back and do step one all over again; she had to suspend blame. How are you doing with step one? Got it in hand? Good.

In the case of the demoted executive, we helped them see that they had never gone beyond the earliest, most rudimentary contract for a marriage. In this type of contract, the man subconsciously says, "I have purpose in this marriage only as long as I am a strong breadwinner."

How many years have you been married? Now, where are you in the parade of passages? To gauge it, you and your spouse might go back through the "How have you passed" exercises at the end of each passage. Or you might each take this quick appraisal by checking the statements below that now apply to your marriage:

Passage 1:

_____ "I can honestly say I've kept the best of idealism while putting aside unrealistic dreams."

_____ "I can honestly say that my spouse and I have a satisfying sexual relationship."

_____ "I can honestly say that I have tried to deal with my parents' incomplete marriage passages."

Passage 2:

_____ "I can honestly say I have a realistic view of my mate and marriage that is not tainted by bitterness."

_____ "I can honestly say that I have recognized the hidden contracts in our marriage and have revised my part of our marriage contract."

_____ "I can honestly say that I have tried to childproof our marriage by reserving special times for my spouse and me without the children."

Passage 3:

_____ "I can honestly say I've come to terms with disillusionment and sameness in my marriage and am working to keep the marriage bond fresh and strong."

_____ "I can honestly say that I have found individual identity within my marriage relationship."

_____ "I can honestly say that I try to truly forgive my spouse for the everyday hurts."

_____ "I can honestly say that I have accepted the inevitable losses of the Third Passage of life—loss of youth, loss of health, loss of some of my dreams."

_____ "I can honestly say that I have tried to help our adolescent become a separate, unique individual."

_____ "I can honestly say that I have tried to maintain an intimate relationship with my spouse despite the obstacles, such as my own self-preoccupation."

We often suggest that a husband and wife discuss their responses to these statements and make some changes if necessary. For instance, Larry had never worked through the Second Passage task of understanding his individual identity within the marriage relationship. He needed to look for other identities in his marriage relationship besides successful breadwinner. He might identify spiritual leadership, companionship, tenderness. A major part of his healing would be to discover these other roles and functions in his marriage.

Finally ask yourself, "How do I think about my mate?" That may be a key to whether you've successfully negotiated the shifts from passage to passage thus far. Discuss it together.

Step 4: Commit to Recovery and Determine to Improve Your Marriage.

That sounds easy. "We wouldn't be doing this if we weren't committed to recovery," you protest. But we didn't say, "Explore the option of recovery." Commitment means you're going to do it, no matter what comes. Exactly how much time are you willing to devote (a generalized "whatever it takes" won't cut it here; be specific)? Exactly what sort of program are you willing to enter? What options will you *not* commit to? Now is the time to put your recovery into clear perspective.

Larry made a verbal commitment to go back and look at his family of origin so he could understand why he had such a one-dimensional view of masculinity. Then he would look for new and different ways to be a part of this marriage team.

We suggest that you make such a commitment yourself by signing this statement if it's true: "I am willing to commit fully to working through this crisis. I don't mean to simply muddle through, but to work diligently toward its resolution."

(signed) _____

Step 5: Assess How Much Deep Sharing Goes On between You: Are Needs Being Met?

Yours, mine, ours. Which is which? When approached with this question, John said, "My marriage is a sharing arrangement. That's not the problem." Everybody says that.

We're not talking about who scrubs the toilet and who mows the lawn. We're talking about letting the spouse know of your needs and expecting to see them met. We're talking about listening to your spouse and trying to meet the needs you hear about.

Frequently, we find people whose needs have gone unmet so long and so often, they have given up asking, or even wanting, anymore. "What's the use? I never get it anyway." People think, "I shouldn't have to ask for it. My spouse should know I need this." Both attitudes are barriers to intimacy. Both spawn crisis where no crisis would otherwise be. With them, anger smolders into resentment and bitterness.

The communication between Larry and Beverly, for instance, had become minimal as her job picked up momentum and as the anger and pain from his demotion increased. No changes had been made in their day-to-day lifestyle even though her responsibilities had increased and his job had scaled down. Together they needed to adjust the household duties to meet these changes.

> What are your needs? More sexual release? Less? More affection? More attention? More trust in matters of finance? Now, what about your spouse? What unmet needs have you and your spouse contributed or are contributing to IT?

> _____

> _____

> _____

Decide which needs are most important and then talk to your spouse about them.

Step 6: Employ Loving Confrontation after You Have Securely and Completely Suspended the Blame Cycle.

Boy, do we hear the jibes and word plays on "loving confrontation"! It is not a boxing match with heart-shaped gloves, or a brawl with a smile pasted on. Only after *both* parties have willingly suspended blame and kept it suspended, can we hope for success here.

One at a time, each expresses concerns and reservations to the other. Each tells the other how that person is or is not meeting needs.

Larry's wife did exactly that. In a counseling session, Beverly told him he wasn't hearing what the company was telling him. Even though he had been demoted and had been told his new job would be less demanding, he had worked longer hours in the last months than ever before. We saw this as a form of magical thinking: "If I just work hard enough or improve my working ability enough, I won't be phased out."

"These added work hours are ripping our marriage even further apart," Beverly said. "I'd like to see you home more, now that you have more time."

In your confrontation, each of you should tell the other what you would like to see.

What action (or actions) do you want your mate to take now?

_____

_____

_____

What actions would have helped alleviate the crisis situation?

_____

_____

_____

Consider also the general marriage state.

What do you feel is missing from this marriage union? Is there anything you feel you have a little too much of?

_____

_____

This is the time to bring up fears about possible chemical dependency or growing estrangement. Gently and with care, you air trouble spots and potential trouble spots you see in the marriage.

What rocks lie in the road to bliss? _____

_____

_____

Step 7: Grieve the Pain in Your Marriage.

"What pain?" John grumbled.

"I don't want to talk about it," Gloria said. In truth, there was deep personal pain. Gloria's first pregnancy ended in miscarriage. It was years ago. Afraid of what to say or do, John said and did nothing. Because men aren't supposed to come all apart over something like that, he refused to recognize any emotional reaction in himself, and he felt uncomfortable when she tried to talk about it.

"That's history. Years ago!" he told her in couples counsel. "You're beating a dead horse." It was history, all right. It was an unmet need in Gloria that had been festering for a long time. Because he refused to participate in the grieving, she herself did not grieve the loss adequately (though, had she realized, she could have proceeded on her own with that). Until they both went back and dealt with that buried issue, it would continue to generate resentment. It was primarily that issue which kept Gloria in a chronic depression. This unclosed bit of history caused much, much pain.

Any chronically unmet needs, as well as pain not dealt with, must be purged in this way, by bringing them into the open and grieving them through. "You're just stirring up issues that would die by themselves if left alone!" John fumed. "No," we assured him, "they will not die if left alone. That's the whole point of this."

"These items hurt at the time, but I put them behind me."

After Beverly confronted Larry he was able to grieve about his job change and to grieve the destruction this crisis had caused in their marriage. Once he grieved the demotion he could accept it and make peace with his new situation.

What is the pain in your marriage?

1. _____

2. _____

3. _____

Deal with these now. Then put them behind forever.

Step 8: Meet Needs through a Series of "Give-and-Take" Sessions.

What am I willing to swap?

Here comes a tense time that usually turns out to be fun.

In a healthy marriage, almost without really thinking about it, the two parties are sensitive enough to each other's needs that they can meet those needs with some honest give and take. In dysfunctional marriages and in marriages that have been damaged by crisis, this process of give and take falls apart. The exchange process is contaminated by resentments and unfinished business. Losses have not been brought to the open and grieved. Unfinished business, working under cover of ignorance or denial, works its mischief. Only when the other seven stages are successfully completed is the couple ready to negotiate some healthy give and take.

John, at first, was unwilling to give up his outside love interest. We insisted that interests of that sort outside the marriage bond be suspended first, before any further progress be considered. The fact that we consider such things immoral is neither here nor there. Distractions of that sort, which are already damaging the marriage bond, work counter to anything that would repair the bond. Gloria was just as stubborn. She clung to her depression; she'd had it so long it felt comfortable, like old slippers that have always been too big and flop when she walked, but she was used to walking funny when they're on and she liked them. Both persons had to make major, major concessions, and stick with them. Gloria had to agree to temporary medical intervention in her depression. She resisted the idea ferociously, until we pressed upon her the damage her depression and a divorce would inflict upon her children. John was absolutely certain his new love could supply his needs and his present wife could not. We had to convince him to give reconciliation a chance.

Some clients actually write their demands and offers on pieces of paper and exchange them. Others keep it verbal. In this situation, oral contracts are to be honored at the same level as written ones. This is not quite the same as when you're hammering out a new marriage contract, though the same techniques apply. In this case, you are trying to correct a dysfunction right now, regardless of the passage you happen to be in or how far you've progressed in it.

Also, give and take may be necessary to prevent possible repetition of this particular crisis situation. Use the negotiation techniques you use for contract-writing to reroute your marriage now.

Beverly and Larry's give-and-take session went something like this:

"I'll agree to work only a thirty-five hour work week. I will prepare our evening meal a couple of times a week," Larry said. "But I'd like some encouragement from you about my job performance."

Beverly admitted that she had been embarrassed to talk about Larry's work. "I know that I've stopped making any comments about it. I haven't known what to do. I thought talking about it—or giving superficial compliments—would only make it worse for you."

Now Larry could admit to himself and to Beverly, "As much as I resent the demotion, as much as I feel I could be doing so much more, I'm still very good at what I do. I need to have you tell me you know that too. And when I tell you about something I've done well, I still need you to say, 'I'm proud of you. I'm pulling for you.'"

Larry was also able to admit a hidden fear, which went something like this: "Since I am no longer the major breadwinner, I will lose control of the financial decisions. In fact, I will have little voice in how the money is spent."

Beverly could quickly dispel that fear. She had no problem with all major finances being a fifty-fifty decision, regardless of the proportions each of them brought in. She'd be happy to swap that for help around the house.

Step 9: Commit to Repairing the Future As Well As the Present.

Part of this commitment includes committing as a team, not as two people after the same goal. Teamwork. In harness together, pulling as one.

Together you must address the major passages of your marriage where you're stuck. You must address the validity of true forgiveness in your lives. In this stage, you commit to mend what is flawed to date.

But there is more. You are also committing to repairs in the future. Once made rosy, no marriage remains that way. New hidden agendas, old ones incompletely vanquished, the tragic and comic operas of life, changing kids, and the changing nature of the marriage itself all contribute to making it a new ball game. You are committing right now to work on the problems these changes will generate.

Neither partner in a marriage can work recovery upon the other person. No partner can rescue the spouse from a stuck spot. Like blowing one's nose or offering up prayer, it's something that must be done individually. The recovering partner can go only so far until and unless the other partner gets with the program. But one partner can do much. And two working in tandem can achieve phenomenal results.

We suggest that the spouses approach this activity as corporation executives work through their one-year, three-year, and five-year plans. The couple needs to talk about each of these time frames. Beverly admitted, for instance, that she enjoyed real estate and making her own money. She wanted to continue that for at least five or more years. Then together Larry and Beverly needed to work out a plan to accommodate her desire. In counseling we call this planning the "ongoing maintenance and repair" of the crisis.

Step 10: Minimize the Stressors in Your Marriage.

This is, in part, akin to the question of boundaries above. Who invades? What invades? Church commitments? School commitments? Service clubs? Social clubs? Committees? The kids' groups such as Scouts and athletic teams? Volunteer organizations? Once-a-year things like the Fourth of July bash or the home and garden show or the fair or the Christmas pageant?

How many Christmas cards do you send out and how tough is it to fulfill that self-imposed commitment? Can you get by with a few thousand fewer cookies and other baked goods this Christmas? How long does it take you to erect the decorations?

Everything mentioned above, and hundreds more categories, are important and worthwhile projects. They should not be shortchanged or dumped. But some of them have to go. You can't do it all. Just because it's a good idea doesn't mean you *have* to incorporate it into your life.

The bad news is, these items don't just splash down upon you like a tidal wave. They come a bit at a time, one here and one there. It's their accumulative toll that gets you.

Ten Steps to Healing Your Marriage

Step 1. Suspend the blame cycle.

Step 2. Acknowledge your contribution to the pain.

Step 3. Examine the status of your marriage: Have you negotiated all the tasks in each passage so far?

Step 4. Commit to recovery and determine to improve your marriage.

Step 5. Assess how much deep sharing goes on between you: Are needs being met?

Step 6. Employ loving confrontation after you have securely and completely suspended the blame cycle.

Step 7. Grieve the pain in your marriage.

Step 8. Meet needs through a series of "give-and-take" sessions.

Step 9. Commit to repairing the future as well as the present.

Step 10. Minimize the stressors in your marriage.

Even the healthiest marriages tend to revert to earlier passages and more primitive coping mechanisms (nearly all of them unhealthy) when these stressors build to overload.

So list all the time-eaters and stressors in your marriage life.
(Because of his recent demotion, Larry felt a sense of economic insecurity. Yet he and Beverly had thought of giving their grandson some money to attend graduate school, and once they did this, they might feel obligated to help the other grandchildren. This, then, became a major stressor for them.)

_____

_____

_____

_____

Now look at these stressors together. If time is one of your stressors, plan to cut back. "Hey, that won't be so easy!" some of our patients say.

And we quickly answer, "What do you mean, 'It won't be easy!'? Of course it won't be easy. It's much easier to pick up another task than to say no, and it's very hard to say no if previously you said yes to something. And you might be walking away from some important chores. You might ruffle some feathers on people who think you should serve on the refreshment committee instead of spend a quiet night with your spouse, building intimacy and mutual pleasure."

In Larry and Beverly's case, some boundaries had to be set. If they wanted to give their grandson some assistance, how much would they give? They needed to set a specific amount that could be given to each grandchild without causing them any financial or emotional stress.

Plan to do this periodically—at least once a quarter—to nip overcommitment in the bud.

18

IS IT TOO LATE
TO ESTABLISH
COMPANIONSHIP
AND UNITY?

*R*ob Millen, husband of Annie War-
den Millen, had no intention of straying, really. At the church picnic he
happened to notice Kerri. She wasn't wearing anything skimpy or revealing, but her shorts and top revealed nice legs and a well-shaped torso. She
ended up just ahead of him in batting rotation at the softball game after
lunch. They got to talking and she seemed sensible enough—not an airhead
or anything. And yet there was a youthfulness about her, a verve and
bounce that he enjoyed immensely. He was forty-nine and very tied down,
she two decades younger and divorced. But then she went to bat and sin-
gled into right field and he struck out, so he didn't talk to her again that
inning.

In the weeks that followed, Rob found himself thinking about Kerri a
lot. She excited him. Annie didn't anymore. Kerri displayed the vigor and
élan of youth. Annie marched purposefully through life with a frown on her
face much of the time. And Annie, forty-seven, certainly didn't display any
youth.

Annie didn't give him much time, either. She was always busy with
something else. She was always too tired at night. She was always thinking
about her schedule tomorrow, when Rob wasn't the least bit interested in
what jobs loomed ahead. He wanted a little snuggling, a little sex right now.
"Just a minute, dear. I need to make these phone calls." And she wasn't

quite through menopause yet. Soon as that happened, she'd be a complete iceberg. An iceberg with crow's-feet around her eyes.

Rob and Annie Millen needed to reestablish intimacy in their marriage or they were obviously headed for trouble. The second task of this passage—Renewing Love—is just that.

THE SECOND TASK: REESTABLISH INTIMACY

At his forty-ninth birthday party, an over-the-hill roast, Rob Millen had received an important-looking paperback book with a tasteful, distinguished-looking cover, entitled *Sex and the Older Man*. All three hundred pages were blank.

The primary task of this Fourth Passage is the intimacy of companionship and unity. That's not the same as sex and romance, particularly if both marriage partners are content. When a couple have been at it all these years, the sexual relationship easily slips into a benign dormancy.

The media doesn't help any. Nearly every ad, every self-help article, every TV show, every film suggests that sex is for the young. Face cream ads tell you to fight aging every step of the way. All the models in the catalogues are slim, even those modeling "older" fashions. Somewhere, somehow, you've been left out of life.

When you look in the mirror and decide a face-lift would require a forklift, when you pinch your spare tire and realize it would fit a road grader, you don't feel very sexy. And the people who know about such things all insist that it is attitude more than anything else that determines whether a man or woman radiates what is called "sex appeal." The first prerequisite for looking good to the opposite sex is a cheerful, upbeat feeling about yourself. That becomes increasingly difficult as age takes its toll on personal appearance and ability.

Then your twenty year old stares at you and exclaims, "Aw, come on, Pop! You don't still do *that*, do you?"

That . . . mumble, mumble . . . young whippersnapper! Hmph!

The vivid, eager sexual dynamic you and your spouse enjoyed at the beginning is probably a thing of the past. The young stud who handled several episodes a day has aged into the old stud who manages a couple a week . . . maybe. You will find some work involved in keeping your sexual union fresh and satisfying.

The Threat of Infidelity

Says Robert Hemfelt, "This Fourth Passage is an extremely vulnerable time for affairs. The line of thought goes *I want to know if I'm still lovable*. Most commonly, though, that thought lies below conscious level. The person becomes insatiably attracted to a neighbor or a fellow employee. It feels like true love or intense romance. Actually, it's a part of that person that's questioning his or her worth in other areas of life. Seeking out a romantic partner provides a strong counterfeit validation of personal identity. 'I am loved for me.' ' "

An affair, whether overtly sexual or only emotional, can also provide counterfeit financial validation or confirmation of youth not yet completely lost. To the persons involved it seems so straightforward—we have found new love again—when it is actually born not of love or even physical attraction but of vague, unspoken inner needs having nothing at all to do with that enchanting other person.

Rob Millen was also fighting another hidden enemy—misperception. Probably no area of life is more poorly perceived, and invites more just plain ignorance and stigma, as sex-over-forty. Even if you make that sex-over-fifty, myths and errors hold sway. Those untruths can ruin your sexual relationship and even open the partners to sexual dalliances with younger persons.

SORTING FACT FROM FICTION

True or false?

_____ Menopause does not actually affect women's sexual desires and performance.

_____ The first sign that the man has lost the capacity for sexual union is when he fails to achieve erection.

_____ Women over fifty eventually become sexually unresponsive.

_____ Talk and boasting aside, very few couples over forty-five engage in regular (weekly or more often) sex.

All the above are false, but the truth is more complex than a simplistic "true or false" permits. Knowing the facts can help you complete the overall goal of the Fourth Passage, to bond together in Renewing Love.

The Woman's Changes

Women have much to celebrate and to grieve.

"My goal is to have a baby in every decade," Mary Alice quips, only halfjoking. With all her miscarriages, it's not a lighthearted issue. "This latest time, when I told people I was pregnant at the age of forty-one, they said, 'Oh, what a surprise!' Or 'Oh, no!'

"The last people we told about this latest pregnancy were my parents. We were afraid they'd get worried and upset because of my age and earlier difficulties. They were so supportive; they just kept on and on. 'You will get such pleasure from this baby,' they said. My mother told me how much her parents had enjoyed my uncle Jack, their seventh child. Uncle Jack went on to be a minister (not every child that comes along late in life will be wonderful like that, of course)."

Susanna Wesley's Charles, the eighteenth child in eighteen years of marriage, survived premature arrival, growing up to write a number of hymns we still sing, such as "O For a Thousand Tongues to Sing" and the Easter favorite, "Christ the Lord Is Risen Today."

But sooner or later, childbearing ends, for many women a bittersweet time. Technically, a woman enters menopause when her periods have ceased for a year. The median age is fifty, but individuals vary widely. The passing of her fertile years is something to grieve. Nothing says "Youth has fled" more forcefully than "You're too old to have babies."

And there is celebration too. No more fear of unintended pregnancy. No more monthly bloating and mess and unpredictable inconvenience. For most women, cessation of menses is Prometheus unbound. For many, their sexual enjoyment *increases* after menopause.

Not that menopause is a picnic in the park. As estrogen levels drop, tissues of the vulva and vagina may become thin and stiff, rendering intercourse painful. Lubricants may decrease, so a woman may have to apply a jelly or estrogen cream to this area before intercourse. And then there are the hot flashes. There may be some decline in the sex drive, but the loss is mild. Doctors have found that if a woman is sexually active before menopause she can continue sexual activity beyond menopause with fewer complications and problems than the woman who has been celibate or nearly so. Sexually active women don't undergo as much change. Many doctors recommend estrogen therapy to not only prevent the physical changes of menopause, but also to retard osteoporosis, that disease of advancing age in which a woman's bones become bent and brittle.

The sex act itself changes somewhat. The woman's arousal graph alters shape. It takes her somewhat longer during the excitement and plateau phases to build to orgasm, and the orgasm itself is shorter. Resolution, the final phase, happens more quickly. But it's all still there, all still giving pleasure, and as far as medical findings reveal, a woman may continue to enjoy the special intimacy of sex until her dying day.

The Man's Changes

Rob Millen didn't see any change in his own sexual responses. After all, he wasn't *that* old. If during sex he was a little slower getting started, and it wasn't quite as wild and satisfying as it used to be, that was Annie's fault, not his. If he had a sexual partner like Annie used to be, he'd perform like he did in the beginning.

Rob Millen was talking himself into sexual self-destruction.

"The man who understands the changes old age brings and adjusts to them," says Dr. Minirth, "will continue to enjoy sexual expression long into old age. The men who refuse to recognize the changes or blame them on outside influences such as old age or illness—imagined illness or real illness, either one—are going to lose their capacity for sexual expression. And that is so unfortunate. You have to be flexible."

What changes can truly be laid at the door of advancing age? Again, let's use fifty as the average age when changes begin to manifest themselves. The man will benefit from longer foreplay. He doesn't achieve erection as quickly, and it may be less firm than it used to be. His orgasm, too, will be shorter and may peak earlier than in the past. His resolution time will certainly be shorter—perhaps seconds instead of minutes. A longer time will elapse before he can begin sexual activity again. Against these losses he will find considerable gain: He can sustain erections longer and will probably have better control. Thus, the sexual experience can be even more satisfying for both partners.

Some problems are medical. Diabetes, prostate problems or surgery, hardening of the arteries, and some types of neurological disorders like arthritis of the back, which can affect the sacral nerves, sometimes reduce a man's sexual desire. Men at risk for heart attack, or who have recently survived a heart attack, may develop a fear of dying during intercourse. As a result they abstain. Such cases of death are extremely rare, however, and there are almost always other factors involved. Sexual activity is actually good exercise, with intercourse equivalent to climbing a flight or two of stairs.

Certain prescription drugs for heart problems, however, such as blood thinners (HCTZ, Lasiz, Spironolactone, and Thiazide) can reduce or destroy the man's capacity to make love, as can some blood pressure medications (Aldomet, Clonodine, and Reserpine). Betablockers, like Inderal, can also reduce desire. Consult your doctor if these drugs are causing difficulty. Other options may be available to you.

Simply increasing a man's level of exercise can raise libido. That's equally true for women.

Adjusting to the Changes

Advisors and counselors recommend these points and others to adjust to the sexual changes of the Fourth Passage.

Time

Since both man and woman require more time to achieve maximum pleasure, relax. Don't rush. Take more time. Also, observe what time of day seems to produce the most satisfying results. Late at night is usually the least satisfying time, and yet it's often the only time available. Experiment, if possible, with midday episodes, perhaps a marital nap before dinner, or early morning activity. What pleases you both the most? The newness of varying the time also increases pleasure.

Other Factors

Know what your prescription medicines do. Ask questions. Understand that alcohol, stress, worry, and fatigue work against you now even more than when you were younger. If estrogen therapy or surgical aids seem indicated, explore their possibility. Hearing aids and eyeglasses compensate for the losses of age. Why stop there?

Exercise

Try to get out and be more active. It improves muscle tone and gets the juices flowing. It also improves the capacity for sexual pleasure.

Talk

Don't assume your partner believes such-and-so, or would never consider so-and-so. Ask. Do you want to do this? Do you want to try that? How can I help you? Experiment with new ways and new techniques.

Dr. Hemfelt points out three levels of communication in sex. First is the physical act itself, a powerful form of communication. Second is talking about sex, setting boundaries and priorities, explaining needs. The third is talking about talking about sex.

Often we hear this dialogue in counseling sessions:

"Every time I want to talk about sex," he complains, "you seem to get angry and tense."

She responds, "That's because every time we bring up the subject, you adopt this accusing tone of voice that suggests I'm not giving you what you want."

They are talking about how they talk about sex. That is actually very important, because you'll notice in the dialogue above that there were misconceptions on both sides. Once those misconceptions are worked out, by talking, sharing sexual needs with one another will be much easier.

Make Contact

People of all ages, but older people especially, over and over again tell us, "I just want the closeness. I want to be held. To snuggle. Sure, sex is great. But physical closeness is great, too, whether it ends up as sex or not." Hold each other. Hug. That simple thing is immensely reassuring and satisfying.

Rekindle Romance

Rob Millen didn't realize it, but Annie also felt estrangement in this Fourth Passage. Once she got Beth Anne married, Annie felt lost—at loose ends—as we mentioned at the beginning of this book. The third leg she had leaned upon so long, wedding arrangements, had just been kicked out from under her stool. Now what? Her husband steamed along on his own track, leaving her to hers. And her train had stalled.

Annie, too, had seriously considered just hanging it up. She'd be neither more nor less happy apart from Rob than with him. She could travel. Do things. For once in her life she could march to her own drummer. Tempting! So tempting.

But . . .

But . . . there was the commitment she had made eons ago at the wedding altar, just as Beth Anne had, just as her parents had before her.

But . . . there was the example she and Rob set for the kids and nieces and nephews and grandchildren. Whether consciously or not, the younger generation looked to them as models.

Those buts were important.

But! She would not continue like this. She would not spend the rest of her days in this emotional vacuum. Either her marriage would again become an important element in her life, or she was going to leave.

Most reluctantly, because the temptation to freedom glowed so brightly, she decided to make a stab at turning her marriage around at this late date.

But how?

She got her first notion when she arrived early for a church bazaar committee meeting at Joan's. Now Joan was not nearly so slim as Annie, and unlike Annie, eschewed hairdressers. To an objective observer, Annie was much more attractive for her age than was Joan. And yet, Joan seemed to have an emotionally satisfying marriage. An emotionally satisfying everything, actually.

Joan yelled, "Come in!" when Annie knocked at her door.

Annie stepped inside. She would have said, "I'm sorry; I may be a little early," but Joan was on the phone. She was making weekend reservations at a bed and breakfast up on the lake.

Joan completed the business and hung up. "Coffee's on the stove. I'm glad you dropped by early. Can you help put out the sticky buns?"

"Certainly!" Annie popped open the microwave and slipped the buns out onto a platter. "So you're going up to that B & B. I've heard of that place. They say it's very romantic. You and your husband?"

"Yep." Joan's eyes twinkled. "To keep the house warm, every now and then you gotta throw another log on the fire."

We suggest now that you rethink and revitalize your romantic love life if need be.

"You don't know my spouse. Everything is cast in cement. We always did it this way, and we're always going to do it this way. You can't imagine the lockstep my mate has settled into in midlife. We're in a deep rut."

We certainly do understand. We see it constantly in counsel.

You are not alone. But remember the rule of the contract. When one person changes, the other cannot remain unchanged. The other must adjust.

In Annie's case, Rob had plateaued at work, even though he considered himself indispensable. He worked a sixty-hour week simply because he'd been putting in extra time ever since he started there. Annie couldn't see that he had anything to prove to anyone. She resented all that time he lavished on his dead-end job. And Annie didn't even know about Rob's attraction to Kerri.

In the past we urged you to be creative about rejuvenating your sexual union and other aspects of your marriage. If you were in Annie's position (and you just might be, if you are in the Fourth Passage), what are some creative ways you might redirect your husband's energies and interests to better support his marriage? There are several ways to approach the problem.

A film actress claimed that her actor husband's obsession with watching newscasts was damaging their time together—wrecking the evening meal, playing havoc with schedules. He had to see them *all* (this was before twenty-four-hour cable news). Frustrated, she emphasized her complaint by draping herself across their TV set, wearing only a rose in her teeth. We are not necessarily recommending that, but it's certainly creative.

Annie was more direct. She unplugged the TV set and cut the plug off. She made an appointment with Rob's secretary at work for an hour of his time. She showed up at his office door one lunchtime with a picnic basket—

he had been planning to work through lunch. From Joan she got the phone number for that bed and breakfast.

She fumed and cajoled and she laid it all out for Rob. "If you want this marriage to survive, you're going to have to start taking an interest in it."

We do not necessarily recommend confrontation of that sort, either. Remember, threats of that sort are one of the sex killers. In Annie's case, it was the only way she could capture Rob's attention. Most important, she was not bluffing. She really was convinced that she had reached the end of her rope. But, also importantly, she did not dump it completely onto Rob. She took positive steps and urged him to join her.

Finally Annie used a powerful bond to strengthen their sexual intimacy: the bond of a shared history. That, too, will help you renew your love during the Fourth Passage.

THE BOND OF A SHARED HISTORY

A few years ago at the annual Old-Timer's Day in Mount Rainier National Park, a ranger in his eighties pointed to a faint stain by the huge fireplace at Paradise Inn. "That's bear grease from the winter of '22," he explained. "Bad snow year. Then during a thaw, but while the snow was really deep yet, a few of the black bears came out of hibernation early. Made a major nuisance of themselves around the residential area and the inn here. We ended up shooting one. It was illegal, so we decided to burn him in the fireplace here. He didn't burn worth zip. All he did was render down to gallons of grease. It came running out of the fireplace, seeping into the floorboards. What a mess."

And the other old-timers nodded, smiling.

Memories

The past calls every person strongly. Times were different and life seemed closer to the edge. And so people put together reunions—reunions of armed forces units or old-timers or the survivors of a momentous event. They get together to share the memories, to keep alive the history.

Your marriage has just that sort of animated history. It includes things not funny at the time but fun now in retrospect. You survived some dreadful (or just dreadfully weird) crises. That's an important bond, no less powerful than the bond that draws old-timers and classmates from hundreds and even thousands of miles away.

Many people will reminisce about anything else but the marriage itself—kids, the cat, the grandkids. Physical ailments get a lot of play. The marriage itself and the memories it generates, hardly any. To put the power of that bond to use, emphasize your marital history. Talk about it. Relive it.

Susan Hemfelt explains about using memories to bond. "We spent our honeymoon at Estes Park in the cabin Granddad built. It's always been an important place in my life. I remember when I was in the ninth grade, sitting on a rock, thinking, 'This is as close to heaven as you can get without being there.' It was there and then that I first grasped the concept of a Higher Power.

"The place grew on Robert also. It means something to him as well. We try to go up there every year. Now the fourth generation goes there. That little house is the locus of so much family history, and 99 percent of it is good history. There's barely enough water; it's rustic; it forces you to take your mind off the frills of life and get to basics. It's a lot of work for Mother."

She pauses thoughtfully. "The bugs are a nuisance, but not too bad. They're supposed to be there.

"We all went up there for Christmas in 1983. My brother-in-law changed the alternator in my dad's car; it was sixteen degrees. The kitchen was so cold the turkey wouldn't bake. My father and brother-in-law tried to seal the cabin with plastic sheets. They got the temperature to rise a bit; it was thirty-five degrees in the kitchen. Mom cooked Christmas dinner in thermals. Later we had T-shirts printed with 'I survived Christmas '83.'

"There's always such a water shortage, we don't flush for everything. But you see, that cabin doesn't just have a history of a string of strange anecdotes. It has a deeper history, of all the people working together solving problems, such as ways to conserve water."

A rich heritage, threaded through four generations. The Hemfelt children are embraced in history, just as the Hemfelt marriage is.

Think about the memories that can bind and renew your marriage. What strange and tragic and delightful and unique things happened in your marriage?

What about the early years before the children arrived (like the times you just took off for a weekend together in the city or for a special day at the shore)?

The birth of your first child?

Your first house?

A special family vacation?

Graduation of a child from high school? From college?

Stitched together, all these patches of recollections form an enchanting crazy-quilt of history.

"Okay," said Annie, "so exactly where and how do I reinforce our trove of memories? Our history?"

The dinner table is an excellent place to begin. Annie Millen never let TV get in the way of dinner again. She and Rob sat at the table and conversed during dinner. Always. (If some family member simply cannot be weaned away from evening news, use a VCR; let him or her watch the news after dinner. It won't get *that* stale in half an hour.) The dinner table is a good laughing place, one of those warm and comfortable places where the family knows it can feel bright and goofy.

Look for small things to celebrate: getting the dog's teeth cleaned; changing the ribbon in your typewriter; the victory of Dad, who's been trying to improve his language at work, making it clear through the day without a single unseemly word; finishing the drywall in the basement . . . there are lots of things.

Play games together. A couple who are friends of ours play three games of backgammon after dinner. It doesn't happen every single night because other things intrude. Sometimes they're not together, or they have company. The person who's behind at the end of each month buys dinner out for the other.

Record your history. Write a letter to each other on every anniversary. Take videos or photographs of both special events and also the everyday ones. In every historical collection, the most valuable and telling photos are not of the prominent people standing around shaking hands, but are of ordinary folk in ordinary situations. It's the same with your family.

Most of all, examine your family traditions. We are a tradition-bound people, all of us, and our traditions in large measure define us. From a *National Geographic* (Feb. 1991) article on a people of southwestern Ethiopia, under government pressure to modernize, comes this quote from the Surma: "We don't want to give up body painting, stick fighting, or lip plates. This is our way of life. We want to keep it and pass it on to our children."

Traditions

Akin to memories are the traditions of your family and the ancestors before you. The culturally conservative Navajo understands that away from his land and his traditions, he cannot truly be Navajo. Not just his traditions shape his identity; his practice of them maintains it. Some people, such as the European immigrants who flocked to America in the early 1900s, tried to put the Old Country behind them, only to find themselves and their children becoming emotionally impoverished. History and traditions kept the Jewish race intact through nineteen hundred years of dispersal and persecution. Today they occupy the ancestral land, speaking a pure tongue that, logically speaking, should have died long ago.

Traditions have that same preserving and bonding power for your family. They will define your family just as powerfully as they define clans and nations everywhere.

Traditions vary from "What we do every Christmas" to "Whether we use cloth napkins at the dinner table." Make sure you savor the traditions that mark you apart as a couple. Celebrate them. Enjoy them. And be sure to pass your family traditions along to your grandchildren.

19

CAN YOU GRIEVE THE PARTICULAR LOSSES OF THIS PASSAGE?

*I*n a space of three years, Robert Hemfelt lost both parents and Frank and Mary Alice Minirth lost his mother and her father. His father is gravely ill. The prior generation is leaving, and their leaving wreaks havoc on the children as much as on themselves. Children may be losing siblings now, as well.

We have in counsel a woman in her fifties whom we'll call Ella. Neither of Ella's parents can bring themselves to accept death. For poor Ella, it's worse than watching a torture chamber because she's getting sucked into it. As death draws closer, those two people, terrified of losing each other, terrified of death, cling piteously to each other and to Ella. They cannot bear to think of temporary separation, let alone terminal separation. No matter how frequently Ella visits, it's not enough.

Ella herself is going to have immense difficulty coming to terms with her own mortality because her parents' fear of death—a major piece of unfinished business—is descending upon her head. In counsel we can help Ella accept her limitations and grieve them. We can help her gain hope in Christ and a measure of peace. But then she goes home to Mom and Dad.

In contrast, if the later Fifth Passage goes well, the passage Ella's mom and dad are now in, husband and wife forge strong spiritual ties with each other and with God (we will talk about those ties in that passage). These ties, however, do not bind and cling. Filled with shared strength, husband

and wife can more easily make peace with reality, enjoy what years or hours they have left, and then let go.

Ella is stuck in the Fourth and Fifth Passages with her parents, and she isn't unique. The next task of the Fourth Passage is to grieve the losses characteristic of these years.

THE THIRD TASK: GRIEVE THE PARTICULAR LOSSES OF THIS PASSAGE

By now you may be thinking, *I've done quite enough grieving, thank you. And quite enough thinking about the losses of my life. Why do you keep talking about them?*

Because life is tough, as the old saying goes. Or as theology says, the world entered a fallen state when Adam and Eve gave in to Satan's temptation in the Garden of Eden. Ever since that time, sin and the effects of sin have been part of our world.

Life is full of losses, and part of the successful completion of each passage is to come to terms with the inevitable losses of that passage. That means grieving them through and looking for the unseen blessings they often bring.

The apostle Paul suffered from the slings and arrows of fortune as much as any person in the Bible. Shipwrecks. Mob violence and persecution. Imprisonment. Yet he could tell the Roman Christians, "All things work together for good to those who love God, to those who are the called according to His purpose."[1]

We like to tell our patients that each good-bye (or loss) has a corresponding hello (or blessing).

Lost Parents

Gerald and his wife came in for counseling when Gerald's father was diagnosed with cancer. They thought the core of their problems was their marriage relationship. After one or two sessions, we thought differently, so we asked Gerald, "How do you feel about your father's death?"

"It's tough, but I just have to face it," he answered.

We could hear undercurrents of denial in that statement, so we pushed him to talk about his relationship with his dad. Slowly the pattern emerged.

"My dad was in control," Gerald said. "We all jumped when he told us to do something." And he described one day when his seven-year-old brother knocked over his mom's favorite lamp because he responded to one of Dad's commands too quickly.

That response told us we were on the right track. So we probed further, asking Gerald to tell us about the close moments he remembered, the times his dad got down on all fours and played with him. Minutes passed. Then tears came to his eyes as he admitted, "None I can remember." Instead, he described the times he yearned for a hug or an "I'm really proud of you" from his father.

Gerald was having trouble saying good-bye to his father because he had never said hello to him. Their relationship resembled the interaction between a sergeant and a private, not a father and a son. His father's imminent death triggered the time capsule of the lack of a loving relationship.

The death of a parent (or the debilitation of a parent through disease or senility) is a powerful transition. We've talked about leaving home and saying good-bye in previous passages. Yet the ultimate good-bye doesn't come, for most of us, until the parent begins to crumble physically or mentally. Unconsciously we think, *This is the person who brought me into this world. This is the person who nurtured me in my early years. I'm losing a part of me.* Even if you've said good-bye to your parents in earlier passages, they still represent the ultimate security symbol for you. You still view them as god-like figures. And you still mourn any lack in your relationship.

We suggest that you say good-bye to your parents now. If you are adopted or grew up in foster care, you have several sets of parents to think about.

With a few words to remind you of the memory, list some good times. Treat the items separately, for each has touched you uniquely.

1. _____
2. _____
3. _____

Now list some bad times with your parents. The bitter as well as the sweet. Each must be recognized.

1. _____
2. _____
3. _____

Now celebrate and grieve each item appropriately. In the movie *Five Easy Pieces,* Jack Nicholson returned home to say good-bye to a dad who had suffered a stroke. He wheeled the old man, who was unable to speak or move, into one of those Kansas cornfields—acres and acres of blue sky and waving cornstalks—and knelt beside him. His conversation with the stone-faced old man went something like this:

"I have no idea if you are in there or not. I have no idea if you can hear me. But I have to tell you why I haven't been back in years." And then the painful memories flowed.

In that monologue, Nicholson was both saying good-bye and hello. Often, saying good-bye can best be done by first saying hello. By talking through their past, the son was able to begin to establish some kind of relationship with the old man. If your parent is still alive and well, you might be able to establish a better relationship with him or her now. We've found that patients who try to establish a relationship in their adult years with a distant parent handle the parent's death reasonably well. Those who run from the anger and pain tend to crumble when the separation is cemented by death.

Even if a parent is senile or comatose or unreceptive, you can say hello and good-bye to him or her with a monologue or a letter. Take the good times and the bad times you remembered above and write about them. Then emotionally wave good-bye to that relationship.

Lost Kids

Say good-bye to the kids? Ask Annie thirteen years ago if she would dread saying good-bye to the kids that morning she walked into her kitchen. Beth Anne, then age seven, perched on a chair at the stove, was making breakfast. Bowls, spoons, flour everywhere. Broken egg on the floor. The dog licked up something over by the fridge. Beth Anne was making pancakes. Jamie, older but less aggressive, was whining that it was his turn. The stove burners still smoked where batter globs had burned. The mixer beaters, perched on the edge of the counter, dripped batter into the open utensil drawer. "Good-bye to the kids? I'll pack this minute!"

Frustrations aside, there comes a day when the fledglings leave the nest. Couples whose nestlings are still home assume that saying good-bye means packing the stuffed toys in the attic, handing the kid his suitcase, and waving him off at the front door. There is much more to it than that.

As the married couple say good-bye to their families of origin by degrees or stages, so do your youngsters. We talked about the steps the departing child/adult takes. There are also steps you take as parents. Consider the following example.

Poor old Mom never accepted her kids leaving home. She had lavished the better part of a lifetime on them and away they went, abandoning her. Daughter does just fine with her own child-raising, until her empty nest comes. The hidden-agenda time capsule, dormant until that time, explodes. Daughter, who was doing so well, falls apart when her firstborn goes to college. She's hit the fifth stage of parenthood, the period of renewal or death in the marriage relationship—the empty nest.

The Empty Nest

How did your parents handle the empty nest? Look first at surface indications (which may all appear just fine). _____

_____

At what ages did you and your siblings leave home:
Residentially (the day you moved out)? _____
Financially (the day you no longer accepted loans from your
parents, like down payments on a house)? _____

List a couple of things your parents said as the first child left.
*("Now that Bobbie's gone, we'll have peace again." "We're so proud of
Bobbie; he's the first person in our family to go to college.")*
1. _____
2. _____
3. _____

What did your parents say when the last one left? *("I don't know
what I'll do without Jane." "We're glad Jane has found such a good
job as a teacher and such a great apartment.")*

_____

_____

Now think about what they did (their overt actions) when the first
child left home. *(How many rooms formerly used by the children were
converted to new uses and how many kept the same—"Still little
Michael's room" when Michael left home five years ago?)*

_____

_____

When the last child left home *(They converted your sister's room into a
sewing room.)* _____

_____

_____

Now look for subsurface attitudes.
What indications, perhaps more felt than seen, tell you your parents

made peace with their children's departure? *(They moved the dining room furniture around to better serve a close couple than to feed a mob.)*

Do any of these words or actions tell you that your parents never quite came to grips with their children's departure? *(Perhaps they left all your brother's sports posters up on his wall, or they refused to change anything in the house, just in case someone should come back home.)* _____ yes _____ no

The patterns your parents set will probably determine your own hidden agenda, the personal attitude your conscious mind doesn't even know about.

Assuming your children have not yet left home, what specific steps do you intend to take to avoid your parents' mistakes or rough spots?

What do you savor about the prospect of your children leaving home, whether it has occurred yet or not? *(I'll have more time to read or do some sewing.)*

And what do (did) you dread? *(Remember the woman in Chapter 1 who looked at her husband, sitting in the recliner and wondered what they had in common now that the kids were leaving.)*

Finally, if your children have left, what would you do differently if you had it to do again?

Should you discuss what you've discovered here with your adult children? Perhaps the insight you've made here will release them from the unfinished business you placed upon them by failing to deal well with their leaving. Consider this very carefully.

Cut the Financial Cord

A large element of good-bye is letting the kids go financially and emotionally, as well as residentially. This is a sticky wicket because no two cases are the same.

Robert Hemfelt relates, "We're trying to help a man now. He has a perpetual student at home. The daughter is twenty-four. The man's problem is his wife. She wants the girl to remain in their home while she finishes her schooling, and Dad wants the kid out.

"This man has to deal with Mom, and somehow convince her it's best for the daughter to become responsible for herself. If the girl had only a semester or two to go, perhaps they could let it slide. But she switches majors, takes light class loads—the end is nowhere in sight.

"It is most important that neither parent act behind the other's back. Undercutting each other will lead to disaster when this couple finally are alone."

How would a counselor help in this situation? Lacking a counselor, how should a couple approach it? Hidden agenda searches come first. The counselor will also look then for signs of emotional incest.

So many times the child becomes a surrogate spouse. When a couple drift apart, one or both may attach to a child for emotional support. But how would a parent see that? We suggest asking yourself these true-or-false questions to help identify the problem if it exists:

_____ "If my spouse and my child are available during my free time, I'd rather be with my child."

_____ "My child and I seem to have more in common than my spouse and I do."

_____ "My child understands my problems better than my spouse does."

_____ "My spouse is unavailable when I most need to talk."

If you checked more than one of the above statements, some emotional incest may be occurring. To take a closer look, fill in the blanks below:

1. If the criterion for the strength of a bond were the amount of time spent with a family member (other than a small child, of course, who requires constant monitoring), with whom would you be bonded most firmly? _____

2. If the criterion were the amount of time thinking and worrying about a person, with whom would you be most strongly bonded?

3. If the criterion were the most emotional response you make—
   being angry with, being proud of, being comfortable with—who
   would win? _____
4. If each family member were in a separate room, which room
   would you likely to find yourself in? _____

Should your child come out ahead of your spouse in more than one of
these instances, start giving a cold, hard eye to your relationship with your
child (if you have children, usually one stands out; emotional incest rarely
happens between a parent and more than one child at a time).

In the case of the frustrated father whose twenty-four-year-old daughter was still living at home, emotional incest had not significantly come into
play. On the practical level, we helped the man negotiate a deal with the
girl. Let her live there, but pay market value rent. Get behind in the rent
and out you go. In negotiations, the parents must also both agree to whatever the deal might be. If one parent sees it differently—and the mother
certainly did—that person must not just shut up and resent the whole thing.
Any negotiation must be mutually acceptable to all involved.

When last Robert Hemfelt heard, the man's daughter had found a
cheaper rent arrangement and was living near the university in a five-
bedroom house with four other girls.

Whatever decisions are made about weaning children away financially,
they must be mutually arranged by the parents. Any other situation invites
friction and resentment.

A healthy friendship with your child, in which the parent is no longer
the primary authority figure, is not the same as the earlier child-parent relationship. Delightful and rewarding as this new friendship might be, the
past must be grieved and put behind. Celebrate the new relationship; grieve
the old one.

Reconcile Any Guilt

A client we'll call Ralph told us, "I started out with a thousand-dollar
debt to the vocational school I attended, and ended up owning the best
transmission place in town, with three locations. We get more business than
the big franchise shops with their fancy advertising. But I lost my family in
the process."

That would generate some guilt. Ralph's priorities cost him his first
wife and their two children. "My girl, Gina. She's so bright. Straight As in
school . . . until she got into drugs and dropped out. And my son. He's in

the Army. Not the Air Force or the Marines. The Army. Seems content to stay that way." Ralph shook his head.

Guilt.

By their Fourth Passage, many fathers feel as Ralph felt, guilty for neglecting their marriage, and especially the kids, in their drive to succeed. Their careers become a powerful third leg to the marriage stool, and the other leg, feeling unwanted, wanders off. The stool collapses.

Very rarely, too, do children meet or exceed the parents' hopes for them. They just don't turn out the way you intended. Ralph's certainly didn't. And guilt is a natural response. So is bitter disappointment. All that must be grieved.

In those cases where the children indeed meet or exceed the parents' hopes, parents must take care. It is easy to blot up a vicarious identity with the successful children, putting your own identity and your identity as a marital partner at risk. They are young, they're making it big, and they're yours. With no trouble at all you might cease to recognize that they are them—another generation, strong individuals, a different family now.

Incidentally, Ralph the transmission man actually has three children: the adult children of his first union and a four year old by his second wife. This time, he's stopping to smell the roses.

The good-bye to your own children has its corresponding hello: the joy of grandchildren.

The Period of Joy

This final stage in the progression of parenthood is often the most enjoyable. Certainly the numerous people who have to look at "pictures of my grandchildren" see a pride that may at times seem overly enthusiastic.

"Children's children are the crown of old men," says Proverbs 17:6. Ask the mother of the first grandchild in the family, any family. Often these tiny bundles resemble the grandparent's own child, so the experience is the closest any of us will ever get to drinking from that proverbial fountain of youth. Any interaction with these miniatures of your son or daughter is like turning the clock back twenty years and recapturing those moments together.

Excitement and joy and love! God designed it that way. And perhaps the greatest joy is that you can spoil them and then send them back!

Lost Finances

We often tell couples in the Fourth Passage of marriage, "You need to come to terms with your financial state."

"I already did that in the Third Passage, didn't I?" they ask.

"You were supposed to reach a realistic appraisal," we reply, "of where you were and where you wanted to be. You still had time then to change things. You don't anymore. You've peaked out now. And that requires grieving and resolution."

A classic example is a couple who suffered massive financial reversal. Thirty years after the husband entered into an arrangement with an appliance distributor and opened a showroom, he had eight showrooms scattered across three Texas counties. Then the Texas economy did its now-famous disappearing act. The man's business collapsed. He salvaged a little something by selling seven distributorships and paring his holdings to one small store in Waco.

As his business telescoped, that man went through the whole grieving process. He denied that he was going to have to scale back even though he saw it coming months in advance. In a literal state of shock, he rationalized that things would pick up soon although no signs said that. Denial didn't work.

He became irritable and highly critical of his wife, turning his intense anger against her (he didn't see it at the time). For six months he drifted into a state of depression and resignation. He thought it was a period of acceptance and that he was through the worst of it. Not so.

Paralyzed by depression, he was unable to act in a business capacity. Things slid downhill faster. There were days when he wouldn't answer the phone as crisis and chaos tumbled around him.

He entered a wild bargaining stage. "If I do more in the office, spend more time on God's work outside the office, somehow it will turn around. If I offer enough sacrifical service, God will salvage my business." That lasted three months until he burned out. Finally, he ended up in true grief. Tears poured spontaneously. Deep sadness engulfed him as he admitted at last that he was going to lose it and couldn't turn it around with any amount of bargaining.

He and his wife accepted the belt-tightening that had to be done. They had to accept that their dream of financial security was lost. At fifty-five they were starting over.

And yet, they didn't lose. They won. Throughout their marriage, husband and wife had substituted busy-ness for intimacy. They were solidly married to the ideal of marriage, but not really to each other. They had never completed the First Passage, let alone the Second or Third. He built the business, served on the church board, belonged to an active civic group. She raised the kids and volunteered in her church and in several service organizations. As painful and tragic as it was, that business collapse gave them the opportunity to rediscover each other, finish what had never been finished.

What was missing was genuine intimacy—knowing each other. They finally invested their time not in business or even so much in service anymore, but in each other. These days they keep their goals scaled back. Both realize that if they had finished the first few passages, they would have had no need to keep so busy. They would not have been seeking false satisfactions and false intimacies. Today they are building a happiness that will last for the next twenty years.

THE NEW CONTRACT

You have seen some of the inner workings of a marriage during this difficult Fourth Passage. Some of the old reasons to stay married have died, or, in the case of the children, moved out. As you forge a new contract, what are the new priorities and needs?

Robert Hemfelt discusses a recent case in his counsel. "It's sad. This person's parents were both terrified of death. Neither of them ever made peace with it, even though one of them met a lingering death due to disease. This person, who is fifty-five now, never made peace with it either. Now he's left his wife of thirty-four years. He's certain he doesn't love her anymore. He's out seeking someone younger. Actually, it has nothing to do with love. He's running away from death, not marriage. He's afraid of getting old."

The man's situation is not all that uncommon. People who have not yet come to terms with their own mortality seek some way to maintain the fiction that they're not old yet. And the more cold reality closes in, the more desperate they become.

The top priority in the new contract, then, may well be some version of "We will do whatever must be done to make it to the end."

Rob and Annie Millen wrote a new contract for their marriage. (Her father Carl, an old-fashioned man unaccustomed to this sort of thing, took a dim view of her efforts. "You made a covenant pact at your wedding. So you honor it. Period. Why a new contract all of a sudden?" "Because, Pop," replied Annie patiently, "details of the old one aren't working for us anymore. This is damage control.")

Their broad strokes included vows to do anything necessary to keep the union from dissolving. Right in the contract, in writing, they reminded themselves that they served as role models for the generations coming up. They renewed the exact pledges they had made before God.

Their broad overview took less than half a page. For the next page and a half, they defined the narrow strokes, the details they planned to make into a formal part of their vows to each other.

Think about what would go into a renewal of your own contract at this stage of your marriage, whether you've actually reached this stage or not. It's fun to project the future, so long as you realize it's all projection. Go back through the sections regarding romance, memories and laughter, and your history together. Your particular situation is unique. What specific items might you write into a new contract to promote romance over the next years? What exactly can both of you do to avoid taking each other for granted?

Think about your history. What can you do to both deepen and transmit your family history and traditions? Write it all into the contract.

And there Annie hit a snag. "It's all very nice to talk about history and laughter and such. But so many of my memories are flat. Rob doing his thing, ignoring me. Some of our best years are lost. We should have been together, enjoying those years, and we were essentially estranged. Emotionally, I mean. I'm very bitter about that."

Annie was right. Much had been lost. She had to sit down and work through grief and forgiveness before she could complete her new contract. You may have to as well. Necessary as they are, these struggles of grieving and forgiveness are never easy. But they are as much a part of your history as the laughter. And properly and completely accomplished, they strengthen the bond as much as do laughter and good nature.

HOW WELL ARE YOU COMPLETING THIS FOURTH PASSAGE?

If you have been married more than twenty-five years, you know that this is a time of either renewal or alienation. Intimacy involves opening up to each other, becoming vulnerable. It also requires learning new things about each other. Use this self-test to help you evaluate your progress toward intimate union and renewal. If you've not yet been married so long, the test may give you ideas for invigorating your marriage now.

1. "One of my very favorite romantic moments of our marriage occurred when _____
   _____."
   "I have talked about it with my spouse since then."
   _____ yes _____ no
2. "One area in which I see myself slowing up physically is _____."

The Renewed Marriage Contract

1. Statement of affirmation; at least one attribute each person admires and appreciates in the other

2. Statement of extent of commitment to the marriage

3. Promise of fidelity

4. Statement of faith, embracing:
   a. Each person's individual statement of faith
   b. Clearly stated common ground
   c. Statement of tolerance (and limits of tolerance)

5. Statement of recognition of old, dysfunctional hidden agendas

6. Declaration of new agendas to redress dysfunctions

7. Sexual contract, including:
   a. Recognition of difficulties or shortcomings in present sexual relations
   b. Steps to improve relations and/or explore new techniques
   c. Details of frequency if frequency is an issue

8. Review of items in first contract, with updates and revisions as necessary

9. Details of everyday life (request for romantic nights out) established through give-and-take (be specific)

"My spouse has noticed it." _____ yes _____ no
"I am embarrassed or afraid to talk about it."
_____ yes _____ no
"I compensate for that slowing-up by doing: _____
_____."

3. "When I am with friends, the topic I tend to talk about most is
_____."

"The human being whom I mention most is _____."
"If it's not my spouse, the reason I don't mention marriage and
spouse is _____
_____."

4. "The last time my partner and I did something truly together
(not watch TV, unless we discussed it as we watched,
interacting with each other as well as the program or video) was

_____
_____."

"If it was more than a week ago, what might we have done
together more recently? _____."

5. "I fear/eagerly anticipate the day our last child moves out (or did
so in the past, when it happened). My major reason for feeling
so is _____
_____."

"I have/have not discussed these feelings with my spouse
because _____."

6. "Fancying for the moment that both my spouse and I live to be a
hundred with mental acuity intact, someone will undoubtedly
ask, 'How did you two manage to stay together so long?' My
answer would be _____
_____."

Young Love, the first two years. Realistic Love, the third through the
tenth year. Comfortable Love, the eleventh through the twenty-fifth year.
Renewing Love, the twenty-six through the thirty-fifth year. You've been
together a long time now. The final passage lies ahead: Transcendent Love.
True love at last.

PART

SIX

The Fifth Passage:
Transcendent Love,
the Thirty-sixth
Year and On

20

WILL RETIREMENT BE A BOON OR A BUST?

*R*etirement. Bah! Twice as much husband, half as much money." Mabel was not pleased as she sat in our office. Her husband, Emery, eight years older than she, faced retirement within two months, and Mabel was not handling it well at all.

"I don't want him underfoot all day," she complained. "No peace, no privacy. Wasting my time because he doesn't have anything to do. No. He was out with a bad back for three months, a couple of years ago, and it drove me nuts."

Mabel was for the first time voicing a fear she had hidden from the moment she learned of Emery's pending retirement. Ever since that announcement she had suffered a series of illnesses—difficulty breathing, migraines, stomach ailments. Alarmed, Emery had checked her into a hospital. It was there she learned that her physical problems, which were very real, stemmed from her emotional turmoil.

Emery had some turmoil of his own. He had planned to work well into his sixties. Here he was, at fifty-three, being put out to pasture. He had started building his retirement nest egg ten years ago, thinking he'd have twenty years, at least, to invest in his future. Now he had a much, much smaller egg than he had planned. That cut deeply. He was proud of the way he handled money. Now he was caught short.

Throughout their marriage, Mabel had remained essentially passive and let Emery run the show. Emery provided nicely for her. He made the financial decisions and she was glad. She didn't really want to be bothered. Also, Emery was pretty well set in his ways.

We asked her, "Have you ever discussed Emery's retirement with him? Have you talked about what your days should be like then?"

What we were asking, in essence, was "Have you rewritten the marriage contract to accommodate this wrenching change in your lifestyle?"

"Why bother?" she replied. "He's a stick in the mud. He settles into something and there he stays. And he's the boss of the house; just ask him. It wouldn't do any good to talk about what I want."

Both Emery and Mabel had their work cut out for them here. Emery would have to deal with his retirement. Mabel would have to become assertive enough to make her wants and feelings known. Both had important good-byes and hellos to say, and many, many adjustments to make. The first task of the Fifth Passage of marriage is to prepare for retirement.

THE FIRST TASK: PREPARE FOR RETIREMENT

Ideally, Emery and Mabel might have made some useful plans for retirement much earlier. Emery had assumed that "preparing for retirement" meant making sure you're going to have enough money. Period. Preparation, however, entails far more than just financial plans.

Psychological Preparation

Emery started as a coal boy on the Jersey Central railroad and worked his way up through steam locomotive engineer to diesel engineer, and eventually to dispatcher. His career spanned nearly five decades and he was justly proud of it. Now he had to say good-bye to a very big chunk of his identity. He also had to acknowledge the sad fact that his income was about to drop considerably. In a culture where worth is too often tied to income, that always comes as a blow. Emery's first big jump, then, would be psychological.

Mabel and Emery viewed retirement as an end. Not so; it is a beginning! It's not hard to see why it might look like the end. Previous generations didn't have the benefits of modern medicine and financial safety nets. Their experience colors our perceptions. Their retirement years too often brought disillusionment and sadness compared with what today's retiree can expect. One random example of many: a few years ago, the man or woman (usually the woman) who broke a hip could expect to deteriorate quickly, wheelchair bound until death. Hip replacement surgery, routine today, puts that person back on a bicycle in a few months. In addition, further strides in medicine are helping us beat the osteoporosis that landed so many women in wheelchairs. Still, the gloom and doom of prior genera-tions often get passed on unconsciously to today's pending retirees. As the first step in their psychological preparation, Emery and Mabel had to fight that.

This is not to say that life will be perfect. Consider Ralph, a retiree who dreamed of playing golf every day. He now suffers joint problems that severely restrict his swing. He must grieve the lost dream. But he can amend it. Still able to walk comfortably, he prowls golf courses not with a bag and clubs but with a bird book and binoculars. He added band-tailed pigeons to his list at the Wawona Golf Course and saw sandhill cranes flying overhead while ambling down the back nine of the Arkansas Country Club.

The second step: Celebrate the new opportunities. Grieve and accept the unavoidable limitations. Amend the dream, if necessary, as circum-stances require. "You have to be flexible or you'll never get anywhere," Mary Alice Minirth is fond of saying.

A third major transition and adjustment is to be mentally prepared for shocks and bumps. A very damaging myth promises that two people, to-gether for decades already, can slip quietly and friction-free into retirement. Expect some surprising rough spots. They're coming. Many psychologists claim that the life change of retirement is as great as that of puberty or of marriage itself.

Mabel and Emery were ahead on this one because they absolutely knew they were facing big trouble.

Persons who have not resolved the control issues and individuation-versus-union issues of the first three passages are going to slam into those unresolved problems right here, at retirement. You may have been able to put off facing certain issues for twenty or thirty years. When one of you reaches retirement, there will be no escaping the problem. Control and per-sonal boundaries are the two big factors in retirement adjustments.

Facing Control and Boundary Issues

Control issues. Boy, do they crop up here when it comes to finances! Persons who would swear they never had a control problem in their lives find themselves saddled with them now. Basically, couples who shared fi-nancial awareness throughout marriage will have the least difficulty as re-tirement looms.

Many books, articles, and folders from financial institutions can help pending retirees sort through the maze of investment and income opportu-nities. Ideally, financial planning by the Fourth Passage of marriage should consist of fine-tuning existing plans in response to the current economic climate. We do not have room here to offer suggestions for financial strategies. But the finances themselves are only a part of financial preparation. There is also the mental preparation to make in this area.

What do you envision as a retirement lifestyle? Do you want to maintain the level of income and activity you have now? Maybe move up a notch? Perhaps you'd rather seize this opportunity to downsize both lifestyle and budget. Now may be a good time to simplify life; take it easy; reduce the housework, chores, duties, needs, and general complexities of modern existence. Set firmly in mind what you and your spouse anticipate and want.

The wise squirrel traveling around in our decision tree will stash nuts away in more than one hollow limb. The wise squirrel will also make sure it has a Plan B, should Plan A fail. Emery thought he had his finances all worked out. But being forced into early retirement, he had ten years less time to build a retirement kitty. That put a serious crimp on his future income. Emery and Mabel had intended to just live in the house they had. That was plan A. But the only bathroom was on the second floor. The house was too big to maintain comfortably should Emery or Mabel get laid up. Besides, Emery needed a bigger nest egg. So he had to shift into plan B: sell this house, buy a much smaller, less expensive one, and dump the money into their retirement fund. Both of them hated the idea. They had to do it, though. Grief. On the other hand, it improved their immediate financial outlook. Celebration. Good-bye and hello.

Emery looked at it philosophically. "I have some friends who live in one room in a downtown hotel. I'm not going to complain about selling our family home when I've got this nice little house on Grove Street."

Many pending retirees look toward an inheritance of some sort from the previous generation. For mental peace as well as financial stability, we advise against that. With inflation, longer life span and extraordinary health care, inheritances stay within the generation longer, often dwindling as the years go by.

Says Susan Hemfelt, "Frequently these days, we see people receiving an inheritance or property when they're in their sixties and seventies. Mother and Daddy live into their eighties or nineties. And they usually use a part of what would be an inheritance for living expenses. That's as it should be. But it also means that someone facing retirement had better not be depending on the family money for a retirement fund."

Emery faced what most workers face; during the First Passage of his marriage, he was making barely enough to establish himself and care for his family. Not until the Fourth Passage was he earning enough to salt away appreciable savings toward retirement. Thus did early retirement hit him hard. He had to mentally adjust to a much harsher reality than he would have had to, had he worked into his sixties.

Building a Mutual Dream

Mabel and Emery, though, were guilty of the most serious of retirement problems. They had never talked about it. This was the first thing we did when Mabel and Emery came to us; we sat them down knee to knee, face to face, to explain to each other their hopes and fears. You should do that too.

Here are some points to start you out. Each spouse answers individually. Compare answers and talk about compromises where compromise is necessary. Answer according to the picture you foresee during your first five years of retirement:

"We will live:
_____ in our present home."
_____ in a smaller/larger home."
_____ in a retirement home."
_____ with one of the kids."
_____ in a recreation vehicle."
_____ in a small apartment."
_____ out of the country."
_____ other—specifically _____."

"We will travel:
_____ a lot."
_____ hardly at all."
_____ now and then."

"We will engage in:
_____ a home business."
_____ no business at all."
_____ volunteer work."
_____ a part-time business or franchise."
_____ something to supplement our income."
_____ other—specifically _____."

"We have the following hobbies to occupy our time and keep us sharp: _____

_____

_____."

There are many other questions to be decided. After you complete this chapter, talk together about what you have read.

Mabel's best friend, Jeanne, planned to lease out her house and travel when they retired, only to learn that her husband was making a list of all the local fishing holes. Emery's pal Gus wanted to sell everything, live in an RV and travel all over. His wife had no intention of giving up her home. Come retirement, the couple literally ripped in half because they had never talked about it. Neither would they negotiate their dreams.

Develop Plan B

Harry reaches mandatory retirement age. His Henrietta does not work outside the home. They save monthly for ten years in anticipation of this time. But it's not enough. Too late they discover that social security will not cover it all. This isn't a case of bad planning, either. Even the best of planners experience a setback in states or areas with an ailing economy.

It's very easy to fall into the role of victim when this sort of thing happens. Harry and Henrietta risk losing these rich later years to bitterness. They must grieve what might have been and immediately and continuously brainstorm options.

A major step in resolving sticky situations is to recognize what you can control and what you cannot. Saving regularly, Harry and Henrietta could control that. They could not control the economy, or things like the death of a spouse, a layoff, or forced retirement. Observe what you cannot control, so as to know how to respond to it, but put it aside as a source of worry. Concern yourself rather with what you can control.

Using what you can control and manipulate, develop alternative plans that provide a workable response to those things beyond control. It sounds basic, an idea everyone should be doing, but we've found that very few people actually do it. When problems loom large, they fumble about, fearful and confused, for solutions that might not have been hiding if they had considered them beforehand.

Harry and Henrietta decided to go to work to support themselves in their retirement. In spite of laws protecting against age discrimination, Harry could not find a job equivalent to what he had been doing. Henrietta faced entry-level work whatever she did. Still the combined income helped to offset their deficit. Now could they reduce their living cost?

The first thought was to sell their old Edwardian house. They resisted the idea vigorously. As plan B they decided to sell some blue-chip stock they held to pay the house off. This would reduce their monthly costs considerably. Then, because living in the house was more important to them than some other niceties, they decided to limit their money for recreation, like eating out several times a week and traveling to far away places. "We've seen enough of the world," Henry said. "A trip every couple of years will do." Their lifestyle and stock ownership was something they could control. Plan B was not preferred, but it was workable. They dropped back to Plan B out of necessity. You may have to also.

No wise squirrel in a decision tree limits itself to one limb. Formulate alternative plans.

Prepare Boundaries

Boundaries were the thing Mabel worried about most. "I don't want him underfoot all day," she said. Mabel for years had been accustomed to having her house to herself during the day, to do as she wished. She did not want to become handservant to a TV-watching couch potato. She didn't want to have to drop what she was doing to help Emery with some cockamamy project out in the garage when he called her. She didn't want his intrusion twenty-four hours a day.

Emery had his boundary concerns too. He didn't want the cholesterol police nagging him when he popped open a bag of potato chips and sat down to watch the sports network. He didn't want the neatness police telling him to pick up his socks and fold the newspaper when he was done with it. He didn't want the liberation police expecting him to vacuum and dust and do the dishes.

Setting the boundaries for everyday life *well ahead of actual retirement* can greatly soften the impact of all the forced togetherness when the time comes.

We suggest you actually put some boundary agreements on paper. Each of you work through the following areas to determine your own needs and what you believe your spouse's response will be. Some surprising perceptional differences show up that way. The two then sit down to compare responses and share views. Here is an excellent exercise in intimacy, as well.

Space

Each person needs his or her own space. There must also be neutral space, shared as a couple, in order to be content with the increased amount of physical and residential togetherness. These spaces may be in or outside the home, but they must exist. Also, each spouse must be willing to respect the other's territory.

His Space

Emery listed the attic for his model railroad (every Jersey Central retiree needs a railroad), the tool end of the garage, and the little office room off to the side of the dining room. These places, of course, were certainly not off limits to Mabel. They were, rather, places where Emery could pursue his own interests by himself, where he could leave possessions as he cared to (either keeping them meticulously neat, or slopping them about, or probably a little of each).

"My space (the husband's) should be _____

_____
_____."

"I think my wife would claim these areas: _____

_____
_____."

Her Space

Mabel claimed the spare bedroom as a workroom for her sewing, needlework, and miniatures. There she could leave her sewing machine set up. She could sort the skeins for her granny square afghan without cluttering the living room. She could put her Victorian farm house on saw horses and work on it at her convenience. Pure heaven! The kitchen, too, was Mabel's, as was the garden-tool end of the garage.

"My space (the wife's) should be _____

_____
_____."

"I think my husband would claim these areas: _____

_____
_____."

Their Space

The living room, dining room, and bedroom. Here Mabel and Emery could expect to interact with each other, disturb each other at will, argue or snuggle, jockey each other for the remote control, do couples things.

"Our space should be _____

_____
_____."

"I think my spouse would expect our space to be:_____
_____
_____."

Time

Time must be reapportioned as his, hers, and ours. Negotiate to agree how much time you'll be spending together and how much will be set aside for individual use. Neither partner ought to feel chained to the other.

Both Emery and Mabel agreed they needed at least six hours each weekday to themselves. Evenings and weekends were negotiable. Weekdays, they stayed out of each other's hair by mutual consent. The value of the chart here, you see, was that Mabel and Emery could both visualize a workable arrangement for maintaining privacy. Seeing the promise of privacy in black and white did much to alleviate Mabel's fears and concerns.

"I think I will want _____ hours each day to myself."
"I think my spouse will want _____ hours each day."
"I believe evenings:
_____ "Should be negotiable."
_____ "Should be spent together."
_____ "Should also have some boundaries. I'd like _____
      hours in the evening."
"I believe weekends:
_____ "Should be negotiable."
_____ "Should be spent together."
_____ "Should also have some boundaries. I'd like _____
      hours on the weekends."

Activities

Activities should be scheduled according to two needs: the universal need to feel needed, and gratification of personal interest. Outline and share activities to participate in daily, weekly, monthly, whatever. Then indicate shared activities.

His Activities and Duties

Emery decided to make breakfast (she was tired of making it after three decades and he got up earlier than she, so he became the breakfast chef), keep up home repair, tinker with the car, and pursue hobbies—his railroad in particular. He also listed hunting, a seasonal activity, and the singing Christmas tree, an annual community project. At last he could attend his men's prayer breakfast regularly.

"My activities and duties (husband's) will be:

_____
_____
_____."

"My wife would like to see me do these things:

_____
_____
_____."

Her Activities and Duties

Mabel listed "cooking on whim." This was as opposed to cooking on demand. When she felt like it, she'd cook. When she didn't, they'd eat out. She also listed gardening, her hobbies, volunteer projects, the household budget (something she'd been handling for years anyway), and house maintenance not including repairs (washing curtains, steam-cleaning the carpet, sorting closets).

"My activities and duties (wife's) will be:

_____
_____
_____."

"My husband would like to see me do these things:

_____
_____
_____."

Their Activities

As a couple Emery and Mabel planned to attend at least one dinner (or host one) each month, go to church, take daily walks, watch certain favorite TV shows together, and make a joint library run at least once weekly.

"Our activities together should be:

_____
_____
_____."

"My spouse would list these activities:

_____
_____
_____."

Goals

Given that retirement is a beginning and not an end, look closely at goals. Husband and wife should each have several. They should share several as a couple. When writing goals, also mention in a few words how those goals ought to be pursued. Goals definitely must provide for each other's needs. Both spouses should establish goals before entering the actual retirement phase. It is far easier to come up with acceptable goals when you're feeling good about yourself, active, and working. If you are lonely, sitting about with time on your hands, goals come hard and assume less apparent importance. "Why bother?" smothers "Let's do it!"

His Goals

Emery, frankly, was quite lax about establishing goals, except for his railroad layout. He wrote short-range and long-range goals for that project, which included building a mountain, installing a whole power substation with wires, poles, and towers all over, building a master control board, and painting and arranging a herd of tiny plastic beef cattle. His non-hobby goals? "Eat." Mabel scowled at him hard enough that he added, "Finish that intensive Bible study I signed up for."

"My goals (the husband's) are:

_____

_____

_____."

My wife's goals are probably:

_____

_____

_____."

Her Goals

Mabel determined to learn something new each day ("or you get bored with life"); volunteer for something a minimum of five hours a week; get all the kids' stuff, stored here and there, out of her house and into the kids' houses. That would mean shipping a couple of large cartons two thousand miles to Sarasota, Florida. She'd do it just to get rid of all that clutter.

"My goals (the wife's) are:

_____

_____

_____."

"My husband's goals are probably:

_____."

Their Goals

Provide daily support for each other (that was Mabel's idea, and Emery liked the notion of programming it right in), keep daily activities varied to avoid boredom, make a new best friend following the death of one of their longtime family friends.

"Our goals together are:

_____."

"My spouse would probably see our mutual goals as:

_____."

Spiritual Growth

Spiritual growth should continue until death, just as temporal wisdom grows. Not only should your spiritual dimension not be neglected, this is the time of life when it should be nurtured.

His Spiritual Needs

Emery wasn't sure he had any spiritual needs, other than that correspondence Bible study he'd been neglecting and his men's prayer breakfast, both already mentioned elsewhere. And as he thought about it, that pleased him. He wasn't separating out his spiritual nature from everything else he did; the spiritual and the more mundane mingled together in his life, each enriching the other. He left that area blank.

"My spiritual needs (the husband's) are:

_____."

"My spouse would probably have these spiritual needs:

_____."

Her Spiritual Needs

Mabel didn't leave this area blank. She signed up for a women's Bible study group, listed her church participation and regular duties, determined to do more for the altar guild, and pledged to bring two new people to church each month.

"My spiritual needs (the wife's) are:

_____
_____
_____."

"My spouse would probably have these spiritual needs:

_____
_____
_____."

The Couple's Spiritual Needs

Emery and Mabel determined to share a prayer time daily and take the neighbors bowling once a month or so. That bowling item was an evangelistic outreach. Their new neighbors, as yet unchurched, seemed eager for fellowship and open to the Word, and they loved to bowl.

"Our spiritual needs together are:

_____
_____
_____."

"My spouse would see our spiritual needs as:

_____
_____
_____."

After you talk about these items together, build a new working outline, not unlike a contract. It then becomes your template for everyday life. The outline in addition offers one more chance to iron out any unresolved issues from previous passages. The plan need not be embedded in stone; but it promotes good solid teamwork right from the beginning.

Both Emery and Mabel found that having planned activities and goals, rather than hampering freedom, actually was very uplifting. They didn't seem to flounder about or drift. They got things done and felt good about the productivity. Emery commented on feeling less useless, whatever "less useless" means.

A friend of ours belongs to a lifelong golf group that has grown despite its older members passing away. They meet weekly at various courses, rain, shine, or occasional snow. They have been known to drive into a forty-mile-an-hour wind on the eleventh hole. The group serves important purposes the retired person must actively seek out. As well as being fun, the group provides companionship, something retired persons especially need.

It needn't be sports. Another friend joins an informal bunch of guys on an SOS hunt. Each Thursday morning at six, they meet at a diner by prearrangement. They've tried nearly every diner in town. Ostensibly, they are seeking the greatest plate of SOS. "SOS", for the uninitiated, is a creamed hamburger (or other meat) mixture served over toast. The SOS is more an excuse than a reason as the men spend time in communal prayer, laugh a lot, and swap both lies and practical advice. "We talk about any-thing and everything," one of the group explains. "Except cholesterol counts. Nobody is allowed to mention cholesterol." He pointed to his plate. "This stuff is a cardiologist's nightmare."

Susan Hemfelt talks of a needlepoint group that started in the 1950s as an opportunity for young mothers to visit while their babies napped. The group is still going strong, for a different reason. Now it's a retirement support group and sometimes a crash course on how to manage with hus-bands in retirement.

Whether a group centers around a sport, hobby, or some other focus, a hidden agenda sustains it through the years; that is the mutual need for support in each passage of marriage.

Might some similar group serve your area? It's never too late to start such a group or join an existing one.

We hope this gives you an idea of how to build a chart for your own retirement plans. Unfortunately, such charts don't fall into place smoothly. Man and wife may balk, at loggerheads over some item that simply will not respond to compromise. Then what?

Trouble in River City

We find that disagreements about major life factors respond to about the same treatment as we outlined in Chapter 3. The couple compromises, or they agree to disagree, or one person offers the other a love gift. Monitor closely, to make certain one partner doesn't do all the love giving and the other partner little or none. That leads to resentment quickly.

An example of agreeing to disagree: She wants to travel and he doesn't. There is no middle ground. So once or twice a year, she goes off with friends from her bridge group and her husband stays home. Once or twice a year, he goes deep-sea fishing. She could not care less to bob on a nauseating little boat trying to entice slimy fish to eat disgusting bait. This is, basically, the agree-to-disagree solution. They also make certain to engage in some activity agreeable to them both, three or four times a year.

Another fount of troubles we find frequently in counsel is the situation where one spouse has had little or no outside interest throughout pre-retirement. The workaholic husband who does nothing else, the isolated homemaker whose idea of recreation is watching TV in the afternoon, suddenly find themselves at sea, confused and aimless. Establishing goals and shoving the horizons out is absolutely essential for situations of that sort. Sit down and think of something new to try, someplace new to explore, a hobby or volunteer project to begin. Deliberately talk about goals and purpose, and then set some.

To avoid trouble of another sort, maintain utmost care in respecting each other's turf. His place, her place, and their place is an immensely important concept.

"He's always breathing down my neck," a client named Sue complained. "I'm in the kitchen, he's in the kitchen. I work out in the yard, there he is. That's bad enough but the criticism is the worst. He's been retired for four months now, and I've been doing my work for thirty-four years. But he thinks he knows how to do it better. Or easier."

Sue was engaged in a battle just like any other military action. Her husband was invading her territory. As an isolated homemaker, she felt suffocated by his constant presence, and yet she felt very alone due to her lack of outside interests and friends. His supposedly helpful criticism delivered the coup de grace.

Sue's husband, bored and restless, took over the chore of grocery shopping. Unfortunately, he didn't consult with Sue. Going to the store was the only time she got out of her home, and he took that away from her. Sue came to us an intensely frustrated and miserable woman.

Our first effort, after evaluating the situation, was to sit Sue and her husband down to work out the orderly reapportionment of household duties. We insisted they put them down on paper—who would do what. This would help prevent hostile takeovers such as when Sue's husband started grocery shopping.

Second, we helped the suffocated wife develop her own interests. Eventually, she gained enough confidence in her ability to influence her husband that she could tell him how much togetherness was comfortable for her. Achieving a comfortable balance between togetherness and apartness is a key to happiness in everyday retirement life, and it comes only with open give and take between the partners.

When dissatisfaction crops up, go back to the chart to pinpoint the trouble spot. And don't expect the same chart to work forever. As people change, so do their needs, and as needs change, so must the spouse. Revise the chart as necessary.

Another trouble spot we find often is the interference in the couple's daily life posed by adult children and grandchildren. "If I had known grandchildren were so much fun, I would have had them first," says the grandmother. But if solid, comfortable boundaries are not in place, grandchildren and adult children can become too much of a good thing. The retired couple find themselves curtailing their own plans as they serve as hosts, baby-sitters, or emergency counselors. To an extent, this is good; older people have a wisdom and balance that youth need. Too much is not good.

How much is too much and what do you do about it? Every situation is unique, including yours. You must work out the boundaries yourself. Some examples to get you started:

"We will baby-sit the grandchildren _____ times per (week) (month)."

"We expect advance notice of _____ (hours) (days) if children or grandchildren plan to visit."

"Children and grandchildren are welcome guests in our home for a period not to exceed _____."

"We have written down a list of house rules and the children/ grandchildren *will* follow them. The list is posted in the

_____."

There is no right or wrong plan when it comes to setting boundaries. Some couples like a total open-door policy. Others cannot live with that. Make your policy known and don't be afraid to stand up to family members who fail to honor it.

LAST ONE IN THE POOL IS A ROTTEN EGG

Usually, when both spouses work outside the home, one retires before the other. An example is Myrtle Speis, age fifty-five. Myrtle put in a thirty-hour work week at a water-testing lab, keeping records and billing. Eight hours weekly she donated to the local library. Then her husband Murphy, seven years older, retired from his job as a mid-level manager, and the friction started immediately.

Murphy Speis wanted to see America next. He bought a motor home and customized it. He took it on a few weekend shakedown cruises. Ready to go, he insisted Myrtle retire also. Now was the time to travel, while they were both in good health.

Myrtle didn't mind travel, but she loved her job. She made good money at the lab and she liked the staff there very much. It was a goofy, competent, lively, Gary-Larsonish place to work, and it made her feel young. She served as grandma to the whole lab crew, dispensing advice, bandages, and brownies as the occasion arose. She was needed. She was loved. She was loathe to give it up.

Murphy, restless and ready to go, recruited several of the couple's friends to his side of the argument. Some of Myrtle's more liberated women friends stood up for her side. The friction spread and got nastier. Before long, Myrtle could not attend a social function or even go to church without hearing that she had no right to mess up Murphy's retirement like that, or she ought to tell Murphy to go jump in a lake. A thousand times, Myrtle wanted to scream, "It's none of your business!" as people volunteered their opinions.

Myrtle and Murphy Speis, at absolute loggerheads, could not hope to solve everything at once. Pain and resentment ran too deep by now. They untangled their Gordian knot by picking at one little loop at a time.

The allocation plan we described in detail earlier worked well for this couple also. The same principles apply for one-retires-and-one-doesn't situations as for mutual retirements. Before assigning them this exercise, however, we counseled them in the steps of forgiveness. Myrtle had much to forgive, and so did Murphy. We led them through the grieving process for they both had much to grieve too. Each was going to have to give up at least a few treasured desires and dreams. We also helped them grieve the pain and trouble their disagreement had already caused themselves and their friends.

One of Murphy's biggest problems was not lack of travel but boredom. Myrtle still did the housework, as she had for years. She did nearly all the cooking. He had scant outside interests other than detailing his motor home. We suggested Murphy take over some household duties. The idea did not sit well. When we pointed out that this would give Myrtle more time for them to do things as a couple, he agreed to try vacuuming, dusting, KP, and half the cooking.

Myrtle now faced a problem many such couples face. She had to assiduously avoid the temptation to take some household duties back when they weren't performed to her liking. And she had to carefully avoid criticism. They made it over that hump with a little jostling and tugging.

Because Myrtle didn't have household chores to do on weekends, she could take off with Murphy on Friday night and not return until work on

Monday. The weekend trips served several purposes, not the least of which was to provide them both a taste of what extensive travel would be like, with the two of them closed into a little box for hours on end.

This surprised Myrtle. The weekend trips fueled and rejuvenated their romance. Also, they needed those trips to adjust duties and roles. They even created a new plan; this one detailed exactly who would do what on the road.

We also got Murphy to extend his interests beyond the camper. A retired spouse must keep his or her day full and interesting. Murphy could not depend on Myrtle's presence in everything; he had to carve out a retirement life of his own, independent of hers. Besides, we pointed out, the more interests people have, the more interesting they are to others. Now was the time for Murphy and Myrtle to get a head start on the day when both would be retired.

Dr. Hemfelt warns that when one spouse retires before the other, two contracts may come into effect. Overtly, the two agree upon the details of the plan. But lurking in the shadows is another, hidden agenda neither may be aware of. The retired spouse sees what seems like a highly productive mate getting paid yet, and harbors a fear of being considered useless. Resentment grows beneath the surface. The couple fight and drift apart and don't know why.

Restlessness and friction serve as signals, especially when they arise over seemingly trivial matters of finance or authority decisions. They indicate that hidden motives and fears lie below the surface. The best solution is to mutually explore one's *own* feelings. Why do I feel as I do? Talk out fears and feelings by acknowledging them. Then build a list of truths to dispel the validity of the fears.

For example, in the case above, Myrtle discovered a need to assure Murphy that he truly was needed. She was committed to him because he was Murphy, not because he had once been a mid-level manager. She pointed out that the reason she was drawing a salary and he wasn't was that her timetable was different; she started working after he did (with time off for motherhood), and she was younger than he. Were she older, she would have retired first and he'd still be drawing a salary.

"This is true; that is not valid. I need you. I value you as a person, just the way you are." Facts and valid reassurances are the best antidote to fear and resentment.

Review the material on hidden agendas at the beginning of this book. Look to iron out any hidden contracts that may be surfacing here.

Murphy began his retirement having no activity or interest outside that motor home. With some encouragement, he developed such a variety of interests that his dream of travel shrank down to a dream of occasional travel. Myrtle could live with that. She worked out an intermittent leave arrangement with her boss, permitting her to turn over her lab duties to a temporary worker for limited periods of a month or two. She could join Murphy then, not for travel stints extending for months and months, but for trips measured in weeks. Neither could have envisioned this compromise when Murphy first retired.

RETIREMENT OPTIONS

Mary Alice Minirth speaks fondly of an aunt and uncle who spend their life in retirement doing things for others. "They left after Dad's funeral to go encourage an uncle in a nursing home. While my dad was undergoing cancer therapy, this same aunt and uncle brought Mom and Dad a motor home so that I could take him to the cancer center in Arlington."

And this aunt and uncle illustrate something else about finding purpose and impact in the Fifth Passage: They enjoy getting creative about it. When they see a need they brainstorm the best way to meet that need, and the idea they come up with may or may not be some tried-and-true pat answer. This is an excellent time in life to encourage new avenues of creativity.

You can no longer get paid to do what you've been doing for so many years. Suddenly, your work, your expertise, your vast experience are no longer welcome. Your whole life, you've been throwing away possessions that were worn out and no longer useful. Now you are the one being thrown out.

Hardly! Millions of retirees will tell you that the good-bye of retirement opens a wonderful hello. Now at last you can do what interests you, what can help others, what can make a difference, what simply pleases you. It may or may not turn a buck, but you're bound to be rewarded.

When the Persian Gulf crisis erupted into war, Cora, trained as a "first responder," gave two days a week to the local military hospital, filling in as her training permitted for the medical personnel in the Gulf. "My war effort," she beamed proudly. Cora is fifty-eight.

Herb, a retired aviation engineer, took up whittling and woodcarving late in life. Now he teaches it at monthly sessions in an inner-city girls' and boys' club. Herb is seventy-four.

The Lacasso Boy Scout Council was going to have to give up meeting in their hundred-year-old cabin because it failed to meet building codes. John knew a thing or two about codes. He'd been a contractor for years. Enlisting the Scouts themselves for labor, he and his crew tore the cabin apart, rewired, replumbed, and installed the required sprinkler system. They even rigged a burglar alarm to protect the half dozen moth-eaten stuffed mammals in a display case. They put the cabin back together and painted it to match a 1911 photo. John turns sixty-four next month.

With the major tasks of life completed—that is, nurturing the next generation and building financial security, couples in retirement are open at last to new sources of creativity and freedom. Again we emphasize that this is not a cookbook from which you can pick a few pat answers and plug them into your life. But we can offer some broad suggestions. Alter and shape them to your own unique needs and preferences. You and your spouse can work together in nearly all these endeavors.

How about:

Your church. The church can always use practical help with maintenance, building and repair, nursery chores, perhaps cooking, library or gift shop work. Do youth functions need chaperones? What better chaperones/examples than a couple who has been together all these years?

Camps. Does your church, denomination, or civic group run a camp somewhere? Worthy medical charities do. Ask around. Ask especially about handicapped camps. The ratio in children's and adults' handicapped camps is often two campers per counselor or even one to one. That's a lot of staff.

Missions. Some of the most urgent needs are found in mission enterprises in our cities. You don't have to travel by camel to Timbuktu. Take the bus downtown for missions opportunities just as rewarding as foreign field service.

Hospitals. Hospital gift shops and auxiliary services use largely volunteer labor. They need responsible help. Many hospitals use people to simply sit and rock the babies in the preemie ward, for babies who are handled and cuddled grow better.

Parks. You quite possibly can spend the summer in a national park. Call a nearby federal agency to get the appropriate phone number. Thus armed, you can call a national park and ask about the National Park Service's VIP program—Volunteers in Parks. A few parks with heavy winter visitation, such as Everglades and Death Valley, need VIPs during cold months. Most use their VIPs in the summer. The National Park Service is a division of the Department of the Interior.

National forests increasingly appreciate volunteer help in a variety of tasks. If no national forest lies nearby, call a federal agency for numbers. The National Forest Service is a division of the Department of Agriculture. You may wish to enquire also into the Bureau of Land Management and

Army Corps of Engineers. They use volunteers during heavy visitation to Bureau and Corps sites such as dams and preserves.

Many state and city parks use volunteer help extensively. Here's a great way to think and act creatively.

Schools. Public and private schools can all use volunteers, especially if you can serve learning-disabled schools and halfway houses.

Public gardens. If you prefer your fingernails with dirt under them, ask if your local public gardens need seasonal help planting spring bulbs or weeding the begonias or handling the annual plant sale.

The county fair, regional exhibitions, and similar expositions. For a few short weeks before and during the event, fairs need tons and tons of people to provide security in exhibition halls, man information kiosks, park cars, take tickets, pick up litter, clean restrooms, mollify lost children, answer phones, stuff envelopes, assist judges, help exhibitors set up and take down (paper work, not physical labor), assist maintenance and repair, prepare flower beds and landscape plantings, paint buildings and equipment, and help out with a hundred other little jobs. Some pay well, others use volunteer labor. Either way, it's fun, and you will be making a difference.

A wealth of other opportunities. Does the zoo need docents? How about the historical museum? You know a lot of history. Can the nature center use help when school groups come through? Would the library like a grandparent type, male or female, to read to small children? Does a political candidate need someone to lick envelopes and if so, how wet is your tongue? Would you like to help an adult learn to read through the literacy program in your area? Do people with arthritis, people who cannot therefore hold a pen, need your help preparing taxes or filling out Social Security forms? Does the local animal control center (that's "dog pound") or humane society employ volunteers?

What do you and your spouse enjoy doing? What are you good at? Think about it. How can you personally capitalize on those things to help others and influence the younger generation with your example and expertise? You'll never feel useless again.

Good old ex-railroad-man Emery caught the idea quickly and easily. Less than a week after his retirement dinner, he lined up a class to teach steam engineers how to run their trains. His clients were the little tourist railroads in the mountains of Colorado, California, and Washington, where they assembled plenty of rolling stock but no one knew how to operate it. He used his diesel skills on a free-lance basis, troubleshooting for a diesel generator manufacturing company. It didn't pay much, and he only got called out a couple of times a year, but it took him all over the country.

Mabel had to grieve and accept the fact that her life was irrevocably changed. But with the grief came ample celebration. When Emery went out on his training and troubleshooting trips, Mabel at first stayed home, rejoicing that she had the house to herself a while. But Mabel, too, found some nice hellos. Now and then she goes along, and she discovered she likes to travel when the trips were not too long. Most of all, she learned that by planting herself right in front of Emery and looking him eye to eye, she could tell him her wants and needs. Sometimes he even responded positively.

In essence, they rewrote their marriage contract (though neither would admit that that's what it was). They stayed out of each other's hair at specified times. They did certain things as a couple and other things independently. With a lot of juggling and shuffling, they arranged a satisfying life together. And Mabel's migraines and stomach problems disappeared.

21

CAN YOU RENEW INTIMACY?

*W*ynn and Maggie had been married forty-two years. After retirement, Wynn worked part time as a night handyman at a nearby nursing home. When something blew up at 2:00 A.M., they'd call him and he'd fix it somehow. He was good at it. But a mild stroke reduced his physical strength in one side and put a reluctant end to his part-time job, and Wynn quit trying.

Maggie had always been a "Nervous Nellie," bustling about, tending to Wynn's needs, keeping the house. Now, thanks to polarization, Maggie did much more. She even cleaned his glasses and cut his meat for him. His horizons ended at sports on TV, and he even went to sleep during the exciting games.

Doctors assigned Wynn exercises to help him become more self-sufficient and build his stamina. Wynn ducked them. He learned quickly that if he pedaled his stationary bike real hard for fifteen seconds, he could lift his feet away from the pedals and coast, putting a good half mile on the odometer with no effort at all. Maggie hit the roof when she found out.

Wynn had closed down his world around himself. Unfortunately, he dragged Maggie's horizons in as well. When he suffered a second stroke and needed a walker to get around the house, Maggie tied herself to him completely, afraid he might try to move around and fall. She wouldn't go out and sit on the front porch if Wynn stayed in the house, and Wynn rarely went out on the porch. Wynn became too heavy a burden for her, of course, for he did fall, often pulling her down with him. He spent his last years in the nursing home where he had once served as night handyman.

So often, in counsel and amid friendships, we see people eyeing the bad as they grow older, hardly ever looking around for the "something good" of late life. Good-byes are coming thick and fast at this stage of life. But good-byes are not so much an end as a beginning. By severing one connection, a good-bye frees you to accept a new connection. Good-byes are more than balanced by hellos. Both will profoundly influence your marriage. "Come, grow old along with me," invited Robert Browning. "The best is yet to be."

We invite you to look upon the changes in this Fifth Passage as another network of good-byes and hellos, of something good linked to the bad. While this is a handy way to look at life in general and your marriage in particular during any passage, now in these latter days is when the philosophy pays rich dividends. Here, too, is a splendid opportunity to deepen intimacy, as you and your mate explore them and talk about them together.

FIGHTING THE IMAGE

It's not just younger people who entertain false attitudes toward the aging: "Set in their ways." "Persnickety." "Slow. You see a line of cars and you can just bet that the car in front holding everybody up is an old person." "Cranky." "They don't tip worth beans. I hate having to wait on them in the restaurant."

Ours is one of the very few cultures in the world that does not honor, even revere, the aged. When Corrie ten Boom, the Dutch woman who spent terrifying years in a Nazi concentration camp for hiding Jews during World War II, traveled into southeast Asia, she was referred to most affectionately as "double-old grandmother," a term of reverence, of extreme respect. Here that would be an insult.

Many Fifth Passage couples enjoy the fruits of a slower lifestyle. They comfortably either ignore or put up with relationship issues that used to irritate them.

And many younger people, looking at the decelerated pace of older couples, don't understand. They see this winding down as giving in to boredom. In a way it is, perhaps, but that's not necessarily negative. There is much to be said for feeling at ease with life. These later years become a real time of contentment and that is much of their purpose. Younger people must come to grasp that. Says Brian Newman, "Until I visited Dad not too long ago, I never sat on our back porch and watched the birds. It was a great experience."

Younger people also tend to condemn the denial older people so often indulge.

"Remember when we played ball?"

"Dad, we never played ball."

"Oh, come on! Don't you remember when?"

"You were always working. You were never there."

For couples in the Fifth Passage, denial serves a special purpose. They are using it to deal with disappointment and personal guilt. By romanticizing aspects of the past (to the point of hallucinating, the kids claim), they bestow an importance and a success to their marriage that it never really had. They cannot go back and change the past literally, so they do it mentally. We always counsel younger people against arguing and hurting them to no good end. In this stage, denial has value.

As one ages, one forgets the bad and ugly, but again that's not a negative thing. Recall the concept we sketched earlier about memories. Positive memories have a powerful influence, whether they reflect the lockstep of fact or embellish it a bit.

Grandkids idolize grandparents, and that can also cause problems, believe it or not, because the parents of the grandkids too often do not. As Bill Cosby says, "You didn't know them when." The children know what those parents were like. If their memories are sour, they have a hard time watching their own children accept the grandparents so freely.

Kathy loved her grandparents. She never understood why her mother despised them. Kathy learned to live a separate life with her grandparents. She visited and helped them as a young adult, but she rarely mentioned them when speaking to her mother. When her mother would ask her where she had been, rather than tell her mother she had been with her grandparents, she often made excuses.

Kathy's mother never resolved her anger with Kathy's grandparents. And she resented Kathy for loving and admiring them. Kathy's grandparents may have been different people as she was growing up than they were when they were raising her mother. She can never know those people as they were then. They've changed. But her mother cannot see them in the same light Kathy does because her perception is so colored by the past.

What others think is secondary. What is important: Do those persons married well over three decades accept the negative stereotypes or do they maintain a strong faith in themselves? What do they think of each other?

If the partners themselves begin believing some of the problem images, they can drift apart by making wrong assumptions. We saw the seed of that in the Fourth Passage, when too often the partners made untrue cultural assumptions about sexual needs and desires. If the partners' marriage has been growing, these latter years usher in a beautiful season of peace. If the partners are frozen up in an earlier passage, unable to mature, the strife multiplies itself.

The second task of the Fifth Passage leads to a peaceful coexistence during these later years: Continue Renewing Love despite so many reasons not to.

THE SECOND TASK: CONTINUE RENEWING LOVE

Powerful deterrents block completion of this task. Plain old stagnation often becomes a major culprit. It's so easy to drift, to close into oneself, to do the same familiar thing, to take all the usual stuff (and that includes the spouse) for granted. Indeed, many older people mistake stagnation for peace.

People who stagnate quit growing. They don't check books out of the library anymore. They never get out to see new things or open the door to new ideas. They don't talk much to each other, and when they do it's usually to recheck the broadcast time of that favorite syndicated game show. Physical deterioration encourages and compounds stagnation. We see among our friends and in the clinic, persons who so gave up on life they died emotionally years before death took them physically.

Antagonism works against completion of the task also. Picture this scene: Grant's sister is going to take elderly Grant and Edna out for a drive. Grant and Edna will be sitting in back. Grant opens the door for Edna. Before he can buck the seatback forward for her, Edna plops down into the front seat. Furious that he must now walk clear around the car to the other door, Grant mutters obscenities at his wife of forty-three years. Half-deaf, oblivious old Edna riffles through her purse, blissfully unaware of the bitterness and anger. Within a few minutes she will snap and swear at him just as viciously. When Edna dies two years later, Grant literally falls apart, unable to face life without the dotty old lady he so openly despised.

This antagonism that develops between couples who have not completed previous tasks is, quaintly enough, not an opposite of love. Both people genuinely in love and those who are codependently enmeshed may become intensely antagonistic of their mates. Little annoyances grow into major grievances. Little habits become burrs beneath saddles. Lack of growth in one brings disrespect from the other; conversely, growth in one can make insecure the one not growing anymore.

By this stage, fortunately, the couple also have a lot going to help advance the task. Their long history together forms a powerful bond. Too, times change rapidly, and here is a couple who can collectively remember a lot of pretty ancient history. Those memories separate and elevate them from the younger generations to whom the word "Hitler" is part of that ancient history. "Remember what we were doing when Hitler invaded Poland?" "Yeah, and we were living on a hundred a month then. Comfortably." Ah, history.

One of the deterrents to completion of this second task is what we call, "Fifth Passage codependency." Younger people sensitive to codependency issues see codependency blossom in aging couples. Indeed, older people may see it in themselves, for the Fifth Passage is an easy place for a codependent relationship to develop or intensify. Friends are disappearing. The kids are gone. Should one of the couple fall into ill health, as Wynn did, they soon find themselves locked in a particularly virulent codependency.

Fifth Passage Codependency

Wynn and Maggie failed this second task of the Fifth Passage miserably. It tripped Wynn and very nearly unhorsed Maggie in the end. Wynn had let his horizons close in. He had worked his whole life. Now was the time to kick back and relax. Watch TV. Sleep. Vegetate.

Maggie didn't want to, but she let Wynn drag her into his enclosing world. She yearned to get out and do something. She didn't, because of Wynn. That was not love. That was enmeshment.

What's the difference? Love does what's best for both partners. Love serves the highest needs—stimulation, health. Once Wynn began to fail, the two became almost totally codependently enmeshed in each other. Wynn let her do everything; she refused to leave his side for a moment. When Wynn entered the nursing facility, Maggie spent months in an intense depression, blaming herself for putting her husband out of his own home. Her head saw that she was too old to physically handle him anymore, but her heart did not. It still loaded up on shame and guilt. She could not see how much he contributed to the situation by giving up. She only blamed herself. If only she had worked harder. If only she had . . . All of that is codependency speaking.

Over and over in our practice we see that persons with flawed love— people codependently enmeshed rather than enjoying Transcendent Love— do not become untangled by death. When one dies, the other almost always will also, three to nine months later.

Especially when debilitation occurs, husband and wife tend to slip into a codependent parent-child relationship unless both guard against it. That is, the "child" becomes dependent upon the "parent" for things the child could do alone if forced to, and the "parent" becomes codependent on the "child" in a desperate grasp at feeling needed, useful, necessary. When the child dies or enters institutional care, the parent is devastated. Should the parent die or be disabled, the child suffers as would an actual orphaned child.

Only a union of equals makes life as good as it can be right up to the end. Only a solid peer relationship, maintained to the end, assures that the surviving partner will make it past the end with a minimum of pain.

The Positive Side of Fifth Passage Codependency

But wait. In many ways, codependency in this passage can be positive. Provided that the codependency does not get too far out of hand, there are good points to it. Each partner gives the other a renewed purpose for living. Each has something to do, someone to take care of. The negative: When one spouse dies, the other loses that purpose in life.

Another positive: Both realize that they're not a burden on the kids (almost always a heavy concern). And their needs can still be met by each other. They can capture, possibly for the first time, a sense of unity, of togetherness.

A second deterrent to Renewing Love during the Fifth Passage is isolation.

Isolation

Since her husband's death fifteen years ago, Liz has been living in the two-story family home alone. She no longer tends the yard and garden. In fact, she no longer leaves the house at all. Her son in nearby Plainfield visits her regularly. He takes care of routine maintenance and brings her groceries. When she answers the door to him she does not say, "It's good to see you, Phil!" She says, "Why are *you* here?" Phil is an intrusion on Liz's life and, quite frankly, at age eighty-seven, she can't see the use of him.

Voluntary isolation, in which the person methodically and progressively cuts off friends, relations, and outside contacts, runs epidemic in the Fifth Passage. A married couple become withdrawn, not just from the world but from each other too. They stop connecting and become introspective.

We believe several things are going on here. Surrounded by painful realities, persons prefer the numbness of depression to facing the pain. Persons having trouble in Passage Five, feeling a fear of leaving and being left, will start shutting down the connections. They pursue the false belief that by severing themselves from all they hold dear, they won't get hurt when they lose it all. Isolation leads to its own depression and its own pain. It's an end run around the paradox of embracing, then releasing, life in order to enjoy it to the fullest.

Self-Blame

Some people go through life getting blamed. A few probably deserve it. Most do not. Many accept that blame for codependent reasons based in low self-esteem. As those persons enter the Fifth Passage and the stakes are raised, they enter a period of deep depression and self-castigation. They feel, we think, that if somehow they devalue themselves enough and blame themselves enough, they don't have to expect anything good or lasting from life.

We find this mind-set often in people who feel powerless about their lives. For example, teenagers, feeling powerless, engage in massive self-blame and self-destructive acts. So, too, do the elderly, who may be even more powerless than teens.

For forty-two years, Joyce lived with a domineering, abusive man. She tolerated it in the prior passages because she could busy herself with the kids, with the house, with their small business. She didn't have to dwell on her own frustration and unhappiness and, most important, she didn't have to work the problem out. When her loud, pushy husband announced to her that she was to blame for this difficulty and that, she accepted it. Why fight it? Now here they were in the final passage, both of them frightened, panicked by what they saw coming. Life had been lousy and now it was over. The only thing Joyce knew to do was put herself down further.

Needless to say, self-blame also leads to depression. As we talked to Joyce we saw her self-blame as a way to squash any spark of hope that life might be better or that the end of life is celebration of all she had. Depression is the most widespread problem among people in their Fifth Passage. It is the great emotional health epidemic. Tellingly, depression is also rife among teens, the other powerless group.

Gerontologists are starting to say that one-third to one-half of what is seen as dementia (a technical term for loss of brain capacity), senility, or early Alzheimer's may be misdiagnosed depression. Sleeping all the time, being unable to think or to concentrate—these are depression symptoms, as well as symptoms of aging problems. The person evidencing those symptoms is often treated like a child. That makes the person more depressed, destroying self-esteem, and that makes the depression worse yet, in turn making the symptoms worse . . . and the spiral descends until the person is considered too feebleminded to function.

Be alert to the fact that depression can be exacerbated by several drugs routinely prescribed for blood pressure and heart problems. But be careful. A dose that is therapeutic in a person aged sixty-five can be toxic to one seventy-five. Metabolism changes with age, and so therefore does drug tolerance. Toxicity can cause depression. We certainly don't recommend that persons throw their pills away, but we do caution you to monitor medications very closely. Adequate vigilance in this regard at sixty may not be adequate at seventy or eighty. Check and recheck with a doctor experienced in gerontology. Check also for contraindications; that is, the effects two or more drugs have when they're mixed together in the system. A heart medication is good. An allergy medication is good. But what do they do together?

The final deterrent to renewing intimacy is blaming your spouse for everything and anything.

Blame the Spouse

Instead of making peace with losses and changes, it's so much easier to just get stuck in the first step of the grief process, anger turned outward, and fire that anger at the nearest target. It's the opposite of self-blame and it does about the same thing! "It's your fault we never have enough money." "It's your fault the kids never come visit anymore." "It's your fault I have heart problems."

Psychologists refer to that as projection. The person who doesn't want to face some reality inside the self projects it onto another person, effectively getting rid of it. It's an effective, albeit twisted, way of handling any problems. Instead of working it out internally, you simply dump it externally onto your partner. Barring that, dump it on someone else—an adult child, perhaps, or maybe even the government.

We find that factors in people's lives predisposing them to this were at work in them from the beginning of their marriage. Through prior passages, this projection simmered, tolerable. Now that real problems loom—death and disability—the coping mechanism escalates into something explosive. The person not willing to go through all the grief steps personally, resolving the pain, suffering through to resolution, can duck the pain in one of two ways: get stuck in the grief step and refuse to go on or project everything onto the spouse.

Rarely is projection displayed as dramatically as a recent case in the newspapers. A minister was counseling an elderly couple when the man pulled out a gun and shot his wife. Projection is usually more subtle. But what went on below the conscious level of that man's mind bears scrutiny. His survival method, his way of dodging death, was to lay all blame on his wife. Then, symbolically, like a true scapegoat or animal sacrifice, she could carry it away into death. Through her he got rid of it all.

We meet many people in Passage Five who do the same thing but without the gun. A woman announces to her spouse on the eve of their fortieth anniversary, "I'm divorcing you." She is killing off the other person symbolically. A man or woman may burn with such anger that he or she blocks the spouse out completely—another symbolic death.

Usually, a person blaming another excessively will at some level feel a lot of self-imposed guilt. It's probably a mix of true guilt and false guilt. Instead of grieving through that, sifting out false guilt from that which is authentic, the person turns it all into anger and dumps it on someone else to get rid of it.

We've looked at the deterrents to Renewing Love, now let's answer that all-important question: *Is it worth investing any further intimacy in this union? It's all going to be gone soon anyway.*

THE INTIMACY INVESTMENT

Mary Alice Minirth has already thought out her answer to this universal question: "Persons on their deathbed don't ask for their banker or interior decorator or old boss from work. They want their spouse. Their best friend. I watched my dad do that."

People in extremity want the company of persons with whom they have developed intimate relationships. Not economic or vocational or even medical relationships. Investment in intimacy offers rich returns when the chips are down.

But when relationships as well as people grow old, when to renew intimacy seems old hat, not to mention a bother, when the sexual aspect of intimacy is grinding to a halt, how does one dream again the old dream? How does one build intimacy at this late stage of the game?

Brian Newman's grandfather commented to Debi about her grandmother-in-law, "I still think she's as pretty as she was at sixteen." They were well into their seventies.

Blindness? No. Appreciation. He saw delicate, translucent skin, not wrinkles; he looked at her form and recalled the allure she had always held for him. He didn't see as a camera sees; history was shaping his vision.

You do the same thing with your flower beds. What do you see in your flower beds on a winter day? Your eyes see a few brown stalks, the grave markers of beauty long dead. But your memory sees the columbines and dahlias that will grow there six months from now. When you admire a rose bush in bloom you see a glorious cascade of color, despite that over ninety percent of the actual two-dimensional plant surface meeting your eyes is foliage. Your eye skips over the foliage to focus on the flowers, minimizing the green and maximizing the color. Brian's grandfather was being honest. He saw what had been and what was still there; he did not bother seeing the ravages of age. He was not in denial; he was simply seeing beyond the eyes, for true vision sees beyond the physical image. That's appreciation.

Sexual Intimacy

Sex at seventy? Eighty? Some wink and dismiss the thought immediately. Others know better. As couples enter the Fifth Passage of marriage sexual interest gradually declines, but rarely disappears entirely, even in the oldest.[1] Most often the decline in frequency of intercourse is due to male sexual dysfunction, usually erectile failure, which is either a normal part of the aging process or the result of disease. Because there is a gradual decline in the conduction velocity of the penile nerves, greater stimulation is required. As a result of this and the fact that blood circulation to the penis is less, the elderly man's penis takes longer to become erect, is less rigid, and remains erect for a shorter period of time.

Yet Passage Five can be an opportunity for sexuality rather than a time to abandon it.

Sometimes, for instance, you may improve an aging couple's sex life by reassuring the male partner of his capacity to perform. That's one conclusion drawn from a study of thirty-two married couples, age fifty to seventy-seven, in which the husband had undergone prostate surgery. If the man believed his sexual function was unimpaired, he had fewer problems with arousal and orgasm.[2]

Another positive factor can be the importance of relationships at this time of life.

At the clinic we often say that relationships are everything to young children. As we mature, material objects and financial security become too important. Now in the Fifth Passage we come full circle again. Couples begin to reorder their priorities. Relationships become most important. Not the mortgage. Or the bank account. Or the membership in the country club. All of that pales in comparison to relationships with other human beings and with God.

Since relationships are everything and since sexuality allows us to better experience a sense of union with another person, my spouse, sexuality in Passage Five can, in fact, be deeper than ever before. Sex in Passage Three, for instance, sometimes has specific goals, like procreating the next generation and relieving tension. Now in Passage Five these two purposes slip away. The emphasis is on union and the joy of that experience.

Couples also have an opportunity for appreciating the interrelationship between sexuality and spirituality, since people of this age are often more attuned to the spiritual than younger people. Experts have long said that there is special interrelationship between these two, rather than a dichotomy. Sexuality and spirituality can be mutually reinforcing.

We believe that sexual intercourse is much more than a biological or physiological function. In the marriage relationship, sex can be a sacrament. During the sexual experience we are able to participate momentarily in a symbolic way in a special type of spiritual union. For example, people tell us they feel:

- a sense of ecstatic surrender and yielding.
- a feeling that time is standing still.
- a special sense of bliss.
- a sense of empowerment.
- and finally a sense of transcendent union during the sexual experience—all emotions of the spiritual experience.

Stop a moment and think about your own attitudes about sexuality in this passage of life. Does your mind tell you, I can't or shouldn't be sexual in Passage Five? If so, think of the roadblocks to sexuality—the messages from our culture, from the church, from your family of origin, and from this marriage—that might be influencing you.

From Our Culture

All of us have seen the cartoons in magazines and newspapers that portray sexual intimacy at this stage of life as humorous. Such jokes build a bias within us that says, "Sex after sixty is a no-no."

What cultural biases have affected you?

_____

_____

Now think about rewriting those biases into new endorsements for Passage Five sexuality. (*"Such cartoons are ludicrous. Sexuality is valuable and important in these years."*)

_____

_____

From the Church

One couple came to us after the husband had undergone urinary tract surgery. The doctor told him that sex was still possible; it would just take a little time and effort to retrain the nerve pathways. His wife rejected the idea so they decided to counsel with their minister. "This is a time when we are to put down our sexuality," the minister told them, "and lift God up."

A couple who accepts this minister's underlying premise—that sexuality will inhibit our ability to reconcile with God—is put in a real dilemma during this passage. Spirituality or sexuality—never both? As we said before, we believe that the two are interrelated rather than dichotomous.

Have you heard some statements about sex after sixty in a church setting? Mention them below:

_____

_____

Now think about rewriting them into endorsements of sex at seventy. (*"I know (or will look for) couples in the church who can be role models to me. Their sexual relationship encourages us to sustain our sexuality."*)

_____

_____

From Your Family of Origin

We also pick up attitudes about geriatric sex from Mom and Dad. If they moved to separate bedrooms in their sixties, the message about sex rang out loud and clear.

Did your parents give you any messages like this? List them here.

_____

_____

Now consider revising these messages with new endorsements. (*"I have chosen to reject my parents' model. My spouse and I shall remain physically close in the same bedroom for the rest of our years or as long as this is possible."*)

_____

_____

From This Marriage

The man who wanted to reestablish sexual intimacy with his wife after his surgery was bumping into his wife's inhibitions.

Is there some resistance in your marriage?

_____

_____

Consider confronting your spouse with new endorsements for sexuality. (*"I love you and me and our marriage enough that I will continue to reinvite you to move back into a sexual union, not because I want to control you but as an expression of my love for you and our marriage."*) _____

_____

We've found that couples in the Fifth Passage can have an unusual perspective toward sex. Their sexual relationship can go either way. If good sexual channels are open (if there is no real physical impediment to sex), this experience can be deeper than ever. If, however, illness or the death of a spouse makes sex impossible, spouses have a better capacity to accommodate that situation.

A true paradox exists here. At this time when we are nearing the end of our story, we can feel greater sexual fulfillment rather than the leftovers, as some would have us believe.

Communion

Another breeding ground of intimacy can also work well: simply sitting down and talking to each other. There are important topics to be discussed in this passage too. When will you transmit your material and financial legacies to the next generations? Have you both agreed to the provisions of a will? Is it up to date? What family history do you want to make certain the next generation knows? How have you arranged for its transmission? Explore each other's thoughts.

"We've been building intimacy for half a century," the old man complains. "Aren't we there yet?"

"Remember we've been talking about growth, as well. Young people can hardly avoid growing. Older people can keep growing. Growth means change. What was true of your partner last week or even yesterday may not be true anymore. Or the truth may have shifted. Intimacy means knowing your partner now. As growth changes the two of you, continuing intimacy keeps both of you caught up on the differences."

Improved intimacy is, in many ways, a form of growth itself.

Horizons

Maggie sat in a little cafe by the city park, watching kids feed popcorn to the ducks. "I thought my world ended when Wynn went into the home," she said to us. "It took me about six months to emerge from the cloud I had wrapped around me. It was a wrenching good-bye." She smiled. "You were talking about good-byes being the opened doors to hellos. It was. My life has been one hello after another lately."

Maggie visits Wynn daily. She brings him treats and talks to him. She shares all the mail. But she has shoved her horizons back out, far beyond the old limits. It was hard at first. The easiest thing is to give up and let the world close in. Maggie had to fight that.

She attended a caning workshop to learn the craft and recaned the seats of those four old chairs that had been hanging up in the attic. "They turned out beautifully," she purred. Now she's weaving new seats for her son-in-law's wood-canvas canoe.

At first Maggie had to make herself join others for lunch somewhere, or invite old family friend Mrs. Smits over for dinner. These days, though, she looks forward to it. "Do you know what that Smits did?" she fumed. (She never referred to Mrs. Smits simply as Smits. It was *that* Smits.) "I made pig stomach and invited—"

"Pig stomach?" we asked cautiously.

"We used to stuff a real pig stomach with it, back when we butchered. I don't use a stomach; I just make up the sausage with celery and potatoes and onions without the stomach part. But we still call it pig stomach.

"I invited *that* Smits over and then I was going to take some up to the home for Wynn. *That* Smits asked if she could have some of the leftovers for lunch, and didn't she pop out a plastic box and take almost the whole thing! So I had to make more to take up to Wynn."

Maggie's disgust was tinged with a smile in the corner of her mouth. Her pig stomach was still the best in the county and worth fighting over.

Check Out Your Horizons

Assuming that you are entering your Fifth Passage or approaching it— it's never too early to expand your horizons—how are your horizons doing? Check the statements below that apply to you:

_____ "There is one skill *(like Maggie's cooking)*—or more—that I can do better than anyone else around. It is (they are):

_____

_____ ."

_____ "My spouse can say the same:

_____

_____ ."

_____ "I have at least one new skill or craft at my command that I didn't know how to do five years ago. It is:

_____ ."

_____ "My spouse can say the same:

_____ ."

_____ "If I needed a friend this minute I could call any of three persons. They are:

_____

_____

_____ ."

_____ "My spouse has three also. They are:

_____

_____

_____ ."

_____ "My spouse and I know the three best places—restaurants or cafes—within a twenty-mile radius to eat lunch. They are:

_____

_____

_____ ."

_____ "We know two excellent little places to buy a good breakfast. They are:

_____

_____ ."

_____ "We have seen at least one Academy-Award-nominated film in the last year. It was: _____ ."

_____ "My spouse and/or I each have our own library cards. The best book I've checked out in the last month is:

_____."

Fifth Passage couples have been given a special gift, the transcendent perspective. We've alluded to that gift in this chapter. We'll talk more about that special blessing in the next.

22

CAN YOU ACHIEVE A TRANSCENDENT PERSPECTIVE?

*N*asal *cannula*. Plural, *cannulae*. Much more official and scientific sounding than *little plastic tubes down your nose*. The Latin name can add much gloss to an otherwise unpleasant item. Carl Warden shook his head and shifted in his easy chair beside Bess's bed. His brain sure came up with some stupid, silly stuff when it wandered.

Bess Warden mumbled something and raised one shoulder. Carl stood. Gently, he helped her roll onto her side. Her spiderweb of nasal cannulae and IVs followed.

He patted the frail shoulder firmly. "Someone at the door, probably Butterfield. I'll be back in a shake, pet."

She mumbled a response as he left the room. His heels clicked hollow in the hallway. The house seemed so much bigger, so much emptier, these last few months. A lot of living happened in this house. A lot of living. And now, a dying.

It was nurse Janis Butterfield, all right, all six feet, two hundred pounds of her. Had Butterfield been a Texan, Santa Ana would never have made it through the door of the Alamo. She marched in without fanfare, a rather nervous young man at her heels. "Hello, Carl. This is Bob McGruder, social services. He kept calling me up with questions about your case so I said, 'Bob, for crying out loud, come along with me this afternoon and ask Carl yourself.' So here he is. Did she sleep last night?"

"Pretty well. Pulse was a little shaky this morning, but she seems stronger now."

Butterfield nodded brusquely. "I'll give her her injections and catch the record up. Keep this McGruder out of my hair, will you?" She charged off down the hall.

"Carl Warden, Mr. McGruder." Carl chuckled and extended his hand. "You look a little, ah, nonplussed. I take it you didn't meet Butterfield before today."

The man grinned suddenly and relaxed as he shook hands. "That obvious, huh? She comes on a bit strong, but I don't think I've ever met a nurse who knows her job better."

"You're right. Butterfield is the best there is. Bess and I are blessed by her. Come sit down. What do you want to know?" Carl led the way out to the patio. A moist breeze tempered the bright Indian summer sun. Beautiful afternoon. Perfect afternoon. Bess's last autumn. Carl settled into a deck chair.

The social worker perched on a wrought iron chair at the patio table and popped open his briefcase. "Ms. Butterfield says you and Elizabeth have been married forty-nine years. Elizabeth is—let's see; here it is—Elizabeth is sixty-seven and you're sixty-eight. Her cancer was diagnosed just a few months ago, is that right?"

"Quite a jolt. She was feeling fine, and then one day she started feeling poorly and bam. We weren't expecting something like this. Guess we should have been, but we weren't."

"Only marriage for both of you, I assume."

Carl smiled. "High school sweethearts. Bess is the only girl I ever really fell for. Married late in '42 when I was on furlough, just before I shipped out to North Africa."

"Three children."

"Four. Our Becky died when she was two."

"Of . . . ?"

"Polio."

Mr. McGruder stopped and looked at Carl a minute. He spoke softly, thoughtfully. "How times change. I've never seen a case of polio. The Salk and Sabin vaccines came into use just before I was born. You've seen a lot of life, Mr. Warden, haven't you? Advances. More than a few reverses, too, I'll wager. A lot of pain."

Carl pursed his lips and thought about that a moment. "Yeah, I suppose you could say that. You could say Notre Dame cathedral is just another church too. Pain is part of it. I'm facing a lot of pain, losing Bess, and she has a lot of it right now. But it's not that. It's so much more than that.

Limiting the measure of a lifetime to pain and joy is like asking a concert pianist to play Tchaikovsky's First with two fingers. It's—'' Carl waved his hand helplessly. "I wish I could convey how very much it all is."

"No regrets? No reservations?"

"I wouldn't trade it for anything."

TRANSCENDENT LOVE

Were you to ask Carl Warden at twenty-five if he loved his Bess, he'd shout "Yes!" exuberantly. Ask him at thirty and he'd say, "Yeah, of course." At forty, the answer might be, "Deeply." Now, at the close of a life well lived, he might reply, "More than the day we married." And he would be speaking the truth, to the infinite power.

When the person who has made peace with life, with its warts and all, bumps into mortality and loss, those seemingly negative realities become fitting and appropriate conclusions to a life well lived. At the very least, they become something tolerable and tolerated. "Well lived" here does not mean brilliantly successful in every facet of life, but a life that is accepted as it is.

Transcendent love is a profound and peaceful perspective toward your partner and toward life. Are your passages, particularly the Fifth, going smoothly or have they been pockmarked with setbacks and tragedy? Transcendent love does not depend upon smoothness. It's not a tidy ribbon tied on the Fifth Passage package. It means, rather, that there has been a quantum shift in perspective. It is not that you somehow become oblivious to pain, that you suddenly can say an easy good-bye to all you cherish, but that you can rise above it.

"Let's say I'm trying to describe how ice cream tastes," Dr. Hemfelt explains. "I can lecture you for hours, and you still won't *really* know what ice cream is like. Similarly, I can hear about the peace of this Transcendent Love in my youth, but I cannot possibly know what it tastes like until I have the maturity, the wisdom, the life experience to get it from my head into my heart.

"It is not a cheap or shallow answer to the inevitable pain of losses. It's a profound dynamic. The older person can tell me what he sees from the top of the mountain, but it will all be abstract until I get there myself. Among the earliest Christian thinkers, there existed a long-standing tradition that as one moves closer to death, life becomes a more grace-filled experience."

Two major components make Transcendent Love what it is. The first is a paradox: The more I am able to let go of things, then ironically the more I can truly value and cherish them. "Things" are human relationships, the bank account, physical health, material things—whatever I hold dear. Many persons facing advancing age feel that the key to transcendence seems to be acting on one or the other. Either I hang on with a possessive death grip (literally), or I have to devalue the things I care about, through estrangement, bitterness, anger. Either/or won't do it. The magic of this transcendent perspective lies in discovering the paradox.

Release things. By that we mean realize how transient they are and that they cannot really be yours. As an example, consider an average couple in the Fifth Passage, their children grown now. Only if they say good-bye to their children's childhood, acknowledging the fact they are now peer adults outside parental control and possession, will that couple really appreciate, enjoy, and cherish their relationship with their children. Instead of spoiling or ending the relationship, releasing the kids allows parents freedom to pursue an easier, broader friendship not possible in any previous passages.

Can you think of friends or relatives who reversed this paradox, thus falling away from the transcendent perspective? Frequently we see an aging parent try to be more domineering and controlling (either through direct control or guilt-generating weakness). "If I can force you to love me, and if I cling tightly," the feeling goes, "I'll never have to face saying good-bye to you."

John Bradshaw, author of *Bradshaw on the Family* and *Homecoming*, reminds his radio listeners that they will leave or lose everyone and everything that they know in this human life. Such an ordinary truth—and yet, how extraordinary it is.

To the person who masters a Transcendent Love toward the spouse and toward life itself, the negative nature of that truth falls away, revealing dazzling hellos and doors of opportunity.

The other major component of Transcendent Love is the discovery of the relative disposition of things. Often people report that a brush with death changes the way they see things. What's important? Not important? What do I value? What counts and what doesn't? The aging process by its very nature forces that new perspective on the person who is willing to accept it.

This is why grandparents can be so much freer and easier about parenting grandchildren than can the children's parents. The grandparents' view of relative disposition has shifted. In the course of eternity, what difference does it make if Junior doesn't drink all his grape juice? So what if some of it lands on the rug? Junior is more important than a million rugs.

In a closing scene in Thornton Wilder's stage classic *Our Town*, the deceased Emily wants to witness one day in her life, something Wilder's dead were permitted to do. She watches a birthday from her past and gapes, stunned at how people attend so earnestly to trivia, allowing small irritations and distractions to spoil the moment. "Doesn't anyone really live life while they have it?" she cries. Her perspective had shifted, you see. From a viewpoint beyond death she realized how valuable each day is. So does the person in Transcendent Love.

The third task of the Fifth Passage of marriage is to achieve a transcendent perspective.

THE THIRD TASK: ACHIEVE A TRANSCENDENT PERSPECTIVE

Carl Warden watched Bob McGruder and Nurse Butterfield ride away in Butterfield's snazzy little sports car. He smiled. She refused to drive the official county car with the emblem on the door; "I look too much like a bureaucrat in those things," she grumped. He went back inside.

Was Bess awake? He walked quietly back to the bedroom. She was.

He rubbed her frail, bony little shoulder. "Chicken for supper?"

"Sounds fine," she murmured.

Why did he ask her when, until he ran down to the store, all they had in the fridge was a chicken? Because he didn't want her to lose her sense of being part of the partnership. Was that it? He thought a moment. That was it. They had always run decisions past each other, usually as a courtesy. No reason to change now.

With a heavy sigh he wandered out to the kitchen to see what else was in the fridge.

Carl was facing a severe good-bye. He knew that. So will you—either you or your spouse, no matter what passage your marriage is in.

We mentioned that Transcendent Love is a perspective toward life. Transcendent Love is not a process people can go through; it's a true shift in perspective. How does one make the shift?

Consider each of two contrasting statements. The first statement can be attributed to a young or immature outlook, the second to Transcendent Love. Where is the link; what was the shift? Apply the two statements to your own thinking and your own circumstance. Which of these statements matches your own perspective?

Suffering is meaningless vs. suffering creates new places in the human heart and soul. "Suffering builds character," the father in the *Calvin and Hobbes* cartoon remonstrates. "I don't want any more character," Calvin pouts.

When suffering looms, a part of us repeats Calvin's protest. Who needs this? But a greater part of us can know that when inevitable suffering comes, it can serve a constructive purpose if we allow it to. Remember the paradox upon which Transcendent Love depends? Only as I am willing to release it can I enjoy and appreciate it. By bringing to sharper focus the finite limitations of human life, suffering helps the sufferer see life clearly. By seeing it clearly and in a way touching it tangibly, the sufferer can more easily release that life. It's hard enough to work in abstracts; fuzzy abstracts are hardest of all to grasp. The end result: the sufferer better enjoys that life which he or she has.

Leon Blau wrote, "There are places in the human heart which do not yet exist. Pain must be that they may be."

Joni Eareckson Tada, while never welcoming quadriplegia, has dedicated her life and ministry to helping others understand the extraordinary blessings that come out of extreme suffering such as hers. Suffering itself helped her make the shift to her transcendent perspective earlier than most. Suffering, then, need not be a roadblock or a barrier, but a facilitator—a point of leverage to push you over into that rewarding and comforting perspective of Transcendent Love.

Aging equals loneliness vs. aging equals greater intimacy. From the transcendent perspective, you've been working on getting to know your spouse better through four passages encompassing many years. Intimacy has been growing. Besides, you now know yourself much better than you did even a few years ago.

An elderly patient of Dr. Hemfelt's offered a wonderful insight. When Robert kidded her, "I see you've put most of your denial down," she replied, "After you've been through all I've been through, you learn not to lie, especially to yourself."

With years of living behind you, you probably have a better capacity to cherish the relationships in your life. As an opposite of loneliness, you find relationships more enriching.

A recent survey asked people in nursing homes what physical possession they valued most. First on the list everywhere was "pictures of relatives." Rob them of their TV and their VCR, but don't dare touch the photos by their bed.

As couples in the Fifth Passage sift through memories, using the measure of relative disposition, they come to cherish relationships more than younger people do. "This is what is important; that is not." Dr. Paul Warren of the Minirth-Meier Clinic in Dallas teaches even very young children in his counsel that relationships are everything. That comes to fruit here.

Physical loss is absolute loss vs. physical loss is spiritual emancipation. Dr. James Dobson commented of material possessions, "Everything I own owns me." There is nothing wrong with having physical possessions, but they all come with a price tag. To the extent we take them on, they drain us, deplete us. They require emotional and spiritual maintenance.

As persons move through this final passage, they either gradually begin to let go of the physical or cling to it inordinately. As the significance of the physical (health, possessions, all things physical) wanes, the persons begin to pump more psychic energy into nonmaterial things, including the hereafter and love itself. Persons making a desperate effort to hang onto the physical are drained by it. This depletes the emotional and spiritual energy needed to shift up into the transcendent perspective.

You can compare this phenomenon roughly with the old "Star Trek" concept of warp drive, speeds faster than the speed of light. In nearly every episode some crisis would deplete the starship's power, preventing it from making the leap to warp speed, condemning it to slog along at sublight.

People make the shift into transcendence in part by gradually surrendering ownership of the material world around them. Instead of feeling like a loss, this surrender becomes liberating. Many couples who planned wisely will start bequeathing some of their money before death. There are often tax advantages, true. But the deeper meaning is to divest oneself of the material, lightening the load.

All through his Fourth Passage, a man named Rader fought with his son over control of their joint business. Dad would hand the reins over to his son so he could retire. Then, he'd seize control again, dissatisfied with the tack his son was taking. Both men ended up in our counsel; it was that or kill each other. Then Rader's wife died suddenly and unexpectedly. Her death was the jolt, the shock, that bumped Rader up into a true transcendent perspective. He realized he no longer wanted or needed control, and could at last turn the business over to his son. His deep regret: Because it came after her death, he could never share that Transcendent Love with his wife.

Time is rushing, slipping away vs. time, being eternal, can slow down. Find a conventional watch or clock face with a sweep second hand. Stare at it for a few minutes. The second hand will visibly slow down. In theory, if astronauts orbit in a particular direction long enough and fast enough, they will return to earth younger than when they left. Time is an amazing flexible phenomenon.

To four-year-old Rachel, the week prior to her birthday is a year long. An afternoon in the park, with plenty of fun and running around, seems like days. Time elongates for children and a year is a long, long time. Not so the person in midlife. The thirty-nine-year-old celebrates a birthday and the next day must celebrate the fortieth. A lot of studio greeting cards and jokes tease about how time speeds up as we get older. But time does an about-face in the Fifth Passage, for those people who can accept life. Instead of flying rapidly, accelerating up to the time of death, time pauses, to let those people smell the flowers.

An acquaintance, Tony, who is well over sixty-five, phrased it this way: "My wife and I do a lot of kayaking. We've ridden some rough stuff—class three water. The cascades spill you this way and that, slam you around, send you shooting down the rapids. Heavy water like that, though, has still spots. You swing your craft around and stick it in the shelter of a boulder, or in a little cove to the side called an eddy, and the water can rush by all it wants. You're on calm water. We call it eddying out. Then you eddy back in and it's down the chute you go again."

People with a transcendent perspective find themselves eddying out of the rush of time now and then. They can savor moments of time; literally, time stands still. "A precious moment when I stepped out of the stream of time," Tony said, "was when I kissed my new little great-grandson on the head. There he was, eight weeks old, and—" Tony's voice catches.

A woman at a bedside vigil with her dying mate reported that during those days, there were many moments when time seemed to stand still.

Another way this phenomenon shows itself is that older people have the capacity to slow down. The reduced pace may be physically necessary to some degree. But also, it reflects the shift of perspective inside. The person no longer has to go faster and faster. If it takes fifteen minutes to walk out to the mailbox, that's all right. The youngster might call it wasting time. The person with a new perspective will not.

"It's like the stream ripping down through the canyon, and then dumping out into a lake or reservoir," Tony relates. "Suddenly it's serene. You go only as fast as you want to. That's what it feels like to me."

What Tony was really doing had far more profound significance than simply appreciating time. He was preparing to move into eternal time. Making peace here with the temporal boundaries, he was starting to leave behind his temporal perspective and shift into the eternal, non-time perspective.

Christian theologians phrase it as, "It's important to try to learn how to live in the eternal now." Long before death, we can discover small ways to step out of the stream of time, providing glimpses and foretastes of what eternity is like. We often do this when we make time to watch the peaceful motion of the rippling waters of a beautiful lake or stroll a lush, green golf course as the sun is setting. We do it in the most significant way when we join in worship of God with others or hold hands together in a circle of prayer. We find profound peace.

Beginning the Journey

We cannot overemphasize the role good preparation plays in dealing with death—your loved ones' and yours.

"That sounds so morbid!" you protest.

"Not at all," we reply. When you expect a baby's arrival you have the diapers, the necessary furniture, the baby clothes ready and waiting. When you go into the hospital for surgery, you make arrangements in advance. You don't troop off on vacation without packing a suitcase. Preparation smoothes the way when any unusual event looms on the horizon.

Mary Alice Minirth's father prepared for his wife financially. He set up funds and accounts for her and put their financial records in order. Mentally and emotionally, they prepared themselves as best they could by talking about what the future held, reminiscing about the past, grieving the approaching end, rejoicing in the safety which their risen Lord promises.

During the last year before his death, Mary Alice's mother received important support from her church. Prayer support was primary. Prayer truly does effect amazing things. If you can do nothing else for friends or loved ones facing loss, pray for them. The pastor and congregation of her parents' church made certain their practical needs were met. In your church, do you have elderly members with everyday needs you can meet?

"At the funeral, that support never faltered," says Mary Alice. "Pastor said to Mom, 'Now, sister Frances, you know that half of you is gone.' He counseled her with facts. 'You have to realize this and this.' He never whitewashed bad points. But he reminded her 'God will sustain.'"

Mary Alice has watched as her mother has adjusted to living alone. She and six other widows in her church support each other. They have lunch together; they attend a seniors' club. Mary Alice calls her, asking about activities, and encouraging them. The daughter is helping the mother to avoid shutting off.

Both of them know that to shut off is dangerous. "Circumstances happen," Mary Alice concludes. "They're not your choice. But your response to them is your choice."

Because Carl and Bess Warden felt in the pink of health, they did not concern themselves with the legal, medical, and social aspects of sudden illness. Somehow, it almost seems like a twisted sort of wish-fulfillment to read up on death and illness. If you ignore it, it won't knock on your door.

It doesn't work that way, of course. Your head tells you so, although your heart still shies away from the subject. So put your head to work. Carl had to come from behind when Bess got sick. He did not know what options were available to him. Did she have to leave her home? Who would pay for what? Was their insurance adequate? What about MediCare? He did a lot of cramming in a hurry, and even then wasn't sure that the perfect solution didn't lie out there somewhere undetected.

A friend of ours confides, "This sounds morbid, but I have a list of things to do in the first three days if my husband dies suddenly. I keep it in the lockbox in the closet. If something should happen to him, I'll get it out and just go down the list. Whom to notify first, whom to write letters to, whom to call about arrangements . . . I figure I'll be in no mental condition to have to work all that out when it happens."

She's being wise, not morbid. Her husband should be doing exactly the same thing.

Preparation—learning in advance what agencies and services are available, what insurance payment plans will and will not cover, what each spouse must do and when—opens several bright doors. One of them is peace of mind. You have the future nailed down as well as you can. You don't have to fret about it and dread it so much, should the time arise. You have just eliminated a whole category of worries. Also, preparation provides you and your children with a solid plan of action, yet not something set in cement. If circumstances alter, the plan can be altered; you have something to start with.

Preparation serves another important purpose. It brings fears and sad thoughts into clear focus. Only when you acknowledge them can you deal with them. That's right. You want to grieve your spouse's mortality (and your own) just as you grieved the other imperfections of life.

THE NEW CONTRACT

"Oh, come on!" you fume. "I'm decades and decades old. Not a new contract at this stage of the game!"

"Sure. Why not?" Whether your future will be two days or two decades, make it the best future possible.

We suggest the new contract might address the following areas as well as others you recognize as being important to you.

Adjust for a Life Without Each Other

Financially

Knowing the end was near, Mary Alice's father set up a good financial plan for his wife. He had handled the finances throughout their life together and he did it now. In your case, you may wish for one person to do it or both to do it together. But write it in.

In practical ways: Can your spouse negotiate the stairs in the house? How about tomorrow? Can your spouse reach the top shelves in the pantry? Can he or she safely use the bathroom facilities? Take care of yard work? Can your spouse do all the ordinary everyday activities without your physical help? Is now the time to look at a smaller, ground-floor-only dwelling? Contract for your future dwelling according to the needs of both. Now's the time to get tough with each other about practical matters.

Brian's grandparents lived in a neighborhood that changed around them. It began as a neighborhood of people their own age, background, and financial status. All that was different by the time of their deaths. Because they owned their home and loved it, they stayed, until the fabric of the neighborhood altered so much they became outsiders. They didn't feel free to visit friends. They weren't as mobile as they might be elsewhere. Consider your own circumstance. If it's similar to theirs, should you bite the bullet and change your residence, your neighborhood, your style of living? Write it in.

Make it a contract item to keep the will up to date, as well as any preliminary funeral arrangements, if you so choose. Most funeral homes will help you make arrangements in advance of need. Though it sounds grisly, it relieves the surviving spouse of much additional stress, confusion, and heartache. If you've not formulated a will yet, by all means do so now. Contract to put everything in writing. Everything. Quite probably your executor will not be able to honor oral requests. Put them on paper.

Emotionally

How do you want your spouse to help you prepare emotionally for what is coming? Write it in as a specific contract point. Listen carefully to what your spouse expresses as needs. Explain your own needs clearly. Then discuss how best you can help each other.

Decide What to Give the World

There are a lot of people and causes who can still use you, and use you in two capacities. You can pray, and you can participate—Lord willing, you can do both.

Wise Christians write their prayer life right into the contract. How exactly will each spouse be accountable to the other regarding prayer? How does the wife want her husband to pray for her; how does he want her to pray for him? What causes and persons are one spouse's concern only, and which are mutual concerns? United prayer works miracles.

Write in your contract just what each of you plans to do (usually on a weekly basis) for a cause or charity. That cause or charity might be something far-reaching and international in scope. It might be your own son or granddaughter right here, who's having problems and needs a temporary hand.

Brian Newman points out, "A lot of men and women in their twenties and thirties seek out the wisdom of elders because they need it so. How do I get along? What do I do now? What does all this mean? Only older, wiser persons can fill that need. Mentoring is an important and valuable gift older people in any passage can give persons younger than themselves."

What is involved specifically? Says Brian, "A mentor has information and emotions in his or her background that were lacking in many people's childhoods, things that ought to be there but weren't. Younger people are looking for guidance from a mature mentor to encourage, support, and direct them."

For years, business has been using mentors to prepare the next generation. The principle extends far beyond business.

"A mentor can help shape your character," Brian explains. "He or she is a coach pushing you to improve. The mentor cares enough about you to kick you in the pants and then put his or her arms around you. So many people either missed it growing up or still need it.

"At each passage, we all desire someone from the next stage. It's a universal need for someone bigger and older, more mature and stronger, who cares and is involved in our life."

Do you see opportunity for mentoring? It need not be in your family. Even if you see none, write in a statement about it, either to seek out a mentoring situation or to accept it.

Contract for Growth

Write in some sort of accountability toward each other regarding horizons. Help each other prevent your horizons from diminishing. Keep each other growing. Sample statements: "We will try at least one new food every month." "We will try a new ethnic restaurant each month." "We will each check out at least two books per week from the library or bookmobile, books neither of us have read before."

Intimacy should still be growing too. You're not too old for touching and hugging, even if sexual potency has abated. Unless you do a lot of spontaneous hugging and caressing, write into the contract a minimal amount of such closeness. Five minutes of hugging a day, at least, or whatever both of you feel comfortable with.

Revision

Make certain you write into the contract a specified time each year to review it. Most financial counselors ask you to review your program annually. Doctors expect you to get an annual physical, a Pap smear, an occasional mammogram. These are all preventive steps designed to catch small problems and correct them while they are still small. It's the same way with your contract.

You should update your will if your circumstances change or when a new grandchild or great-grandchild enters the family. Update your contract as well.

HOW WELL HAVE WE DONE?

Check the statements below that reflect your situation in Passage Five.

_____ "I have put away my old dream that my spouse can fulfill every need I have. Completely put it away."

_____ "I sure don't look forward to it, but I'm prepared to lose my spouse when the time comes."

_____ "I can picture three things I would do for myself, should I lose my spouse in the next ten years:

_____

_____

_____."

_____ "I can name three friends with whom I'd like to spend the day. I can trust them with most (but not all) secrets.

_____

_____

_____."

Now discuss these four points with your spouse. How can you help each other come to terms with the future to the best possible degree?

GOOD-BYE . . .

Carl Warden wandered down the street to the park and the quiet duck pond. His house was bustling just now with friends, neighbors, kids, and grandkids. He wanted to get away a few minutes. Then he'd jump back in, making the final arrangements.

The Renewed Marriage Contract

1. Statement of affirmation; at least one attribute each person admires and appreciates in the other

2. Statement of extent of commitment to the marriage

3. Promise of fidelity

4. Statement of faith, embracing:
   a. Each person's individual statement of faith
   b. Clearly stated common ground
   c. Statement of tolerance (and limits of tolerance)

5. Statement of recognition of old, dysfunctional hidden agendas

6. Declaration of new agendas to redress dysfunctions

7. Sexual contract, including:
   a. Recognition of difficulties or shortcomings in present sexual relations
   b. Steps to improve relations and/or explore new techniques
   c. Details of frequency if frequency is an issue

8. Review of items in first contract, with updates and revisions as necessary

9. Details of everyday life (request for romantic nights out) established through give-and-take (be specific)

They had talked about this day, Bess and he. They speculated what it would be like. They joked about it. Joking helps relieve the pain of reality. On one occasion, Bess explained what she wanted in the way of final rites. On another, Carl talked about what he wanted. Neither of them bound the other to their wishes with idle promises. Each knew what the other wanted; that was enough. They discussed which children would receive what among their personal possessions. Bess wanted Annie to have the mantel clock her own great-grandfather brought from the old country. Annie appreciated that kind of thing. Carl would see to it.

Bess had also asked Carl to sing at her funeral. He decided he would not do that. His voice no longer had the quality it used to. He'd let his buddy Al do the singing; Al was still a hearty baritone. Besides, his voice would probably break. His heart had already.

Al would fly in this afternoon; Rob was probably already on his way to the airport to pick him up. Not everyone was as lucky as Carl, who would have all his family around him at the funeral. In fact, Carl was twice lucky. Between him and all his kids and grandkids there were no rifts, no factions, no guarded hostility.

That wasn't true for Al and his son. Maybe one of these days Carl would talk to Al about how important relationships had become to him. He knew for a fact how much happier Al would be were that rift repaired.

He reached the pond shore. The resident ducks, goofy-looking mallard-and-something mixed breeds, came gabbling over to him. Carl had forgotten the stale bread. No matter. These fat, saucy ducks certainly weren't depending on Carl for their next meal. The water slapped and sloshed at his feet, churning and yet peaceful.

Bess.

23

CAN YOU ACCEPT YOUR ONE AND ONLY GOD-GIVEN LIFE?

*I*n the classic Disney film *Old Yeller*, the lead character, a charming scalawag of a dog, captures the hearts of a pioneer family whose father/husband must leave for a time. The dog acts heroically and, in the process, contracts rabies. The teenage son destroys his beloved companion to spare it the agony of slow suffering and a certain, horrible death.

The father returns, and his words of wisdom to ease his son's heartache can be applied far beyond the circumstances in that motion picture. They also frame a philosophy that describes this Fifth Passage to a tee. With that philosophy, the whole of your history and experience work together to strengthen what can be the best years of your life.

Father and son converse beneath a tree on a hill.

The father: "Thing to do now is try and forget it—go on being a man."

"How, Pa? How ya gonna forget something like that?"

"I guess I don't quite mean that. It's not a thing you can forget. Maybe not even a thing you want to forget. What I'm trying to say is, life's like that sometimes."

"Like what?"

"Well, now and then, for no good reason a man can figure out, life will just haul off and knock him flat, slam him against the ground so hard it seems like all his insides is busted. It's not all like that. A lot of it is mighty fine. You can't afford to waste the good part frettin' about the bad. That makes it all bad. You understand what I'm trying to get at?"

"Yes sir. It's just that—"

"Sure, I know. Saying it's one thing; feeling it's another. But I'll tell you a trick that's sometimes a big help. Start looking around for something good to take the place of the bad. As a general rule, you can find it."

FRETTIN' ABOUT THE LOSSES

Is the person who loves transcendently freed of the need to grieve? Not at all. There still remain the anger, fear and depression, bargaining, sadness, and acceptance. But the acceptance, the fruit of grief, extends to satisfying new dimensions.

The fourth task of the Fifth Passage is to come to terms with your own death. We phrase the task this way: My acceptance of my own death requires that I have accepted my one and only God-given life. If you, like Carl Warden, lose a spouse early in the Fifth Passage, your spouse's death will force you to accept your mortality early in the passage. The sooner you make peace with your own mortality, the more joyous this passage will be.

THE FOURTH TASK: ACCEPT MY ONE AND ONLY GOD-GIVEN LIFE

The extent to which I have trouble accepting my own death may reflect a major way in which I have not accepted some past or present aspect of living. Trouble includes exaggerated fear, depression, anger, and bitterness. Moreover, if I have much exaggerated fear, anger, or denial about my inevitable losses and good-byes, that tells me that I have failed as yet to make peace with (that is, accept) some aspect of my living.

Getting Stuck

A woman, Grace, in our counsel took her mother into her home in 1968, when her father died. Until last year she cared for her mother, providing everything for the woman (Grace is also widowed). Then Momma broke a hip and Grace could not physically take care of her. Necessity forced Grace to place Momma in a nursing home. The first thing Momma said when Grace walked in the door to visit her was, "You betrayed me." A quarter century of constant care and effort meant nothing. In her mother's eyes, Grace had abandoned her. What went on here?

As we took Grace into counsel, we explored the probability (a very high probability) that Grace and her mother both had become mired in one of several possible swamps: Either they had become stuck in a prior passage of marriage, or they had become stuck in some step of the grieving process.

People who are stuck in a previous passage cannot achieve the Transcendent Love of the Fifth Passage. If they get bogged down in a stage of grieving, they cannot reach resolution. Resolution and acceptance are critical parts of Transcendent Love. Grace's Momma got stuck in the bargaining phase of grief, and Grace was suffering the fallout just as much as Momma was. We find it very common for people in the Fifth Passage to get stuck in the bargaining stage.

Perhaps, instead of accepting that life is coming to an end and possibly taking appropriate steps to distribute their estate, a couple starts hoarding money even more. How often do we hear of elderly persons, living alone in penury, who have stashed thousands of dollars in their mattress? The bargain there is "If I can hoard enough financial security, somehow, I won't have to face the final losses." It's not a conscious bargain. It certainly makes no intellectual sense. Bargaining is neither conscious nor intellectual.

Another couple may take up a fanatical preoccupation with physical health. "If I can only remain vigilant enough about my health, I won't die." (And the clincher: "It's worked so far, hasn't it?")

Had Grace's dad not passed away, even if Momma had not spent twenty-some years under Grace's roof, Grace's mom would probably be stuck at the bargaining stage anyway. "If I can just cling closely enough to my daughter, her youth will carry me through. I won't lose everything." Grace's problems and her mother's arose out of their past. Grace's mother had never really wedded well to Dad; they never established a close emotional bond. Grace's mom drew from Grace to meet her intimacy needs, particularly after Dad died. Grace, with scantly met emotional needs of her own, became a party to it. Their final years were simply a magnification of what had been going on for most of their lives.

Beware also the contingent life. The person living a contingent life is always waiting for life to start. "When I graduate from high school, I can really live. No, wait; make that after I graduate from college. Actually, when I get married is when life really starts. But I have to get the career going first, then I'll really enjoy life. . . . When I retire I'll really be happy. . . ." The person living a contingent life never admits, "This is my life now, and I will enjoy it now." Life is not a dress rehearsal. When that person arrives at the Fifth Passage, deep, deep bitterness and anger boil up as the truth hits: "My life is coming to end and I haven't lived yet."

Persons overcome by that realization may go through a period of agnosticism, doubting the value of everything in life from God on down.

"What happened to dear old George?" the neighbors ask. "He used to be so dependable. So regular. Now here he is consumed with bitterness. What kind of example is that for the younger folks?"

Dodging Death

"Can't be done," you say. "Spiritually, yes. Not physically."

We agree. "But that's just your head speaking. A lot of people, unable to come to terms with losses, make strange pledges in their heart where their head has no say." Dodging death here includes not just physical death, but symbols of impending death such as deteriorating health, departed youth, loss of a driver's license—those things that serve as mileposts to the final day.

Seven common pitfalls, seven "death dodgers," bar a person from reaching Transcendent Love. Which one a person picks depends on which way that person's family of origin shaped him or her. Even more so, how that person negotiated the previous passages of marriage will determine whether the person gets hung up in one of these death dodgers. See if any of these death dodgers have ever occurred to you.

Hypochondria

Hypochondriacs constantly imagine illnesses or inflate existing illness. The symptoms and the pain are absolutely real, but they are not caused by the agents normally associated with them. Stress and emotion generate them. We call this psychogenic illness. Gerontologists agree that they have to sift through a lot of psychogenic symptoms to find organic problems.

Hypochondria serves two purposes. It is a way to dodge death and mortality: "If I can be vigilant enough, I will outmaneuver death. Lethal problems cannot sneak up on me." Also, hypochondria is a way to indirectly grieve death. Long before she (or he) dies, she has grieved, literally, hundreds of little illnesses. It's the mind and body's way of staging a miniature death experience over and over, preparing for the big one. In a way, it works. The grieving process is served. But it's not a good way, for the pain is real, and fear and worry drain away happiness. There is no calm and peace for the hypochondriac. Thereby it is only an escalation of pain and fear as the end actually comes.

Bitterness and Cynicism

Anyone in any passage of marriage can become bitter and cynical, but the persons dodging death raise it to an art form. These persons are headed in the opposite direction from Transcendent Love. Instead of serenity and acceptance, they promote friction and refusal. We believe the underlying, unspoken motivation here can be expressed, "If I cannot reach a perspective of Transcendent Love (because of failure to complete prior passages), I will move radically in the opposite direction." It's exceedingly common in the elderly.

Ebenezer Scrooge in Dickens's *A Christmas Carol* is the quintessential example. So is Silas Marner. If their perspective is turned upside down—reversed by ghosts or by circumstance—they are quite capable of achieving acceptance and serenity.

Bitterness does two things. It channels off the anger and frustration about not being able to reach a transcendent perspective. Too, it becomes in a way almost a rationalization for avoiding the transcendent perspective. "If I can poke enough holes in tranquility and become cynical enough about God and meaning and life, I don't have to mourn the pain of not having all that."

Health Obsession

Twenty thousand units daily of Vitamin C is the key to life or perhaps two slices of whole wheat bread or maybe blackstrap molasses. There is an immense and profitable (for the producers) body of literature available for and by people who buy into super-health for prolonging life. An offshoot of this is the practice of freezing a body until such time as a cure is found for its terminal illness or other problem, or until rejuvenation has been perfected.

Suicide

This is the flip side of health obsession. Suicide includes slow or passive suicide. For example, an elderly person might stop eating. It happens often. "Why?" you ask. The person shrugs, at a loss for a valid reason. "No appetite. Nothing tastes good anymore." That person is moving away from Transcendent Love.

Instead of accepting the brevity and transience of life, enabling them to appreciate and cherish it, such persons say deep inside, "Life is transient and fleeting, and that is so frightening that the only way I can handle it is to shorten it deliberately. If I can't master it, I shall take the power of life and death into my own hands." The dread of uncertainty makes them want to seize the power to end it on their own terms. When the doctor tells the person to walk a mile a day, and the person doesn't; when the person consciously fails to take prescribed medicine—all are manifestations of this. The person who can accept the transitory nature of life, we've found, will be a better steward of life, living it sensibly and well.

Counterfeit Change

All through life, Herb's faith had been, at best, lukewarm. He limited it to Sundays in a mainstream church and didn't think about it much the rest of the week—until he moved into the Fifth Passage. His parents died. His sister died. His wife became ill. His arthritis became so bad he had to give up golf. Suddenly Herb became pious. "Religious fanatic" was not too strong a label for him. "Religiously addicted" hit the nail on the head. He embraced a fringe church some would call a cult because it offered a promise of healing. If Herb just had enough faith, he could escape misery.

Hate God, Fate, and/or Circumstances

Brett's father lost the family fortune during the Depression. Brett salvaged a snip of the family business and worked hard for nearly fifty years to keep it afloat. When Brett retired he sold the business, but not for much. Brett had never fully grieved what his father had lost, nor had the father. Brett did not grieve and celebrate the heroic struggle he himself had made. Now in Brett's Fifth Passage, what had started out as anger about the family business had mushroomed until it encompassed everything. Brett was angry and suspicious of all things. We call it agitated paranoia.

If you yourself feel overwhelmed by the unfairness and pain of the past, look for losses you and your family accrued earlier that might not have been grieved and worked through. Those unresolved losses earn interest over time, growing and magnifying, so that by the Fifth Passage they burst forth in highly magnified form.

Those Time-Release Capsules

When Franklin Delano Roosevelt died, his wife grieved deeply, picked up the pieces, and went on to greatness in her own right. When Prince Albert died, Queen Victoria descended into a sorrow and depression from which she never recovered. A man in our counsel, married forty-five years, left his wife. It took a while to uncover his deepest, darkest motivations. The man was terrified of death. He never made peace with it. His mother and father, his brothers and sisters all experienced extreme difficulty saying good-bye. He was running away from marriage, but what he really was running away from was death.

Even now in the Fifth Passage, forty years or so after your departure from your childhood home, those time-release capsules still influence you; often they are not activated until you reach the age your parents faced these issues. You may, in fact, be trying to dodge death in the way they did. How did your parents and grandparents come to terms with mortality? Think about your siblings' attitudes, too; they are subject to the same cross-generational influences you are.

Have you made peace with your own mortality? You will wrestle (or are wrestling) with this yourself. Know that your family's attitudes shape your own. Take a moment now to look back.

"When did my parents sit down with me to discuss illness and death?"

_____ "When my favorite pet died."

_____ "When my grandfather or grandmother died."

_____ "When my brother or sister died."

_____ "When my mom or dad died."

_____ "When a playmate died."

"What did they say to me at this time?" *(They said, "Grandpa has gone to a better place." Or they said, "He's gone to be with the Lord, and we will see him again some day.")*

_____

_____

"If a grandparent(s) has died, how old were my parents then?"

_____

"How did my parents treat it?" *(Did Dad talk about the fun times he had with Grandpa fishing or playing ball? Or did he refuse to talk about him? Or did Mom cry every time someone mentioned Grandma for a couple of years?)* _____

_____

_____

"Has my parents' attitude toward death influenced my own attitude?" _____ yes _____ no

One male patient inherited the attitude, "When a man stops working, he dies," from his father. Prior to the man's retirement, he and his wife joked about that legacy. One year into his retirement, that became a reality. The man was gorging himself with food, but he had stopped playing golf or walking or doing much of anything else.

His wife confronted him with that old family legacy and suggested counseling. In the next weeks the man realized he was, in fact, living out that legacy. He was startled by how powerful that time capsule had been. He had not planned to neglect himself in those first nine months.

Could you be living out an old family legacy? Could your attitude toward death reflect that of your parents? If so, how? _____

_____

_____

Like this man, you have a choice. You can choose to replicate that attitude, or you can choose how you wish to die. This man decided that he wasn't going to live a living death for ten or twenty years. Instead he determined to find new interests to pursue and to commit himself to renewing his marriage.

Once you've freed yourself from the temptation to dodge death, you are ready to look at your own life from a perspective that sees beyond the immediate, which will help you complete this task of accepting your one and only life.

THE PERSPECTIVE THAT LIVES

We talked about the perspective that sees beyond the immediate, as we considered the death of a spouse. That perspective is just as important as you make peace with your own mortality. As before we will express that perspective by giving you two dichotomous statements—one, the immature outlook; the other, the transcendent perspective.

Death Is an End Vs. Death Is a Beginning

When Annie Warden Millen watched her mother slide downhill, Annie believed the first statement. She saw Mom leaving; she saw an end to a woman she loved very much.

In contrast, Carl Warden watched his Bess walk down a road he himself would take. He would grieve, of course. The sadness would rip his heart and soul. But he could celebrate, too, that death was a gate for his beloved Bess into eternal life.

Many who study death and dying claim that death should be celebrated just as much as a birth. Both are the starts of a new life. This is reflected in trends recently of people requesting an upbeat atmosphere at their funerals. Texas statesman John Tower requested that the "Hallelujah Chorus" from Handel's *Messiah* be sung at his funeral. He wanted something joyous and triumphant.

In times past, when most people died at home, the persons in attendance could sense the dying's attitude about life and death just in the way they physically let go.

Some people near to death have been known to question, as they slip in and out of consciousness, whether they are still on earth or are in heaven.

So eager are they to make the transition from life to death to new life, they become frustrated when they keep coming back to consciousness.

In contrast, attendants have reported that some dying persons grab the sheets, grab people—literally, physically struggling to avoid that final, fearful moment. Decades before their physical deaths, persons may grab onto spouses, adult children, friends, or material things, and intensely fear letting go.

Wynn, the man who spent his last years in the nursing home where he was a handyman, was unconsciously wrapping himself up completely and codependently in his wife: "If I hang onto people around me tightly enough, I'll never have to say good-bye." Anything that pried Wynn loose from that grip, such as his residential removal to a nursing home, placed him in the mortal danger he so desperately tried to avoid.

We invite you to think about this time of grief and celebration, not in a morbid way but in anticipation. Discuss with your spouse what you would like your own funeral to be and listen to your spouse's feelings on the subject. Here, believe it or not, is still another opportunity for improved intimacy and oneness. Rites of passage are properly planned by the persons undergoing those rites, whether funerals or weddings.

Death Invalidates Life Vs. Death Completes Life

Let us tell you the story of two patients. The first woman had devoted her whole life to nurturing her children, her grandchildren, occasional nieces and nephews, and a foster child as well. Through time she became less and less necessary to the younger generation. There came a day when they didn't need her at all. They didn't want her to baby-sit; too old, they implied. They didn't need her cookies. Her quaint clothes and clicking false teeth embarrassed the teenage grandkids. What was the use of living like this?

The second grandmother, equally as dedicated to the children and grandchildren, took another view. She celebrated that the children didn't need her anymore. That indicated she had raised them well, sending them out into the world fully equipped to take what comes. She had done a good job; she had completed her tasks. She could relax now and enjoy the peace of not having to take care of youngsters.

Both women's circumstances were identical. Each saw their role in life as a caregiver, a nurturer. When that role was no longer applicable, one felt her life was no longer valid. The other, instead, was able to surrender that role without being threatened. The difference in their responses? Perspective.

The second woman saw this passage of her life as a time of transition, not between passages, but between this life and the next. She seemed to see God as she never had before.

Obviously, none of us can see God directly. God Himself told Moses that the Israelites would die if they saw Him directly. That's a condition we have to accept as part of our mortality. In this life we see Him indirectly through images.

We've found that many people in Passage Five see five images of God as they never have before. What was pure theology in their twenties and thirties becomes the essence of their existence in their seventies and eighties. This is the transition period where I've not left earth yet, but I am beginning to experience God and the Holy Spirit within me in a deeper way. That's why many cultures reverence older people. They instinctively know they are more spiritual than younger people, a bonus of Passage Five.

Image One: God As Father

To patients who've missed Dad's parental nurturing, to those who've had an especially difficult marriage or childhood, to those who've had to say a premature good-bye to their spouses, this image of God is particularly reassuring. It's as if they are coming full circle. They emerged out of the womb and into a family headed by earthly parents. Now they are returning to join their heavenly family. Good-bye to the stern, remote earthly father. Hello to the loving heavenly Father.

The second grandmother saw herself returning to that family rather than ending her life. Her heavenly family was becoming as important—if not more important—than her earthly family. She knew the crossover would be scary, just as the birth of her children was scary and painful, yet joyous. God was increasingly near.

Image Two: God As Shepherd and Leader

Often it's difficult for older men and women to surrender their positions of leadership and responsibility. The man or woman who was the head of a corporation or a department or a region of the country is now without that challenge. Those grandmothers were no longer responsible for their children or grandchildren. They were no longer shepherds.

Once older people come to see God as their shepherd, they no longer maintain a death grip on the rod and staff. They're not humiliated to lay down those symbols of power. Instead, they see this as a natural transition and feel a tremendous sense of relief since they no longer feel false guilt about not being superproductive. It's not difficult for them to allow God to shepherd them through Passage Five and back home again.

Image Three: God As Physician and Healer

Those in Passage Five obviously feel their physical mortality. Some are just slowing down. Others live with constant pain or are confined to a wheelchair.

Chronic or terminal illness doesn't seem like a dirty trick to people who know they can trust God to ease their pain and feel it may soon be time to lay down their physical bodies. They know that as part of their salvation they shall have new, purified bodies in eternity.

Robert Hemfelt remembers his mother, who in her mid-seventies suffered hip pain, teasing about her aches and pains. "I'm getting ready to lay down this body," she would say. "After all, it's got a lot of mileage on it. It's time to put it down."

After she suffered a heart attack and experienced kidney failure, the doctors told her they could keep her alive indefinitely on dialysis. She and her husband prayed about the alternative. She opted to forego heroic measures and let nature have its way. Said she, "My body is a vehicle I picked up at birth, and I'll lay it down at death." Together the elder Hemfelts began a two-week death watch, a peaceful waiting for her home-going.

Image Four: God As Judge

It might seem strange for this image of God to be comforting to someone who knows eternity is all too close. Yet we find that patients are often relieved of bitterness during the Fifth Passage. One acquaintance, for instance, spent years feeling angry because his cousin inherited oil-rich land from a family member and he received pasture land from that same relative. For years he was obsessed by the injustice of it all. "Now in my sixties, it doesn't bother me so much," he tells us. "I can't explain why. Nothing has changed, legally or physically. She still has the oil; I still have rocks and grass. Yet it doesn't matter as much. God might just have a perspective on this that I can't see." People who have been wronged by other people clearly picture that Judge whose justice is beyond human justice. All these inequities are known to Him, they know, and are being worked out on a cosmic level we someday will understand.

Sometimes in our group sessions we tease patients. "Sitting here in group, we're experiencing a little taste of heaven. Together we can look back on our lives—including the pain of our childhood—and realize, 'We're all doing the best we know how.' Instead of bitterness, we can forgive each other and feel a sense of justice and resolution and forgiveness about what happened. Someday we will all face each other in heaven and be able to forgive even more completely."

Image Five: God As Savior and Redeemer

Where does it all end up? The non-Christian possesses no good hope at all. The Christian? All the Christian's life, he or she has been talking about faith in Christ. Have faith. Help faith grow. It's almost all talk, but not because of hypocrisy. Only in these last years does spiritual surrender become truly possible. All friends, all relatives, perhaps even the spouse, all fall away. No more props. Far fewer distractions.

"Uplifting disillusionment," Dr. Hemfelt calls it. It's the final grief and acceptance that no earthly savior or parent or spouse will ever completely fulfill your needs in life. At last you can turn your hands and heart completely to God.

People in Passage Five also become very aware of what they have done to others. For years they may have rationalized—or denied—their physical abuse of one of their children, but now, as they watch their grandchildren go through the same rebellion, they are flooded with waves of guilt and remorse and shame. They are ready to say, as the prophet Isaiah did:

> "I, even I, am He who blots out your transgressions
>   for My own sake;
> And I will not remember your sins."[1]

Spiritual resolution of the deepest sort, the sort that leads to a true and abiding love of God, comes only when the person has said all the other good-byes, made peace with his or her life, and has put away all the false idols that used to call so temptingly.

All the substitutes are at last put away; will the real God please stand up?

If this passage goes well, a strong spiritual base permits peace. Carl Warden could say good-bye to Bess. He could face his own pending death honestly and squarely. The last good-bye. A new and Transcendent Love and peace with God: the ultimate hello.

HOW WELL HAVE WE DONE?

Take a moment to consider your own situation. Check the statements below that apply to you.

_____ "I can still give the world something. It is _____."

_____ "I can picture myself as an old person and (barring unpredictable catastrophic illness) can pretty much estimate what my physical and mental limitations might be. I may not be completely at peace with the vision, but I can see it. Those limitations might be:

_____

_____

_____."

_____ "God's role in my life, particularly as it applies to death and illness, is *(Some of our patients feel that God has been guiding each day of their life. They are often able to face death well because they know He has held them before through difficult situations and they know He will hold them again. They trust Him as they trust no one else.)*

_____

_____

_____."

"My attitude toward death is:
_____ I am petrified of death. It seems like the final end."
_____ I'd rather die now than live another year of misery."
_____ I am prepared for my own death when that time may come."
_____ I look forward to saying hello to my God."
_____ I believe Jesus Christ saved me from my sins and that I will live with Him forever."

If you are afraid of death, you need to ask yourself why. We always find that someone who is haunted by a strong apprehension about death has an underlying fear about life and living. One woman referred her mother to us. The mother had become possessive and paranoid about money. She was afraid someone was going to swindle her. She was afraid her money wouldn't last the rest of her lifetime. She was afraid someone was trying to get control of her money.

In reality the woman had more than enough money to last a lifetime, and she couldn't put her wealth in a U-Haul and attach it to a hearse. In counseling she realized that her fear of death and her paranoia about money reflected her childhood fears of not having enough to eat during the Great Depression. She grieved that former fear and accepted her mortality.

You are now well familiar with the grieving process. Hardly morbid, grieving your mortality frees you to accept God's ultimate plan for you. No longer fretting and dreading the inevitable, you are able to live the years ahead with a new freedom.

THE YEARS AHEAD

Carl Warden hated to see a grown man cry, himself least of all. But the tears ran freely down his cheeks now as Diane came down the aisle. Praise God, she was beautiful! Warm, suntanned skin, with far fewer wrinkles than you would expect on a sixty-two-year-old woman; long silver hair swept back in elegant waves; that uncertain, nervous smile. She was almost as beautiful as Bess had looked.

He, with a married granddaughter, was himself getting married! He glanced over at his daughter, Annie. The daughter of the groom still had that look of I've-got-it-all-together, and Carl knew that now it was genuine. Annie had come to terms with her marriage and her life, and was making them both work.

Diane stood at his side now, and Carl almost got cold feet. Almost. Diane wasn't taking Bess's place. No one ever could. Bess had been gone more than a year now, but she was still as much a part of his life as his memories. She was so many of them. But Diane . . . beautiful woman, sprightly companion. For the last year Carl had felt like a centenarian with a hundred-pound backpack, incredibly burdened and incredibly empty. Then he met Diane.

Man is not meant to be alone, the Scripture declares. Carl knew that now. Marriage is so much more than a legal union or a sexual union or a melding of minds and families. Infinitely more. "I don't plan to marry again," Diane told him when first they met. "It's just too difficult to break a new one in." And she was serious when she said it. Now here she stood. She felt the pull as much as he.

Exasperating, elating, horrible, wonderful, shackling, freeing—the human being's single most intimate source of conflict and of joyous intimacy is marriage.

Carl slipped the ring on her finger.

NOTES

Chapter 2   Can Two Independent Persons Become One Unit?

1. Jerry D. Hardin and Dianne C. Sloan, *Getting Ready for Marriage* (Nashville: Thomas Nelson Publishers, 1991), mss. pp. 171–200.

2. Ibid.

3. Ibid, mss. p. 204.

4. Ibid., mss. p. 208.

Chapter 4   Is Your Brain Affecting Your Sexual Experience?

1. Hardin and Sloan, *Getting Ready for Marriage,* mss. pp. 216–241.

2. Ibid.

3. Ibid., mss. pp. 246–7.

Chapter 7   Hidden Agendas: Their Cause and Cure

1. Hardin and Sloan, *Getting Ready,* mss. pp. 216–241.

Chapter 9   Can You Childproof Your Marriage?

1. Hardin and Sloan, *Getting Ready,* mss. pp. 251–276.

2. Ibid.

3. Frank Minirth, Ike Minirth, Georgia Minirth Beach and Mary Alice Minirth, *Beating the Odds* (Grand Rapids: Baker Books, 1987), 67.

4. Genesis 29:20.

Chapter 14   Is the Adolescent in Control, or Are You and Your Spouse?

1. Wayne Gretzky and Rick Reilly, *Gretzky: An Autobiography* (San Francisco: Harper & Row, 1990).

Chapter 19   Can You Grieve the Particular Losses of This Passage?

1. Romans 8:28.

Chapter 21   Can You Renew Intimacy?

1. A. Verwoerdt, E. Pfeiffer, and H.S. Wang, "Sexual behavior in senescence: Patterns of sexual activity and interest," *Geriatrics* 24 (1969), 137.

2. L. Creti L and E. Libman, "Cognitions and Sexual Expression in the Aging," *Journal of Sex and Marital Therapy* 15 (2) (1989): 83.

Chapter 23   Can You Accept Your One and Only God-given Life?

1. Isaiah 43:25.

APPENDIX

THE MAJOR TASKS OF THE PASSAGES OF MARRIAGE

THE FIRST PASSAGE—YOUNG LOVE
The First Two Years

Task 1: Mold into One Family
Task 2: Overcome the Tendency to Jockey for Control
Task 3: Build a Sexual Union
Task 4: Make Responsible Choices
Task 5: Deal with Your Parents' Incomplete Passages

THE SECOND PASSAGE—REALISTIC LOVE
The Third through the Tenth Years

Task 1: Hang On to Love after Reality Strikes
Task 2: Recognize the Hidden Contracts in Your Marriage
Task 3: Write a New Marriage Contract
Task 4: Childproof Your Marriage

THE THIRD PASSAGE—COMFORTABLE LOVE
The Eleventh through the Twenty-fifth Years

Task 1: Maintain an Individual Identity along with the Marriage Identity
Task 2: Say the Final Good-Byes
Task 3: Overcome the Now-or-Never Syndrome
Task 4: Practice True Forgiveness
Task 5: Accept the Inevitable Losses
Task 6: Help Your Adolescent Become an Individual
Task 7: Maintain an Intimate Relationship

THE FOURTH PASSAGE—RENEWING LOVE
The Twenty-sixth through the Thirty-Fifth Years

Task 1: Combat the Crisis of This Passage
Task 2: Reestablish Intimacy
Task 3: Grieve the Particular Losses of This Passage

THE FIFTH PASSAGE—TRANSCENDENT LOVE
The Thirty-Sixth Year and On

Task 1: Prepare for Retirement
Task 2: Continue Renewing Love
Task 3: Achieve a Transcendent Perspective
Task 4: Accept My One and Only God-Given Life

BIBLIOGRAPHY

I. BUILDING SELF-ESTEEM
Rainey, Dennis and Barbara. *Building Your Mate's Self-Esteem*. San Bernardino, CA: Here's Life, 1986.

II. COMMUNICATION
Augsburger, David. *Caring Enough to Hear and Be Heard*. Ventura, CA: Regal, 1979.

Crabb, Lawrence. *The Marriage Builder*. Grand Rapids, MI: Zondervan, 1986.

Wright, H. Norman. *Communication: Key to Your Marriage*. Ventura, CA: Regal, 1979.

_____. *How to Speak Your Spouse's Language*. Old Tappan, NJ: Revell, 1988.

_____. *More Communication Keys for Your Marriage*. Ventura, CA: Regal, 1983.

III. CONFLICT RESOLUTION
Carter, Les. *Good 'n Angry*. Grand Rapids, MI: Baker, 1983.

_____. *Will the Defense Please Rest*. Grand Rapids, MI: Baker, 1986.

Mace, David. *Love and Anger in Marriage*. Grand Rapids, MI: Zondervan, 1982.

Stoop, David and Jan. *Refresh Your Marriage with Self Talk*. Old Tappan, NJ: Revell, 1984.

Talley, Jim. *Reconcilable Differences*. Nashville: Nelson, 1985.

Wright, H. Norman. *How to Have a Creative Crisis*. NY: Berkley, 1987.

IV. FORGIVENESS
Smedes, Lewis. *Forgive and Forget*. San Francisco: Harper & Row, 1984.

Stanley, Charles. *Forgiveness*. Atlanta: Oliver-Nelson, 1987.

Wangerin, Walter. *As for Me and My House*. Nashville: Nelson, 1989.

V. KEEPING BALANCE IN MARRIAGE
Fowler, Richard, Jerilyn Fowler, Brian Newman, and Deborah Newman. *Day by Day: Love Is a Choice*. Nashville: Nelson, 1991.

Hemfelt, Robert, Frank Minirth, and Paul Meier. *Love Is a Choice*. Nashville: Nelson, 1989.

Hemfelt, Robert, Ph.D., Frank Minirth, M.D., Paul Meier, M.D., Dr. Deborah Newman, and Dr. Brian Newman. *Love Is a Choice Workbook.* Nashville: Nelson, 1991.

Minirth, Frank, Paul Meier, Frank Wichern, Bill Brewer, and States Skipper. *The Workaholic and His Family.* Grand Rapids, MI: Baker, 1981.

VI. KEEPING LOVE ALIVE

Dobson, James. *Love for a Lifetime.* Portland, OR: Multnomah, 1987.

Swindoll, Charles. *Strike the Original Match.* Wheaton, IL: Tyndale, 1990.

Wheat, Ed. *Love Life for Every Married Couple.* Grand Rapids, MI: Zondervan, 1980.

VII. SEXUAL DISTINCTIONS/ROLES

Carter, Les. *Push-Pull Marriage.* Grand Rapids, MI: Baker, 1984.

Crabb, Lawrence. *Men and Women.* Colorado Springs: NavPress, 1991.

Dobson, James. *What Wives Wish Their Husbands Knew about Women.* Wheaton, IL: Tyndale, 1977.

Harley, Willard F., Jr. *His Needs, Her Needs.* Old Tappan, NJ: Revell, 1986.

Smalley, Gary. *The Joy of Committed Love.* Grand Rapids, MI: Zondervan, Date not set.

Wheat, Ed. *Love Life for Every Married Couple.* Grand Rapids, MI: Zondervan, 1980.

VIII. SEXUALITY

Dillow, Joseph. *Solomon on Sex.* Nashville: Nelson, 1982.

Meredith, Don. *Becoming One.* Nashville: Nelson, 1979.

Minirth, Frank, Paul Meier, and Richard and Lorraine Meier. *Sex in the Christian Marriage.* Grand Rapids, MI: Baker, 1988.

Penner, Clifford and Joyce. *The Gift of Sex.* Dallas: Word, 1987.

Rainey, Dennis and Barbara. *Questions Book for Marriage Intimacy.* Family Ministry, 1985.

Wheat, Ed and Gaye. *Intended for Pleasure.* Old Tappan, NJ: Revell,1981.

Ziglar, Zig. *Courtship after Marriage.* Atlanta: Oliver-Nelson, 1990.

IX. OTHERS

Carter, Les. *Broken Vows.* Nashville: Nelson, 1991.

Meier, Paul. *You Can Save Your Marriage.* Grand Rapids, MI: Baker, 1988.

Meier, Paul and Richard Meier. *Family Foundations.* Grand Rapids, MI: Baker, 1981.

Minirth, Frank, and Paul Meier. *Worry-Free Living.* Nashville: Nelson, 1989.

X. MARRIAGE AND FAMILY SEMINARS

The Association for Couples in Marriage Enrichment is a resource organization promoting effective communication to help couples increase intimacy, negotiate differences, express appreciation for one another, and deal creatively with emotions. Through the bookstore and bi-monthly newsletter members receive books and publications specifically developed to lead them to identify and develop their strengths, recognize their weaknesses, learn new family-life skills, and promote growth of their relationship. Trained leader-couples hold retreats, facilitate local support groups, and demonstrate new ideas at regional conferences throughout the country. A.C.M.E. resources are designed for couples in all stages of marriage. The popular Newlywed Program builds positive interaction patterns during the critical period soon after marriage. For further information contact A.C.M.E.; P.O. Box 10596; Winston-Salem, NC 27108; (800-634-8325).

Family Life Conferences, sponsored by the Family Ministry of Campus Crusade for Christ, are marriage enrichment and marriage preparation conferences where couples are equipped with proven solutions within a flexible framework that addresses practically every component of "how to build a better marriage"—from communication skills, conflict resolution, and leadership roles, to sexual matters and true intimacy. For more information, write Family Life Conferences; P.O. Box 23840; Little Rock, AR 72221-3840; (800-333-1433).

ABOUT THE AUTHORS

Dr. Frank Minirth is a diplomate of the American Board of Psychiatry and Neurology. Along with Dr. Paul Meier, he founded the Minirth-Meier Clinic in Dallas, Texas, one of the largest psychiatric clinics in the United States.

Mary Alice Minirth is a homemaker and the mother of five children.

Dr. Brian Newman is the clinical director of inpatient services at the Minirth-Meier Clinic in Richardson, Texas. He received his M.A. in counseling from Grace Theological Seminary and his Doctorate of Philosophy from Oxford Graduate School.

Dr. Deborah Newman is a psychotherapist with the Minirth-Meier Clinic. She received her M.A. in counseling from Grace Theological Seminary and her Doctorate of Philosophy from Oxford Graduate School.

Dr. Robert Hemfelt is a psychologist with the Minirth-Meier Clinic who specializes in the tratement of chemical dependencies and compulsivity disorders.

Susan Hemfelt is a homemaker and the mother of three children.

THE MINIRTH-MEIER CLINIC OFFICES
The Most Trusted Name in Christian Counseling™
Established in 1976

National Headquarters
MINIRTH-MEIER, CLINIC, P.A.
2100 N. Collins Blvd.
Richardson, Texas 75080
(214) 669-1733

1-800-229-3000
OUTPATIENT SERVICES
DAY TREATMENT CENTER
HOSPITAL PROGRAMS

MINIRTH-MEIER TUNNELL & WILSON CLINIC
Centre Creek Office Plaza, Suite 200
1812 Centre Creek Drive
Austin, Texas 78754
(512) 339-7511

1-800-444-5751

OUTPATIENT SERVICES
DAY TREATMENT CENTER
HOSPITAL PROGRAMS

MINIRTH-MEIER CLINIC WEST
260 Newport Center Drive, Suite 430
Newport Beach, California 92660
(714) 760-3112

1-800-877-4673

OUTPATIENT SERVICES
DAY TREATMENT CENTER
HOSPITAL PROGRAMS

MINIRTH-MEIER CLINIC, P.C.
The Grove, Suite 1510
2100 Manchester Road
Wheaton, Illinois 60187
(708) 653-1717

1-800-848-8872
1-800-545-1819
OUTPATIENT SERVICES
DAY TREATMENT CENTER
HOSPITAL PROGRAMS
NATIONAL COMMUNICATIONS
DIVISION

MINIRTH-MEIER-RICE CLINIC, P.A.
Koger Center in the Shannon Building
10801 Executive Center Drive, Suite 305
Little Rock, Arkansas 72211
(501) 225-0576

1-800-488-4769

OUTPATIENT SERVICES
HOSPITAL PROGRAMS

MINIRTH-MEIER BYRD CLINIC, P.A.
4300 Fair Lakes Court, Suite 200
Fairfax, Virginia 22033-4231
(703) 968-3556

1-800-486-HOPE (4673)

OUTPATIENT SERVICES
DAY TREATMENT CENTER
HOSPITAL PROGRAMS

For general information about other Minirth-Meier Clinic branch offices, counseling services, educational resources and hospital programs, call toll-free 1-800-545-1819.

National Headquarters: (214) 669-1733   1-800-229-3000